We Have Seen
The Future
And It
Looks Like Baltimore

Also by
Craig R. Smith

Rediscovering Gold in the 21ˢᵗ Century:
The Complete Guide to the Next Gold Rush

Black Gold Stranglehold:
The Myth of Scarcity and the Politics of Oil
(co-authored with Jerome R. Corsi)

Also Co-Authored by
Craig R. Smith and Lowell Ponte

Crashing the Dollar:
How to Survive a Global Currency Collapse

The Uses of Inflation:
Monetary Policy and Governance in the 21st Century

Re-Making Money:
Ways to Restore America's Optimistic Golden Age

The Inflation Deception:
Six Ways Government Tricks Us...And Seven Ways to Stop It!

The Great Debasement:
The 100-Year Dying of the Dollar
and How to Get America's Money Back

The Great Withdrawal:
How the Progressives' 100-Year Debasement
of America and the Dollar Ends

Don't Bank On It!
The Unsafe World of 21st Century Banking

We Have Seen The Future And It Looks Like Baltimore

American Dream vs. Progressive Dream

By Craig R. Smith

and Lowell Ponte

Foreword by Pat Boone

P2 Publishing
Phoenix, Arizona

We Have Seen The Future
And It Looks Like Baltimore
American Dream vs. Progressive Dream

Cover art by Dustin D. Brown, KrypticEye.com
Editing by Ellen L. Ponte

Portions of this book originally appeared in
the following projects by Craig R. Smith and Lowell Ponte:
Don't Bank On It! The Unsafe World of 21ˢᵗ Century Banking;
The Great Debasement: The 100-Year Dying
of the Dollar and How to Get America's Money Back;
Crashing the Dollar: How to Survive a Global Currency Collapse and
The Great Withdrawal: How the Progressives' 100-Year
Debasement of America and the Dollar Ends;
as well as in various White Papers and Studies.
Copyright © 2010, 2011, 2012, 2013 and 2014 by Idea Factory Press,
All Rights Reserved.

Library of Congress Data
ISBN Number 978-0-9968476-0-5
First Edition - October 2015

P2 Publishing
15018 North Tatum Boulevard
Phoenix, Arizona 85032

Table of Contents

Dedication

To my wonderful wife and best friend
Melissa Smith, who makes me better
each day and raised our daughters
Holly and Katie to love the Lord
with all their hearts.
Also to my Pastor Tommy Barnett,
who taught me that doing the right thing
is always the right thing to do,
and to always hold onto the vision.

Foreword
by Pat Boone

"When just leaders are in power, the citizens celebrate;
but when evil people gain control, their joys become moans....

"A king gives stability to the land by justice,
but one who imposes heavy taxes tears it down.....

"When the wicked are in authority, sin flourishes,
but the godly will live to see their downfall."

– Proverbs 29: 2, 4, 16 [1]

Leaders shape the future of every nation, state, city and family. When you see decline, look at the actions and values of those who lead.

In this book my long-trusted friend and advisor Craig Smith and former *Reader's Digest* Roving Editor Lowell Ponte look at Baltimore, once the second most popular destination for immigrants seeking the American Dream. By 2015 it has become a city of heroin and welfare addiction, riots, looting and murder. More than 60 years of Progressive rule took Baltimore on the downward path many other American cities are now following.

Craig and Lowell also examine a country that for decades was divided into capitalist and communist states. New research reveals that those raised under socialism lie, cheat and steal more than do people from a free economy. [2]

Baltimore has a saving remnant that could restore the virtues of work, morality, individual responsibility, thrift and honor that once made it great. Those virtues – including saving – build strong families, too, where nation-saving leaders are raised. This is a mind-opening, heart-opening book.

– PAT BOONE

*"[Most people] cannot grasp the concept of liberty.
Always they condition it with the doctrine
that the state, i.e., the majority, has a sort of
right of eminent domain in acts, and even in ideas –
that it is perfectly free, when it is so disposed,
to forbid a man to say what he honestly believes....*

*The overwhelming majority of citizens....
especially the liberals, who pretend –
and often quite honestly believe – that they
are hot for liberty...never really are.*

*They...advocate only certain narrow kinds of liberty –
liberty, that is, for the persons they favor.
The rights of other persons do not seem to interest them.*

*If a law were passed tomorrow taking away the property
of a large group of presumably well-to-do persons –
say, bondholders of the railroads – without compensation...
they would not oppose it; they would be in favor of it.*

*The liberty to have and hold property is not one they recognize.
They believe only in the liberty to envy, hate and loot
the man who has it."*

– H.L. Mencken
Journalist "Sage of Baltimore"
1925. [3]

Introduction
by Craig R. Smith

"...We also gave those who wished to destroy
space to do that as well, and we work
very hard to keep that balance..."

– Stephanie Rawlings-Blake
Mayor of Baltimore
regarding its 2015 riots [4]

Baltimore has become a culture-war battlefield between two dreams – the individualist American Dream of our nation's Framers, and the collectivist utopian dream of Progressives.

What we saw in the rioting, flames and smoke of Baltimore in 2015 was one small skirmish in this war. It was also a look at what soon might be coming to a city near you.

We remember the televised news coverage:

Police were ordered to retreat before a mob of young people who were hurling threats and hunks of concrete at them.

Police, along with a City Council member married to the State's Attorney, stood by while a few feet away rioters smashed business windows and looted a liquor store.

The councilman seemed unconcerned that he had sworn to uphold the law, but on police faces you could see the pain of being ordered by self-serving politicians not to defend the people and property of their community.

Dark smoke poured from the windows and roof of a looted and torched CVS Pharmacy that neighbors had spent years trying to get built in this inner city.

As firefighters tried to put out the blaze, one news camera showed a young tough trying to cut a fire hose.

Adolescent thugs jumped on the roof and kicked in the windshield of a police car, while none of the authorities nearby moved to stop them.

It was obvious that Baltimore bosses had made a decision and issued orders: let the mobs rob and torch as many stores as they wish. Forget the property loss and financial devastation to local business owners. Do not lift a finger to protect private property. Avoid using any force or firepower that might risk killing one of the rioters, which would lead to more protests, lawsuits and rioting.

Let Baltimore Burn

The message from politicians was clear: Do not confront the criminals. Just let the poorer parts of Baltimore be looted and burned.

This might have saved a life or two in the short run, and it certainly made things easier for city politicians who favored protestors and gangbangers over a few business owners.

The decision, however, had consequences. The rioting led to 200 injured police and more than $20 Million in other damages.

By signaling to looters that store goods were free for all, these Progressive politics created a free-for-all. Surveillance cameras used to identify thieves, many of whom brazenly did not bother covering their faces, identified two Baltimore female corrections officers who had casually joined in the looting of one store.

The police felt shame at not being allowed to protect the community. In the wake of similar rioting in Ferguson, Missouri, and elsewhere, police officers risked having their careers and lives ruined if they put traditional force behind law enforcement. Progressive politicians and media would throw them to the mob.

In Baltimore, demoralized police began an apparent "work slowdown" that reduced their risk of violence or political backlash, but left the community with far less pro-active police protection. Baltimore's murder rate soared.

The Progressive mayor, rather than take responsibility for offering "those who wished to destroy space to do that," instead made a scapegoat of her African-American police chief, while replacing him with a white officer.

The mayor had turned to gang leaders to help curb the rioting, and later said they had been helpful. This happened *after* she tied the hands of city police.

New York Times reporter Ron Nixon spoke with a self-described Crips member who told how "he and some Bloods had stood in front of black-owned stores to protect them from looting or vandalism. He said they had made sure no black children, or reporters, were hit by rioters. They pointed them toward Chinese- and Arab-owned stores." Baltimore peacemaking.

Local gangs such as the Crips, Bloods and Black Guerrilla Family are rumored to be involved with the illicit drug trade in Baltimore. While rioters kept police distracted, not only the CVS Pharmacy but also up to 30 other Baltimore drug stores were targeted and their morphine and other restricted prescription drugs were looted. One analyst concluded that enough drugs were stolen during the riots to keep local drug dealers in business for a year.

The longer-term costs of Baltimore's 2015 riot are impossible to calculate, but they will be high for many years to come. How many investors will it deter from funding new enterprises and jobs here? How many more inner city lives will this drive to frustration, despair, drug addiction and violence?

We perceive that widespread addiction to the drug of welfare can make it easier to fall into illicit drug addiction. Medical authorities estimate that nearly one of every 10 Baltimoreans is a drug addict.

What will it mean for tourism, investment and community optimism that the first thing most Americans think of when they hear the name "Baltimore" is this rioting? How many of Baltimore's best and brightest residents and companies are now planning to flee, as happened after the city's 1968 riots?

Dream War

For much of America's history, Baltimore had been a city of enormous beauty and achievement. Yet after more than half a century of Progressive political rule, Baltimore is burning.

The Progressive dream is rapidly spreading and spawning nightmares. By looking deeply at Baltimore as a leading example of what Progressivism does, we can see how this collectivist ideology corrupts and is replacing the traditional American dream of legal equality, life, liberty, prosperity and the pursuit of happiness.

Writing shortly after the dawn of Progressivism in America, Henry Louis Mencken, an astute journalist and thinker known as the "Sage of Baltimore," understood that what we now call its Politically-Correct politics and values – which in 1925, just after the Marxist Russian Revolution, he saw rising up around him and becoming intellectually fashionable -- were a mortal threat to liberty, free speech and private property. (See what he wrote on the page facing this Introduction.)

The American Dream and Constitution are being dismantled by this alien ideology, by the radical activists infected with it, and by those addicted to the mind-altering and soul-destroying drugs it peddles.

In our 2013 book *The Great Withdrawal: How the Progressives' 100-Year Debasement of America and the Dollar Ends,* we examined how the great city of Detroit and its residents were dragged into economic stagnation and violence by Progressive interference with its economy and values.

In Chapters One and Two of this book we look at the rise and fall of Baltimore, where seeds of both the American Dream and the Progressive nightmare are fighting for control of our nation's future.

In Chapter Three we show the tangled roots of the rival dream of Progressivism, where this alien collectivist ideology came from and how it has been invading our institutions.

In Chapters Four, Five, Six and Seven, we explore ways that Progressives are systematically undermining four cornerstones of the American Dream, the same dream that so many immigrants were drawn to in an earlier Baltimore.

In Chapters Eight and Nine, we examine how Progressive policies and institutions have debased the U.S. Dollar, hamstrung our economy, and fundamentally transformed our once-free marketplace into companies and institutions addicted to and dependent on Progressive government favors and largesse.

In Chapter Ten, we consider whether a "Third Dream" that combines the American and Progressive Dreams is possible, and we show why sustaining the internal contradictions of such a hybrid would likely in the long run prove impossible. We look at how Progressive attempts to combine free market individualism and socialist collectivism are failing in Greece and Puerto Rico.

We also show you ways to protect yourself and your family from the severe turbulence and shocks that will come from both the struggle to reclaim the American Dream and from being pulled deeper into the Progressive collectivist nightmare and a worsening economy as this War of the Dreams continues.

Our Epilogue returns to Baltimore and discovers seeds of hope that even this riot-torn city, dragged down sooner and harder than most by Progressive politicians and policies, has surprising ways to achieve a successful, prosperous tomorrow.

The Key to America's Future

The future looks like Baltimore, but will that future be of a city destroyed by looters, arsonists and Progressivism – a place whose burning embers spread via the media and ignite fires in many other American cities?

Or will Baltimore again become a shining example, the once and future beautiful city of success and creativity where the long nightmare of Progressivism ends and the American Dream is reborn and restored?

Baltimore could be the key to America's future, but which future will it be?

We are now suspended between the two dreams. Progressives have succeeded in creating an America where 94 million Americans are without full-time work, the worst job participation rate since the malaise of Progressive Democratic President Jimmy Carter in 1978.

Roughly 101 million Americans still have full-time jobs, but 108 million receive one or another kind of means-tested government benefits. At least 49.5 percent of American households include someone who receives government benefits.

America is at a tipping point. If a majority of households begin benefitting from welfare, then future elections could become mere bidding wars won by whichever side offers the most free goodies as a *de facto* bribe to voters.

"It's hard to run against Santa Claus," as former Speaker of the House Newt Gingrich has said. This is especially true in a society where Progressives are willing to give away limitless amounts of other people's money, taxing the makers who work to buy the votes of the takers who do not.

As the old saying goes, if you want less of something, tax it. If you want more of something, subsidize it. Progressives now tax work, success and achievement, and subsidize failure and laziness.

Economic growth in America has been slowing for decades because taxes and regulations keep diverting the lifeblood of capitalism, capital, out of the private sector and into the non-productive sector of our society, the government.

The bigger government gets, the more from us it devours. And the more Progressive politicians "tax and tax, spend and spend, elect and elect" (the motto of President Franklin Delano Roosevelt), the less overtaxed investors have to build new enterprises or create more jobs.

If the Progressive nightmare wins, then you need to protect yourself and your family against a bumpy downhill future with severe, predictable risks.

If the American Dream wins, the long-term future can be bright – but between today and this better tomorrow will be the economic shocks and dislocation of tens of millions of people and corporations experiencing withdrawal symptoms.

After decades of Progressive welfare addiction and brainwashing designed to infantilize them under a paternalistic government, many of these Zombies will need time to recover their minds, hearts, work ethic, and personal responsibility....things that Progressives took away in order to make millions helpless and utterly dependent on government.

Whichever dream wins, you will need to be prepared by being diversified in ways that might be new to you.

This is our sixth book. Millions have read one or more of the earlier five as well as additional White Papers. Our aim is to empower you with facts and ideas that could help save your family's future, if you are ready to take prudent but decisive action. The time to do this may be much shorter than you think.

We do not share the view of the Progressive Democratic Mayor of Baltimore that the forces of destruction, the looters, takers, gang members and rioters, should be elevated to the same stature in our society as producers and protectors, our firefighters and police.

"In the end", as the international television series *Highlander* says, "there can be only one."

The individual freedom of the American Dream and collectivist Progressive authoritarian dream contradict one another and cannot coexist much longer as rulers of the same city, nation or world. One of these two visions and value systems will prevail, and the other will lose.

What you do will help determine the outcome, one way or the other.

Despite the many failures of their ideas, Progressives continue to undermine the American Dream. All they need to triumph is for good people to do nothing.

May the winner be the American Dream.

– CRAIG R. SMITH

*"Our contemporaries are constantly excited
by two conflicting passions:*

They want to be led, and they wish to be free.

*As they cannot destroy either the one or the other
of these contrary propensities, they strive
to satisfy them both at once.*

*They devise a sole, tutelary and
all-powerful form of government,
but elected by the people.*

*They combine the principle of centralization
and that of popular sovereignty....*

*By this system the people shake off
their state of dependence
just long enough to select their master
and then relapse into it again.*

*A great many persons at the present day
are quite contented with this sort of
compromise between administrative despotism
and the sovereignty of the people;*

*And they think they have done enough
for the protection of individual freedom
when they have surrendered it
to the power of the nation at large.*

*This does not satisfy me:
The nature of him I am to obey
signifies less to me than the fact of
extorted obedience."*

– Alexis de Tocqueville
Democracy in America (1835)

Part One

Baltimore's Rise & Fall

Chapter One

Beautiful Baltimore

"I came to America....
And then I came to Baltimore.
It was the most beautiful place
You've ever seen in your life."

– Barry Levinson
Baltimore-born Director
from his movie *"Avalon"*

When the American Dream was young, Baltimore was second only to New York City as the port immigrant dreamers picked as their destination.

Sailing ships carried them through the Chesapeake – waters rich with blue crabs, oysters, clams, fish and waterfowl, even porpoise and whales – then turned left into the mouth of the Patapsco River to safe harbor at one of the most inland of East Coast seaports, far from the fierce shores of the wild Atlantic Ocean.

Like Philadelphia and many other Eastern cities, Baltimore was built at the "Fall Line." Here the rocks remember when the Appalachian Mountains were as tall as today's Himalayas. The geology has weathered them down, and the sea-level Chesapeake washes up against a wall of higher land called the Piedmont, the French word for "foothills" or "foot of the mountain."

Rivers flowing eastward from these inland mountains plunge at this Fall Line, turning into waterfalls or steep rapids that ships cannot navigate, so this was where settlers stopped and made their harbor and home.

Much of Baltimore is near sea level, but one part of this city has a toehold on the Piedmont and an elevation of 454 feet.

Entrepreneurs looked at Johnson Falls and other waterfalls that stopped ships, and they smartly saw the fresh water, and later the steam it could produce, as energy to power machinery and factories.

Soon this enterprising city was using abundant wood and water power to build ships such as the Baltimore Clipper, a favorite craft – light, fast and heavily armed – for privateers who ran blockades or, with government approval, captured and looted the ships of hostile powers.

Baltimore became a center of American technological innovation. This is where our first railroad began with the Tom Thumb engine and the Baltimore & Ohio railroad.

This is where Samuel Morse in 1844 sent his famous pioneering telegraph message "What Hath God Wrought?" down roughly 38 miles of wires between the Capitol Building in Washington, D.C., and the B&O station in Baltimore.

If the telegraph was the high-tech Internet of its day, then one of America's Silicon Valleys of that time was Baltimore, a can-do city bursting with energy, new ideas and innovations.

Lords Baltimore

Maryland began as a colony granted by the British King Charles I in 1632 to George Calvert, 1st Baron Baltimore, no doubt in part because both the king and Calvert were Roman Catholics in what was an increasingly Protestant England.

Much as Virginia next door had been named for Queen Elizabeth I, known as the "Virgin Queen," the new Maryland colony was nominally named after King Charles' wife and queen consort Henrietta Maria.

Calling this colony the land of Mary, however, was a clear sign throughout Europe that this was a New World refuge that welcomed Catholics, much as Massachusetts welcomed Puritans. Maryland became a magnet for these faithful, especially from England, Germany and Ireland.

Lord Baltimore, who was also proprietor of a colony in Newfoundland he called "Avalon," died five weeks before the final charter for Maryland was completed. His sons would control it, and today the Calvert flag with its two distinct crosses is Maryland's state flag.

King James I, for whom Calvert served as a Secretary of State, had raised him to the Irish Peerage with the title Baron Baltimore, from Irish Celtic words meaning "town of the big house," the name of the family's estate in Ireland's County Longford.

King Charles would eventually lose his head, literally, and the Calvert family would eventually lose Maryland's special status as a haven for Catholics, even though these immigrants kept coming. The colony was a successful commercial venture that had always accepted religious tolerance.

But in Baltimore the European religious battles between Protestants and Catholics were reflected as one additional source of tension among the city's various ethnic groups.

Giving Birth to D.C.

In 1776 Maryland joined the other 12 English colonies in declaring and winning independence from the mother country.

The first "President of the United States" came from Maryland.

This was John Hanson, who was the first to serve a one-year term as the President – the one who presides – over the Continental Congress. This was his title under the Articles of Confederation that came before our Constitution – and which later may have inspired the name of the Confederate States of America. Hanson was the first of 14 such Presidents before George Washington.

Under the Constitution, Washington's Treasury Secretary Alexander Hamilton and Secretary of State Thomas Jefferson agreed that the new country needed a new and neutral capital, not an already established city in any of the states. They agreed to situate this capital midway between the northern and southern states.

For this capital, Maryland donated a ten-mile-square parcel on its side of the Potomac River. This is the land where Washington, D.C. stands today. (Virginia also donated land for the new capital on the opposite bank of the Potomac, but this was returned to Virginia in 1846.)

A debate in recent decades has been that residents of Washington, D.C. have no empowered representative or Senators in Congress. As the local license plate says, they have "Taxation Without Representation."

Democrats have long advocated granting statehood to the District of Columbia, which the Framers intended to be a politically-neutral meeting place. The reason is obvious. Those who serve Big Government will overwhelmingly vote for the Big Government Party and elect only Democrats.

Republicans have replied that if District of Columbia citizens want representation, then for purposes of voting D.C. can be legally "retroceded" to Maryland and residents can cast their ballots for Maryland's two senators and a member of Congress.

Having given birth to Washington, D.C. out of its own territory has been a mixed blessing for Maryland, as we shall see.

Leeward

The decision by President James Madison, a protégé of Thomas Jefferson, to fight the War of 1812 against the British caused great disagreement between the Jeffersonian Democratic-Republican Party, which evolved into today's Democratic Party, and the more aristocratic Federalist Party.

In 1812 near Baltimore, this issue led to blows, as Brown University historian Gordon S. Wood tells in his study of America's early Republic, *Empire of Liberty*:

Shots were exchanged between Federalists in their house and a mob outside. This confrontation ended only when the Jeffersonians got a cannon and threatened to blow the home to splinters with Federalists inside it.

One who suffered a severe wound during this shootout was "Light-Horse Harry" Lee, a Revolutionary War hero and former Governor of Virginia who had famously eulogized George Washington as "First in war – first in peace – and first in the hearts of his countrymen."

Lee at the time had a five-year-old son named Robert Edward, who one day would be offered command of both the Union and Confederate armies in the War Between the States. As a Virginian, Robert E. Lee chose to remain loyal to his state and became the Confederacy's military commander.

This shootout that left "Light-Horse Harry" hampered for the rest of his life became a symbol throughout the states of just how quick to violence and mob behavior the people were in Baltimore.

Mob City

America's Civil War began in Baltimore…and, some say, it continues there today.

Historians will tell you that the War Between the States actually began in South Carolina when that self-proclaimed secessionist state shelled the U.S. troops President Abraham Lincoln ordered to hold Fort Sumter in Charleston harbor. No soldier, however, was killed or injured by those two days of shelling.

Six days after Sumter surrendered, however, on April 19, 1861, a pro-Confederate mob in Baltimore clashed with members of the Massachusetts militia who were slow-marching through in response to Lincoln's order to end local insurrection.

The mob blocked the militia's route, then attacked rear companies of the regiment with "bricks, paving stones, and pistols." Several soldiers fired into the mob.

As the gunpowder smoke cleared, Corporal Sumner Needham and three other soldiers lay dead, and 36 others too injured to continue had to be left behind. Twelve civilians were killed and an untold number were wounded.

This war that over the next four years would end more than 620,000 American lives began that day in Baltimore, the city's Mayor George William Brown later wrote, "because then was shed the first blood in a conflict between the North and the South; then a step was taken which made compromise or retreat almost impossible; then passions on both sides were aroused which could not be controlled."

Hearing of the carnage, James Ryder Randall wrote a poem titled "Maryland, My Maryland" that, set to the tune of the Christmas song "O Tannenbaum," quickly became the unofficial state song (made official in 1939).

The song urges Marylanders to "Avenge the patriotic gore / That flecked the streets of Baltimore" during this riot, while its nine stanzas denounce the Union as despots, tyrants, Vandals and "Northern scum." It urges Maryland to join neighboring Virginia in secession, and uses the words "Sic Semper" from Virginia's state seal.

In 1865, actor John Wilkes Booth shouted the Latin words *Sic Semper Tyrannis*, "Thus always to tyrants," after fatally shooting President Lincoln.

Booth was born and raised in Maryland.

"Know-Nothings"

Baltimore is America's northernmost "Southern" city.

In 1860, Maryland's tobacco plantations were worked by roughly 90,000 slaves, and Baltimore was home to 25,000 free African-Americans.

Maryland culturally identified with the South, and, then as now, voted overwhelmingly Democratic, the political party of the slave owners. On the eve of the Civil War, Baltimore was a city torn by racial and political tension and dissention.

Rioting in 1856, 1857, 1858, and 1859 had reinforced Baltimore's hot-tempered reputation and nickname as "Mob City."

Part of the agitation behind this was influenced by the nativist "Know-Nothing" third party. In 1855 it had changed its official name from the Native American Party to the American Party. This party's odd nickname is said to have come from the typical secretive member response when asked about what the party did: "I know nothing."

Former President Millard Fillmore left his disintegrating Whig Party to make a run as the American Party's presidential candidate in 1856. Baltimore elected a "know-nothing" as Mayor.

This new party called for restricting immigration, fearful that America was being transformed by a flood of new Roman Catholic ethnics, Germans and the Irish, who in the late 1840s and early 1850s had fled the potato famine that starved up to a million people in Ireland. Many recent immigrants feared having to compete for work at the bottom of the job ladder with freed slaves.

In the 1860 presidential election, Lincoln won a plurality of national votes among three candidates. In Baltimore, however, he won only 1,100 votes out of 30,000 cast.

The route to Washington, D.C., for his inauguration took Lincoln through Baltimore. His Pinkerton security agents, however, had picked up rumors of a plot to assassinate the President-elect in Baltimore and feared what a mob of secessionists might try to do.

Rather than have him give a speech to locals as happened in other cities, the Pinkertons moved Mr. Lincoln through Baltimore unnoticed in the dead of night. Opponents for years repeated the tale that Lincoln sneaked through Baltimore hiding in a railway cattle car.

While several other states seceded from the Union, President Lincoln was determined to prevent Maryland from doing so. One reason is obvious: it surrounds Washington, D.C. on three sides, with the fourth side being Confederate Virginia. If Maryland joined the Confederacy, the Union capital would be cut off from the rest of the country.

No Secession For You

This could have put Mr. Lincoln in the embarrassing position of having to move the union capital north to a safer city – much as happened during the American Revolution when the Continental Congress for safety moved itself from Philadelphia to Baltimore for more than two months in 1776-1777. Baltimore during these months had been the temporary capital of the newborn United States.

Baltimoreans on May 13, 1861, awoke to find that a thousand of Lincoln's troops had overnight erected and occupied a fort atop Federal Hill and had cannon aimed down at the city's business district.

Lincoln poured not only state militias but also national troops into Maryland and Baltimore. The message was clear: despite its sympathy with the Confederacy, Maryland would not be permitted to secede from the Union.

Even after its state legislature voted against secession, Maryland remained under *de facto* military occupation for the duration of the war, as if it were enemy, or at least rebellious, territory.

Under this occupation, a third of the state assembly, the Mayor of Baltimore, one member of Congress and others were jailed in violation of *habeas corpus*, an American's Constitutional right to be formally charged and tried.

Lincoln did not rush when U.S. Chief Justice Roger Taney ordered their release. Taney in 1857 had authored the Dred Scott decision that slaves were not citizens and remained their owner's property even if they reached a free state. Taney, who came from slave-state Maryland, inherited slaves but as a young man freed them.

Lincoln had asserted the Union claim to Fort Sumter. Lincoln now had troops heavily reinforce Fort McHenry, whose cannons controlled Baltimore's harbor.

Maryland did not escape the horror of the war. Its bloodiest battle, Antietam, was fought only 70 miles from Baltimore. On a single day, September 17, 1862, nearly 23,000 Confederate and Union troops were killed, wounded or missing in action.

Antietam was a Pyrrhic victory, one so costly to both sides that the Union's nominal win might have meant only that it had halted General Robert E. Lee's advance into a northern state that had many Confederate supporters.

President Lincoln, however, used this victory as an opportunity to publish his first Emancipation Proclamation. Lincoln restricted emancipation to the territories in rebellion, Confederate territory that his troops did not control. It gave slaves in these states added incentive to rise against their slave masters, and to assist and join Union troops that arrived.

However, in the slave states that never seceded – Maryland, Delaware, Kentucky and Missouri – slave owners continued legally to own their slaves. Maryland's new state constitution abolished slavery on November 1, 1864, before the U.S. Constitiution did.

In the spring of 1861 Union troops from Ohio had rushed into western Virginia, largely to secure the Baltimore & Ohio Railroad lines there. This was a region of subsistence farmers, few of whom owned slaves. Under Union control, this region was deemed to have separated from Virginia and on June 20, 1863 was admitted to the Union as the state of West Virginia.

"O'er the Land of the Free"

In 1814 a British fleet and ground forces tried to seize Baltimore but failed to overcome Fort McHenry, despite bombarding it with thousands of cannon shells and new-fangled Congreve rockets.

From a nearby ship, Francis Scott Key – a lawyer whose sister was the wife of Roger Taney – watched the giant American flag still flying over this fort through the night by the light of explosions and the red glare of the Congreves, and then by the dawn's early light.

Inspired, Key dashed off a poem that would become America's National Anthem, "The Star-Spangled Banner." Ours may be the only national anthem that ends with a question that all Americans need to ask themselves: "Oh, say, does that star-spangled banner yet wave o'er the land of the free and the home of the brave?"

Today you might be arrested at an airport merely for quoting our anthem's lyrics about rockets and bombs bursting in air. And Political Correctness now threatens our free speech in many other ways, as we shall see.

During the Civil War, in Maryland Lincoln jailed not only potential Confederate sympathizers – but also those who questioned the constitutionality of his actions. For writing such an editorial, one Baltimore newspaper editor was jailed without trial in Fort McHenry. This young "political prisoner," as he described himself was Frank Key Howard, the grandson of Francis Scott Key. In 1863, when he wrote a book about this, *Fourteen Months in the American Bastille*, two of the publishers selling the book were arrested.

A century after Francis Scott Key wrote this poem, a distant relative named after him, novelist F. Scott Fitzgerald, would pen one of his most famous novels, *Tender Is The Night*, in Baltimore County.

After the War

Baltimore factories were major suppliers to the Union during the Civil War, but after the war the local economy began to decline. New York City redoubled its power as both the immigrant's preferred destination and America's economic capital.

Immigrants who once came to Baltimore to stay now increasingly saw the city and its burgeoning African-American population as a transit point, a steppingstone to the Ohio River and cities of newer opportunity such as

Cincinnati, Detroit, Chicago and St. Louis to the West via the Baltimore & Ohio Railroad.

One long-term problem was that being close to Washington, D.C. meant being close to Washington, D.C. While other cities worked hard to attract private companies, Baltimore often looked for deals and money to the Federal Government.

As a result, while other cities like Detroit became more self-reliant, Baltimore was slowly becoming a less industrious welfare state with high local taxes and greedy politicians. In 2015 the city will probably get more than 40 percent of its revenues from Washington and from the state capital in Annapolis.

Baltimore remained vibrant, and its population continued to grow, but in the 20th Century the Great Depression hit the city hard. Industrial jobs declined, and were replaced with service jobs that either paid less or required higher skills than factory work.

During World War II Baltimore rose to the challenge and proved it could still be, like Detroit, an arsenal of democracy. Bethlehem Steel churned out Liberty Ships, and another factory manufactured Martin B-26 Marauder bombers.

In 1950, Baltimore reached its population peak of around 950,000 residents, 24 percent of whom were African-Americans. The city efficiently integrated its schools, but this increased white flight moving to the suburbs beyond the reach of city tax collectors. Falling revenue made it harder for Baltimore to deal with problems.

Baltimore had been home to or influenced so many who enriched humankind. Baseball great Babe Ruth was born here. So were filmmakers like Barry Levinson, whose movies "Diner," "Tin Men," "Avalon" and "Liberty Heights" are set in B'More, as are several films of eccentric Baltimorean John Waters, whose movie "Hairspray" begins with the cheery song "Good Morning, Baltimore."

Gothic author Edgar Allen Poe died of a mystery ailment in Baltimore in 1849, at age 40. His poem "The Raven" inspired local football fans to name their NFL team The Ravens, another bird to join their baseball Orioles.

Humans are not the only great athletes who come here. Baltimore is home to Pimlico, where the Preakness Stakes began in 1873 and have been run every third Saturday in May since 1908. This grand "Race for the Black-Eyed Susans" is the second of the three legs in horse racing's Triple Crown.

Baltimore-touched stars range from journalist H.L. Mencken to philosopher John Rawls, Progressive activist Upton Sinclair, singer Billie Holiday, musician Frank Zappa, and hundreds more.

Baltimore still runs, but for decades it has seemed to be running downhill.

One reason is the Progressive political rule that has controlled the city almost without break since the end of World War II.

"Let me offer you my definition of social justice:
I keep what I earn and you keep what you earn.

"Do you disagree? Well then tell me
how much of what I earn 'belongs' to you – and why?"

– Dr. Walter Williams

"The average American family head will be forced
to do twenty years' labor to pay taxes in his or her lifetime."

– James Bovard
Lost Rights

Chapter Two

Baltimerica

"The word 'campaign' is a war term,
so when you go into a campaign
you just prepare for war.
If you think this is an exercise
in civic activity...then you
are going to be surprised."

– Nancy Pelosi
Co-founder, Congressional
Progressive Caucus

In 1948, when Nancy D'Alesandro was eight, her dad Big Tommy, the Mayor of Baltimore and Democratic big boss of its Little Italy neighborhoods, was said to have begun putting her on the telephone with those calling for favors.

We can imagine what Nancy might have said: "You want that building permit for your project? Here's what you need to do for us."

Such machine politics used to dominate and corrupt many American cities. They live on in Baltimore, and have made the city what it is today.

Big Tommy learned his politics by working for the city's Democratic boss Willie Curran. One Curran or another has been on the city council almost without a break for more than 60 years.

Tommy D'Alesandro, however, was ambitious. At age 22, he defied the machine to win a seat in the state assembly, then in Congress, and then was elected Baltimore's mayor. His son and Nancy's brother Little Tommy would later also become mayor.

Another who became Mayor of Baltimore, as well as Governor of Maryland, after he married into the Curran family, is Martin O'Malley.

O'Malley in 2015 became a declared candidate for the Democratic presidential nomination, but by September he was barely a blip in the polls and was accusing the Democratic Party of rigging the process in former Secretary of State Hillary Clinton's favor by scheduling only a few candidate debates.

Progressive O'Malley's class warfare tax on Maryland millionaires caused a quarter of them to leave, costing the state $1.7 Billion in lost revenue.

Another who became Mayor of Baltimore is Stephanie Rawlings-Blake, daughter of the late longtime Democratic boss of the city's black neighborhoods and a powerful state legislator, Howard "Pete" Rawlings, an ally of the D'Alesandro family and O'Malley. Nearly two-thirds of Baltimore residents are now African-Americans, and as many as 9 in 10 vote Democratic in this one-party town.

Rawlings-Blake was, as head of the city council, given the position of Mayor in 2010 when the elected Mayor Sheila Ann Dixon quit amidst allegations that she had "fraudulently misappropriated" gift cards for the city's poor. Mayor Dixon cut a deal with prosecutors that let her keep her $83,000 per year pension.

How Progressive is Mayor Stephanie Rawlings-Blake? As noted in the Introduction, during the summer 2015 riots she told reporters: "…We also gave those who wished to destroy space to do that as well, and we work very hard to keep that balance…"

Mayor Rawlings-Blake had been a rising political star and already held one of the highest positions in the Democratic National Committee. In September 2015, however, she announced that she was cancelling plans to seek re-election as Baltimore Mayor.

Pelosiland

This is the tough Baltimore where Nancy D'Alesandro Pelosi -- the future Speaker of the House of Representatives and co-founder of the Congressional Progressive Caucus when it was openly allied with the organization Democratic Socialists of America – learned to think of politics as mortal combat. She would employ Baltimore political tactics to impose Baltimore Progressive political values nationwide.

As Mayor, Big Tommy D'Alesandro was popular for fixing streets as well as for building schools and parking garages. He had even resurrected the Baltimore Orioles major league baseball team. He was preparing to run for Maryland Governor when circumstances forced him to quit the race. As *Time* Magazine reported on April 26, 1954:

> "A contractor named Dominic Piracci, who seemed to have a corner on the city's garage-building business, was convicted of fraud, conspiracy and conspiracy to obstruct justice. Piracci and Tommy had long been friends, even before Piracci's daughter, Margie, married Tommy D'Alesandro III."

> "Piracci had erased some names from his ledgers. Among the names deleted: Nancy D'Alesandro [Nancy Pelosi's mother]. On the witness stand in Piracci's trial, Nancy admitted getting six checks totaling $11,130.78 from Piracci. But she swore that $1,500 of it was a gift to their newly wed children, Tommy III and Margie. The rest, she claimed, Piracci lent her to pay off debts incurred in her feed business and a venture with a skin softener called Velvex."

A decade later Little Tommy would become mayor like his father. But a riot erupted on April 6, 1968, following the assassination in Tennessee of civil rights leader Dr. Martin Luther King. Over the next few days six people died in the rioting, 700 were injured, 1.200 fires were set, and 1,000 small businesses were damaged, destroyed or looted while Mayor D'Alesandro seemed unable or unwilling to respond.

As would happen in 2015, Maryland's Republican state governor in 1968 stepped in and brought the chaos decisively to a halt. This former Baltimore County Executive was Governor Spiro Agnew.

"I call on you to publicly repudiate all black racists," Agnew told African-American leaders. "This, so far, you have been unwilling to do."

Black leaders were angered by this, even though the Governor had signed Maryland's first open-housing laws and helped repeal its law banning interracial marriage.

With longtime Alabama Governor George Wallace a potential spoiler in the 1968 presidential contest, GOP candidate Richard Nixon named Agnew as his running mate.

Wallace would cut deeply into Democratic standard-bearer Vice President Hubert Humphrey's votes in 1968, but the Governor's campaign was severely hampered after a would-be assassin shot and partly paralyzed the candidate at a shopping mall in Laurel, Maryland.

Agnew in 1973 resigned the Vice Presidency in a plea deal involving more than $100,000 in alleged bribes when he was governor. Welcome to the politics of Maryland.

Shades of Gray

In 2015, as protests swelled over the death of Freddie Gray from a neck injury suffered in a police van, cynics noted that such "Ferguson Effect" mobilization of African-American upset and anger, as happened months earlier in a Missouri town, could be useful to Democrats with a presidential election looming in 2016.

When the *Washington Post* quoted another arrestee in a separate compartment of the prison van saying that he heard Gray hurling himself against the van's walls when it was not in drastic motion, this story was quickly followed by the witness on television saying he heard nothing and knew nothing.

It was not hard to imagine that this now-visibly-nervous witness had been reminded of what happens to "snitches" in the gang-infested sections of Baltimore.

The Progressive mainstream media also downplayed or ignored evidence that Gray was a longtime dealer in heroin and other illicit drugs who had been arrested 17 times.

How sympathetic would America be if the victim in this case turned out to be a *de facto* urban terrorist who for years had been waging chemical warfare by selling such mind-altering, health-destroying dangerous illegal drugs to the children and infantilized adult addicts of Baltimore?

The media downplayed autopsy evidence that Gray had heroin and other illicit drug residue in his body when arrested.

The media also buried hints that Gray may have considered deliberately injuring himself and then accusing police in hopes of getting a big payday in court, as others may have done.

Freddie Gray clearly was a victim – perhaps of the police, but unquestionably of the Progressive Democrats who have ruled Baltimore as a one-party machine-controlled city rife with corruption for several generations. We could almost say that Progressives killed Freddie Gray.

Casting Blame

The mainstream media, of course, share the ideology of those who have governed Baltimore since World War II, and went to great lengths not to blame Progressive policies or corruption for the problems Gray exemplified.

Instead, the media poured out an assortment of other explanations for such problems in Baltimore's African-American neighborhoods.

Republicans were to blame for Freddie Gray's death, the liberal media suggested, for creating harsh criminal prison sentences that removed fathers and other male role models from the community. These men had made women pregnant but not married them in 70 percent of births.

Yet this city for nearly six decades has had a Democrat as mayor, a city council made up only of Democrats, a police department run by Democrats, and a state legislature controlled by Democrats. The state has two Senate seats, both filled by Democrats, plus eight House seats, seven of which are occupied by Democrats. Only four state governors in more than half a century have been Republicans, and only one of those served more than one term, yet the media found a way to imply that Republicans are somehow responsible for Baltimore crime and what happened to Freddie Gray. Amazing.

Baltimore is a city of roughly 620,000 people, more than 63 percent of whom are African-Americans. Baltimoreans account for just over 10 percent of Maryland's state population, but are one-third of state prison inmates.

"An estimated $220 million is spent incarcerating people from just 25 communities in Baltimore each year," according to *Money/CNN*. [5]

Gray, the media reported, may have been a victim of teething as a baby on brain-damaging lead-based paint in the home where he grew up. If his brain was addled, blame the environmental poison of a capitalist product used many decades ago.

Poor Baltimore

Or, America was told, Gray was the victim of inequality and poverty, like many in Baltimore's black neighborhoods where the unemployment rate for men up to age 24 is 37 percent.

The economic disparity can be dramatic if one does not take welfare and other government benefits into account.

Maryland, because it borders Washington, D.C. and the Federal Government's vast influx of tax revenue, has some of America's wealthiest counties where federal employees and lobbyists live.

The state is home to the National Institutes of Health, with their large staff of medical doctors and highly-paid researchers, as well as other important federal government facilities.

Maryland thus has the highest median household income in the United States – $73,538. [6]

In Baltimore itself, however, median household income is $60,550 for whites. It is $33,610 for blacks, less than half the median statewide income. Nearly a quarter (24%) of Baltimore's population – and 35% of its children – live below the poverty line, which is $20,090 per year for a family of three. [7]

The median value of owner-occupied housing units in Maryland is $292,700, but in Baltimore itself is just over half that amount: $157,900. [8]

In 1904, the Great Baltimore Fire destroyed 1,545 buildings across 70 blocks in the heart of the city. The blaze threw 35,000 people out of work. The then-vibrant and optimistic city rebuilt almost entirely within two years.

The Housing Authority of Baltimore City has estimated that in 2015 Baltimore has 16,000 vacant buildings and 14,000 vacant lots. Many were abandoned during or after the city's 1968 race riots and have not been repaired or rebuilt. [9]

Money/CNN reported that "in the blighted neighborhoods of Sandtown-Winchester and Harlem Park, the area where Gray reportedly lived, almost a quarter of buildings were vacant in 2011, according to the city." [10]

Much as happened in Detroit, as we documented in our 2013 book *The Great Withdrawal*, the 1968 racial upheaval was followed by a huge exodus of middle and upper-middle-class black and white residents, as well as many businesses, fleeing to safer suburbs outside the city.

This rapidly shrank Baltimore's population from almost a million to today's 620,000 and sent home prices plummeting in the city. The 2015 riots caused another immediate drop in property values.

As we documented about Detroit, extremely low home prices are attracting some "urban pioneers" to seek home bargains in Baltimore. In Charm City it is now possible to find huge Victorian mansions for the price of a tiny condo in New York City. Local colleges and universities entice student applicants by saying how low the price of housing is in Baltimore...but then add the caveat that it may be unsafe to walk around such housing, day or night.

Such derelict neighborhoods can be hazardous to health in other ways, too.

One comparison of two Baltimore neighborhoods – upper-middle-class Roland Park and lower-class Upton/Druid Heights – found that life expectancy is 83 years in Roland Park, but only 63 years in Upton, where the risk of being murdered is 15 times greater; being infected with HIV/AIDS is 20 times greater; the chances of having diabetes is eight times worse, and heart disease three times worse. [11]

In Baltimore, Progressive policies and politicians can kill you.

How and why did things get this bad?

Baltimore "Fix"

Addiction to welfare money and the dead-end hopeless life such dependency causes might make the step into drug addiction easy.

Baltimore is the heroin capital of the United States. Almost 10 percent of Baltimorons are addicted junkies, many of whom then turn to selling the stuff. Men commit burglaries and other crimes, and many young women sell their bodies, to get their next "fix" of the drug. The cable TV drama "The Wire" was set in the streets of Baltimore, where its creator had been a crime reporter for the *Baltimore Sun* newspaper. The opening of this series gave the city its latest grim nickname: Bodymore, Murdaland.

The sap of opium poppies, from which heroin comes, goes back a long way in Baltimore. Some of its ships were involved in the lucrative opium trade from Turkey to China, where smoking this addictive drug ruined millions of lives and devastated the Chinese economy and culture during the 19th Century. [12]

In 1988 the recently-elected first African-American Mayor of Baltimore, Kurt Schmoke, testified before Congress that he favored legalizing possession of illicit drugs.

"Providing legal access to currently illicit substances carries with it the chance…that the number of people using and abusing drugs will increase," said Schmoke. "But addiction, for all of its attendant medical, social and moral problems, is but one evil associated with drugs. Moreover, the criminalization of narcotics, cocaine and marijuana has not solved the problem of their use." [13]

Schmoke proposed making marijuana legal and, for certified adult addicts, making heroin and cocaine available through doctors.

New York City Mayor Ed Koch disagreed, noting that heroin addiction in Great Britain had doubled after its government tried a similar policy. [14]

Congress rejected Schmoke's proposal, but the Mayor had Baltimore authorities ease up on enforcement of the drug laws.

"Decriminalizing" Crime

Mayor Schmoke was doing what has become almost standard practice nowadays among Progressives. We call it "decriminalizing crime," and President Obama is a master at its use.

Are illegal aliens a problem? Simply stop enforcing the immigration law and they become *de facto* legal. Create "sanctuary cities" where the authorities agree not to enforce nor help federal authorities enforce, such laws and they effectively vanish.

Baltimore, by the way, is a Sanctuary City.

Others such as San Francisco have seen residents murdered by undocumented immigrants, and had numberless Americans die from exposure to diseases such migrants sometimes bring to the U.S. with them.

Or pipedream that you are a Progressive who wants to control people as was done in Aldous Huxley's dystopian novel *Brave New World* by destroying their will with a drug he called "soma." Then you can applaud President Obama's refusal to enforce federal law prohibiting possession or use of pot in Colorado, Washington State and Oregon. These three states have declared the recreational use of marijuana legal and become "sanctuary states" for high-potency cannabis intoxication.

Some other states such as California have reduced the penalty for marijuana use to little more than that of a traffic ticket. California, where whites in 2014 officially became a minority of the population, is also a *de facto* sanctuary state for illegal aliens.

Mayor Schmoke was unable to repeal the drug laws officially, so he in effect decriminalized the drug laws by reducing enforcement. Unfortunately, Mayor Koch proved to be right. Drug addiction skyrocketed in Baltimore, and so did drug-related crime. They have remained high ever since.

We know where that road paved with Progressive good intentions leads: to hell and to serfdom.

Years ago Mayor Rudy Giuliani drastically reduced crime rates in New York City by using, among other things, the theory of broken-window policing. If a store or home has a broken window left unrepaired, would-be thieves can see this as a sign of vulnerability and become more inclined to rob such a place.

Recidivist criminals are almost always predatory. What others offer them as compassion, most hardened criminals see as weakness. New York's current mayor, Progressive Bill de Blasio, wants to stop arresting people for what he sees as petty crime, such as jumping the turnstile to ride the subway without paying. This will eventually raise fares for those who do pay.

Meanwhile, not enforcing the laws encourages young criminals – and other young people who see them getting away with this – to break more laws.

Selectively enforcing the laws our politicians took an oath to uphold creates disrespect for the laws and police.

Maryland State's Attorney Marilyn Mosby has advanced diversion programs to help young drug offenders avoid the lifelong stigma of a criminal conviction. One can see this as wise compassion, or as helping neophyte criminals avoid full responsibility and punishment for their crimes.

Schmoke helped Mosby, now 35, win election as the youngest such government attorney in America.

15 Minutes of Fame

Mosby's position has involved her deeply in the Freddie Gray case after barely 100 days in her new job, but from the outset critics have said that the inexperienced prosecutor seems to be in over her head.

"I have heard your calls for 'No Justice, No Peace,'" she told a crowd of protestors. "However, your peace is sincerely needed as I work to deliver justice on behalf of Freddie Gray."

Critics responded that justice is justice, blindfolded and impartial, and is not to tip the scales to either political side. Did Mosby not understand that the slogan "No Justice, No Peace" was generally regarded as a call for convicting the police charged in this matter?

Mosby and her City Councilman husband Nick then joined pop singer Prince on stage at a weekend concert. While the Mosbys silently assented, Prince then sang his new song "Baltimore" that repeated "No Justice, No Peace" and urged "Let's take all the guns away" – even though guns were not involved in the Gray case. [15]

The artist Andy Warhol said that in the future everyone would have 15 minutes of fame in his or her life.

Mosby's sudden 15 minutes of stardom in the Gray case has included an interview in *Cosmopolitan* Magazine in which she said: "As young people, we need to utilize this moment and make it into a movement to address some of the structural, socioeconomic, and systemic issues that plague our communities all across the country, not just in Baltimore." [16]

This is rather grandiose for someone whose job is to seek simple justice in one case. Mosby's sudden jolt of fame appears to be intoxicating, judgment-impairing, and a stimulant to her personal and political ambitions.

Mosby also did a *Vogue* Magazine interview that included her glamorously posed image by famed celebrity photographer Annie Liebowitz. [17]

The *Vogue* piece prompted Fox host and attorney Greta van Susteren to say "You really lose confidence when you look like you're more interested in yourself than you are in the case."

Mosby rejected demands from the accused police officers' attorneys that she recuse herself because of conflicts of interest. Mosby's husband represents what was Gray's district on Baltimore's City Council. Ms. Mosby took a $5,000 political campaign contribution from the attorney who now represents the Gray family.

On September 9, one day before a judge was to decide whether the officers charged in the Freddie Gray case would be granted a change of venue, Mayor Rawlings-Blake announced that the city had reached a huge $6.4 Million settlement with Gray's family.

Critics noted that it was extremely unusual for any city to announce such a settlement before officers had faced criminal charges in court. Such a settlement, said author and veteran Judge Andrew Napolitano, was tantamount to the city saying the officers were guilty. It also, as the mayor came close to saying, was an attempt to buy off potential violence if the trial were moved out of Baltimore or the officers were acquitted.

According to Judge Napolitano, under Maryland law the most that such a settlement usually can give for the pain and suffering of loved ones in such a case is $950,000. Other legal analysts set this number as low as $400,000.

The rest of the settlement, said Napolitano, must therefore be to compensate for the loss of lifetime income by Freddie Gray. Gray, noted Napolitano, was a drug seller and addict whose legal income was zero and personal worth was zero. The settlement, said the Judge, was far too high.

How much the Gray family's attorney will receive from this settlement has not, as of the time of our writing, been made public. If it is a conventional attorney share of one-third of the money, then famed Baltimore lawyer William H. "Billy" Murphy, Jr. – whose $5,000 was reportedly the single biggest contribution by an individual to case prosecutor Marilyn Mosby's election campaign – might, perhaps at the expense of Baltimore taxpayers, be paid more than $2.133 Million.

This settlement of $6.4 Million is greater than the combined 120 such police-related liability settlements that Baltimore has made since 2011.

Mosby has been accused of "judge shopping" while gathering evidence about the police in this case, as well as withholding evidence from defense lawyers.

Mosby's behavior arguably has made it easier for these police officers to be granted a re-trial if convicted. She also strengthened their case for a change of venue to another city because a fair trial might be impossible in Baltimore after the Mayor's settlement made the officers appear guilty. What Baltimore juror would dare vote to acquit in a city where mobs might react violently against jurors and their families if the officers are not convicted?

In August 2015 a former Baltimore prosecutor, Roya Hanna, charged that Mosby, by going easy on criminals and firing veteran prosecutors, has a role in the city's increase in violence. [18]

Mean Streets

For many who have lived in inner-city Baltimore, violence can become a major influence in their lives.

"Fear ruled everything around me," writes *Atlantic* Magazine national correspondent Ta-Nehisi Coates of his experience growing up the son of a veteran Black Panther leader in the Mondawmin neighborhood of Baltimore during the 1980s crack cocaine epidemic.

Now a Progressive intellectual, Coates in his 2015 book *Between the World and Me* tells his adolescent son that somehow the White American Dream is to blame for the problems of inner-city African-Americans. [19]

"Historians conjured the Dream. Hollywood fortified the Dream," he writes, and because the American Dreamers will not wake up, "We are captured, brother, surrounded by the majoritarian bandits of America. And this has happened here, in our only home, and the terrible truth is that we cannot will ourselves to an escape on our own."

Coates was radicalized through the fatal shooting of a black friend by a policeman. He has struggled to persuade himself that this was caused by white people. However, both the police officer and the elected officials above him were all African-Americans.

Clearly Coates' mind has been captured, but by racist Progressive ideology. His belief is not in an idea but in a cult of radicalism that his self-professed atheist mind may have substituted for religion.

Racism, as Ayn Rand observed, "is the lowest, most crudely primitive form of collectivism." This is why Nazism could so easily combine the evil of racism with collectivist national socialism. They ultimately are the same philosophy, the rejection of the individual for Orwellian groupthink.

The American Dream is freely available to those who see and respect human beings as individuals. Coates needs to free himself from despair, infantile helplessness and excuse-making by throwing off the mental slavery of paternalistic Progressivism.

A good place he could start is by re-reading his own 2009 memoir, *The Beautiful Struggle*, about growing up in Baltimore with his father's support and love.

Welcome home, Ta-Nehisi, to the American Dream.

The Logic of Redistribution

A closing thought for this chapter:

Why did the rioting and looting in "Mob City" Baltimore surprise anyone?

Did no one hear President Barack Obama's first White House Chief of Staff – and now Chicago Mayor – Rahm Emmanuel say that "a crisis is a terrible thing to waste," that it offers opportunities to do things that would not otherwise be available?

When young protestors are manipulated by Progressive radicals into violently attacking the police and setting neighborhoods ablaze, this, not coincidentally, provides a smoke screen for opportunistic gang looters.

When a welfare state empowers and justifies its vote-buying by class warfare – by telling people that the rich are evil exploiters who deserve to be robbed via taxation, confiscation and wealth redistribution to them – why should anyone be surprised when welfare recipients decide to eliminate the politician middlemen and simply rob the rich themselves directly?

Why, such looters logically reason, should they split their "take" from robbing the rich with self-serving, patronizing Progressive politicians?

If robbing the rich is justified, then why let government be the only one to steal their wealth and decide how the loot will be divvied up?

The hate rhetoric of Progressive class warfare has already justified robbing the rich.

Progressives have also said that the wealth taken from the evil rich should be given to those who have little.

The only thing left to decide is whether privateers, as in the days of old Baltimore, are allowed to do the robbing.

The answer from Progressives like Baltimore Mayor Rawlings-Blake, whose police were ordered to "stand down" while looters plundered her city, seems to be that Baltimore is a city where freelance piracy is now welcome.

"Make yourselves sheep
and the wolves will eat you."

– Benjamin Franklin

*"The whole aim of practical politics
is to keep the populace alarmed
(and hence clamorous to be led to safety)
by menacing it with an endless series
of hobgoblins, most of them imaginary."*

– H.L. Mencken
Journalist "Sage of Baltimore"

Part Two

Killing the American Dream

Chapter Three

Two Dreams

*"It was always about
the progressive economic agenda...."*

– Nancy Pelosi
Former Speaker,
House of Representatives

The United States and its success have been built on ideals that we now call the American Dream.

According to our Declaration of Independence, in this American Dream individuals are created equal and have a God-given, not government-given, unalienable right to life, liberty and the pursuit of happiness.

In concrete terms, this means that the law is supposed to treat all of us equally, not tax or punish some one way and some another. It means that Americans of ordinary birth could by their own hard work acquire and own property. This especially meant a home that, as English Law held, was your own castle with property rights even the king was bound to respect.
The American Dream means that an individual can rise as high and become as rich as his or her ability and effort can achieve.

No requirement of aristocratic birth prevents the child of any American citizen from becoming President or the head of some great enterprise. In practice, this promise of social mobility has become manifest as each generation did better than its parents. A prime example of this was going to college, something that in Europe centuries ago was a privilege largely reserved for the children of the rich and powerful.

In the American Dream, accomplishment is supposed to come by hard and smart work, not as the gift of political privilege or the king's redistribution to his favorites of what others have earned.

The American Dream assumes that you will be able to keep what you earn, spend part of your life in retirement enjoying the fruits of your labor, and have the right to pass on your property and savings to your children or others of your choosing without government confiscating it.

The American Dream is that your life belongs to you, to do with as you wish. You will succeed or fail based on effort and merit, and almost always this means on how well you serve others by selling products, services or ideas they wish to buy.

The Progressive Dream

Around 1800 in Europe the rational philosophy of the Enlightenment was giving way to the emotional ideals of the Romantic Age. The American Revolution in the cause of individual liberty had replaced a king with a democratic republic, fortunately electing exceptional leaders such as George Washington and Thomas Jefferson.

The French Revolution then made its emotional appeal to equality and fraternity, and soon the mobs of Paris were cutting off the heads of both aristocrats and dissenters. Order would be restored by the nationalistic dictatorship of a charismatic military genius, Napoleon Bonaparte, whose attempt to conquer Europe caused social upheaval.

Out of this continental chaos a new radical utopian dream emerged that today in the United States we call Progressivism.

In this ideology, the old religious order was to be replaced by communion with pagan or pantheistic nature and its sublimity. And nature was to be understood through the new priesthood of science, which if given unlimited government power could solve all problems.

The American Dream was based on freedom of the individual. This new Progressive Dream was based instead on collectivism, on seeing people only as members of groups such as nations or races.

The American Dream was based on you choosing what to do with your life.

In the new Progressive Dream, individuals were "equal" but were also mere cogs born to live or die to serve the group interests of the collective, which in practice usually meant the state.

The state embodied the collective, the cultic new substitute for God to which mere individuals could be sacrificed. As Ayn Rand noted in *Capitalism: The Unknown Ideal*, "the smallest minority on earth is the individual. Those who deny individual rights cannot claim to be defenders of minorities."

In Europe, the Progressive philosophy metastasized into Communism, Nazism, Fascism and today's socialist welfare states.

In the United States, this collectivist ideology metastasized into Progressivism.

Some confuse Progressivism with liberalism, but genuine liberalism believes in individual liberty, small decentralized government and free market capitalism. A 19th Century liberal is essentially what today we would call a Jeffersonian or Libertarian.

(And because American conservatives are conserving the revolutionary ideals of 1776, they are also in many ways Jeffersonians….unlike European Tory conservatives, many of whom dislike the dynamism and constant change of free market capitalism.)

Nanny Nancy Statism

Even the most benign Progressives have an elitist tendency to want the state to impose their values on everybody else.

One of the first Progressives may have been the Greek philosopher Plato, who 2,400 years ago wrote of an imaginary utopia in his book *The Republic*. This society would be run by an elite of the smartest, most highly-educated people, whom he called "philosopher kings."

These kings would decide what was best for all, and everyone would obey their orders. This society, that today we would call totalitarian, controlled how everyone lived in even the tiniest matters – such as what music people were permitted to listen to.

Sound crazy? Think of Michael Bloomberg, who when he was Mayor of New York City used the power of the government to control how large a glass of soda pop customers were permitted to order.

Or remember First Lady Michelle Obama telling school cafeterias across America what they could, and could not, serve to students for lunch. Yes, telling kids to eat apples might be good advice, but more than 80 percent of those apples were thrown uneaten into trash bins.

What such Progressives believe in every such case is that:

1. They are imposing their values for your, and society's, own good; and

2. They are far smarter, a superior ruling elite, and you are too stupid to know, or be permitted to decide, what is best for you or for the collective.

Almost all of today's Progressives exhibit similar clinical symptoms of arrogant, control-freak megalomania.

They generally accept the Darwinian assumption that humans are just one of many species of animals in a natural environment where no God exists, that we are merely the result of billions of years of evolution.

Many Progressives, including politicians who in public pretend to be religious, regard those who believe in God as inferior and lacking in intelligence. Progressives routinely accuse religious believers of "imposing their morality on others."

Progressives and other leftists, however, hypocritically never hesitate to impose *their* morality on others via laws, regulations, and government redistribution of wealth taxed away from those they envy or look down on, and transferred to those whom Progressives favor.

Progressive Priesthood

Progressives embrace science, perhaps because its white-robed practitioners are the closest things that today's usually-atheist collectivists have to a religious priesthood possessing deep knowledge and authority.

Progressives believe that if Science and State are given limitless power, they can create a new Eden and a perfect human species free from greed, want and war.

In this human-made paradise the only God will be Humankind. The genetically-modified vegan lion will lie down with the genetically-modified fearless lamb, and re-tribalized Age of Aquarius hippies will beat their swords into iPhones.

To bring about their vision of the future, Progressives have no compunction about sacrificing us as expendable pawns in their coercive, secular-humanist social engineering.

Because only the collective matters to them, Progressives have been willing to sacrifice more than 120 million individual human beings to advance the cause of totalitarianism during the last 100 years.

In the United States, Progressives, eager to perfect the human race via science, embraced eugenics, the idea that we should breed humans as we do race horses and other animals to amplify their "best" traits and weed out what Progressives saw as defects.

The Naked Face of Progressivism

President Woodrow Wilson, who earned his Ph.D. at a Baltimore university, supported the eugenics movement, later discredited because Germany's Nazis based their racist theories and genocidal mass murder on it.

Yet eugenics was a fashionable Progressive cause in 1907 when Woodrow Wilson "campaigned in Indiana for the compulsory sterilization of criminals and the mentally retarded," recounts historian Paul Rahe, "and in 1911, while governor of New Jersey, he proudly signed into law just such a bill." [20]

Margaret Sanger was co-founder of Planned Parenthood, which thanks to Leftist lawmakers has received billions in taxpayer funding and for decades has been America's largest abortion services provider.

Sanger was one of the most outspoken Progressive leaders of the eugenics cause. The Public Broadcasting System reported that Sanger in 1920 said that "birth control is nothing more or less than the facilitation of the process of weeding out the unfit [and] of preventing the birth of defectives." [21]

Sanger, embraced as a heroine by today's Progressive feminists, believed that she and other eugenicists had a shared mission to "assist the race toward the elimination of the unfit." [22]

In her book *The Pivot of Civilization*, Sanger called for coercion to prevent the "undeniably feeble-minded" from having children. [23]

Who did she have in mind? Judging by her proud speech before the Ku Klux Klan, one group she wished to expunge was African-Americans.

Since the 1973 Roe v. Wade Supreme Court ruling that legalized it, an estimated 57 million abortions have happened in America. Planned Parenthood has located 70 percent of its clinics in predominantly African-American inner cities such as Baltimore's.

African-Americans comprise approximately 12.5 percent of America's population, but 25 percent of abortions since Roe v. Wade – more than 14 million human beings, more than double the number of Jews murdered in the Holocaust -- have been African-American babies.

We are horrified at expert evidence that at least 4,000 to 6,100 African-Americans were lynched by the Ku Klux Klan and other Progressive racists in what scholars have called an "African-American Holocaust" during the 85 years of Jim Crow and the segregated Democratic Party-controlled South following the Civil War.

If these numbers are correct, then since Roe v. Wade legalized it, the 14 million black babies aborted amount to between 2,300 and 3,500 unborn black babies killed for *each one* of these lynchings.

From video by reporters using hidden cameras, America in 2015 saw evidence that Planned Parenthood was selling the body parts of aborted babies. In order to sell intact baby body parts for maximum profit, this organization subjected many of these unborn babies to crushing techniques that caused agonizing pain at least as terrible as that suffered by the victims of lynchings.

Why have the Progressive media not reported this horror, committed by their ideological comrades, to the African-American community and all other Americans?

This "disparate impact" of African-Americans being aborted at double their proportion of the population strongly suggests that Progressives have targeted black Americans for population reduction in a modern genocide, just one more elitist Progressive act of "social engineering."

Why would Progressives want to reduce a population that overwhelmingly votes with them ideologically? That same question arose when Democrats changed from being a party of mostly white voters to one whose typical voter is a person of color. (The last Democratic presidential candidate to win a majority of white male voters was Texan incumbent Lyndon Baines Johnson in 1964.)

Could it be that the Democratic Party's behind-the-scenes bosses and billionaire funders are shifting their allegiance from African-Americans to Latinos? The Obama Administration has been an economic nightmare for millions of black Americans, in part by allowing in a flood of millions of low-wage immigrants from Latin America. Mr. Obama then gave these newcomers work permits to compete against African-Americans at the low end of the job ladder, a treacherous stab-in-the-back to loyal blacks who elected him.

Democratic politicians such as Hillary Clinton and President Obama, who have received large Planned Parenthood contributions that doubtless came in part from the ghoulish profits of selling baby body parts, have refused to condemn or defund this taxpayer-enriched entity.

Both have said that women should have the same rights to an abortion that they have in Progressive Europe. European welfare states permit abortion, but in almost all cases only during the first trimester after conception; most seldom allow the abortion of a seven-pound baby only days from natural birth, as today's American Progressives have made legal here.

With regard to abortion, said Ronald Reagan, "there's one individual not being considered at all. That's the one who is being aborted. And I've noticed that everybody that is for abortion has already been born."

"Three Generations of Imbeciles Are Enough"

Progressives continue to lionize their ideological comrade Supreme Court Justice Oliver Wendell Holmes.

In his 2006 book *How Progressives Rewrote the Constitution*, New York University Law Professor Richard A. Epstein wrote:

"Holmes had some sympathy for the great Progressive cause of eugenics; his notorious decision in *Buck v. Bell* [1927] declared that '[t]hree generations of imbeciles are enough,' and thus allowed the state to railroad a helpless woman of normal intelligence and poor background into forced sterilization." [24]

Progressive Justice Holmes elsewhere wrote: "It is better for all the world, if instead of waiting to execute degenerate offspring for crime, or to let them starve for their imbecility, society can prevent those who are manifestly unfit from continuing their kind." [25]

Genetically Engineering Humankind

Surely today's Progressives could not so arrogantly play God, could they? Yes, they could, even in President Barack Obama's White House. Mr. Obama's Science & Technology Advisor is John P. Holdren, an appointment heralded by the liberal media as proof that the new President's views were far advanced beyond those of troglodyte Republicans.

Holdren in the 1977 book *Ecoscience,* which he co-authored with Paul and Anne Ehrlich, raised the possibility of controlling population size by "Adding a sterilant to drinking water or staple foods" or by "Involuntary fertility control....A program of sterilizing women after their second or third child."

Under President Obama, this is the mind shaping and controlling America's science and technology policies. [26]

Holdren's co-author Paul Ehrlich became famous as author of *The Population Bomb,* which predicted that global overpopulation would cause mass famines and world wars late in the 20th Century. Like almost all Progressive doomsaying, his prediction proved false.

Ehrlich in subsequent speeches discussed the use of such a sterilant in food and water supplies, with government in control of the only antidote. Ehrlich proposed that those wanting children could enter a government lottery to win a dose of antidote, so that no political favoritism would be involved.

Given the megalomaniacal lust for power that tempts Progressives to sterilize the rest of us in the first place, however, imagine a future dictatorship whose citizenry is thus sterilized. This would be a dream come true for such racist Progressives. Genocide would for them be as easy as the government deciding which Aryans would receive the antidote, and whose DNA would be weeded out of the gene pool by refusing them the reproductive antidote.

Even without such a sterilant, Charles Darwin could tell you that when a Progressive government politicizes everything, giving subsidies and other benefits to certain groups while heavily taxing others, this also creates an evolutionary tilt that re-engineers humankind. It increases the success and survival prospects of some, while reducing these chances for others. This is what, in small scale, was happening when tax breaks were given to Progressive political groups and were denied to conservative groups.

Progressives Take Power

We raise these facts not to preach, but to show that the arrogance and power-madness of Progressives know no bounds.

How did such people ever come to power?

In the years leading up to 1913, America was undergoing a huge transformation that changed both of our major political parties, our government, our economy and our society.

Thirty-two million of America's 92 million people, according to the 1910 Census, lived and worked on farms. Their way of life was being replaced by agricultural machines so rapidly that within a century America would be producing four times more food than we consume with only two percent of Americans farming. Fifty-four percent of Americans lived in communities of 1,000 or fewer people.

People from rural farms and foreign lands were flocking in pursuit of happiness to factory towns and big cities. Most found jobs and a rising standard of living, yet they also found cities run by corrupt political machines, and industries owned by the corporations and trusts of the wealthy and powerful.

The spirit of the age was "progress" and change. Scientists and inventors were remaking the world with electric light, gasoline-powered vehicles, radio communications, phonographs and flying machines.

In this era of upheaval, from turbulent pre-revolutionary Russia to rural America, many well-intentioned people began asking if government and society could be improved. Many wondered if the old ruling elites should remain in control of this new world.

"Progressivism" became the umbrella label that brought together populists suspicious of private or public concentrated power and wealth, a variety of social reformers, and recent immigrants, some of whom came to America bringing European socialist ideas of class warfare and expropriating the rich.

Bull Moose Mess

In 1912 former Progressive Republican President Teddy Roosevelt, after being denied his party's nomination, sought re-election to the White House on his own Progressive Party ticket. No one had persuaded him to sign a Donald Trump-like pledge to support the Republican nominee.

Roosevelt's "Bull Moose Party" platform advocated women's suffrage (unlike either of his rivals, Progressive Democrat Woodrow Wilson and Republican incumbent William Howard Taft). It also called for a National Health Service; social insurance for the disabled, elderly and unemployed; an eight-hour workday; an inheritance tax; and a constitutional amendment permitting an income tax, among many other things.

Above all, Roosevelt's Progressivism centered on his "New Nationalism" – his ideal of a paternalistic, muscular central government to regulate businesses, create great national projects such as the Panama Canal and national parks, extend American values to other lands, and protect working people and the middle class.

"To destroy this invisible Government, to dissolve the unholy alliance between corrupt business and corrupt politics is the first task of the statesmanship of the day," declared Roosevelt's 1912 platform.

Power-loving Progressivism

Democratic Progressive Woodrow Wilson won the presidency with 42 percent of the national vote. Roosevelt split the Republican vote, winning 27 percent of the popular vote to his one-time friend President Taft's 23 percent. Socialist Party candidate Eugene V. Debs won 6 percent.

The following year, 1913, President Wilson began a fundamental transformation of America by signing an income tax law made constitutional by the new 16th Amendment. He also signed the act creating the Federal Reserve System, the quasi-private entity that has grown to control America's banking institutions, money supply, economy and more in fulfillment of an evolving Progressive ideology.

He also signed a new 17th Amendment that undid the Framers' requirement that U.S. Senators be elected by state legislatures, which made Senators representatives of states' rights and prerogatives. The new Constitutional amendment required direct popular election of Senators, which turned them into glorified Congressmen with longer terms and whole states as their districts. This meant that Senators were no longer elected by lawmakers of their entire states and could win merely by campaigning in one or two of their state's biggest cities.

Wilson signed into law the Clayton Antitrust Act to regulate corporations and trusts, and the Federal Trade Commission Act giving government far-ranging powers to intervene in business.

Most remember Woodrow Wilson, who earned his doctoral degree in Baltimore and became President of Princeton University, as America's only professional intellectual President.

Most also remember that Wilson took the United States into World War I only months after being re-elected in November 1916 on the slogan "He Kept Us Out of War." Wilson would use the involuntary servitude of conscription to impress soldiers for this European war, where one Allied European official boasted that his country was "prepared to fight to the last American."

After that war, Wilson and his "Fourteen Points" helped establish the League of Nations, forerunner of today's United Nations; the U.S. Congress, unwilling to relinquish a measure of America's sovereignty to the international body, refused to ratify Wilson's agreement to join the League.

Klan Fan

Wilson was fashionably Progressive, pro-organized labor and anti-Big Business. Yet his smug Progressivism was also eager to impose his eccentric morals on others.

Wilson cracked down on the free speech of those who opposed his entry into the war. Recreating his own version of the Alien and Sedition Acts that Thomas Jefferson had abolished, Wilson unleashed his Attorney General A. Mitchell Palmer, who rounded up 10,000 reds and other radicals and deported many of them.

Wilson, born in Virginia and raised in Georgia, was the first Southerner to be President since 1869. His father was a slave owner and Confederate chaplain. One of Wilson's earliest boyhood memories was of standing next to Robert E. Lee and looking up at the Confederate general's face.

As a Progressive president, Wilson re-segregated the federal civil service that Republicans had racially integrated. African-American federal employees were required to eat in segregated dining rooms and use "Blacks Only" bathrooms.

Wilson also enthusiastically praised and encouraged Americans to see the D.W. Griffith movie "Birth of a Nation," which was openly pro-Ku Klux Klan.

This made perfect sense because the Democratic Party had always used racial polarization to win power; it was the party of the slave owners, the Klan, Jim Crow and Bull Connor.

In places such as Baltimore, the Democratic Party would eventually switch which race it favored – but has never changed the polarizing, divide-and-conquer appeal to racism that has always been its political bread and butter.

As Democratic President Lyndon Johnson of Texas reportedly said after passing civil rights and welfare laws in the mid-1960s, "Those Ni**ers will vote for us for the next 200 years!"

This seemed odd, since a higher percentage of Republicans than Democrats in Congress had voted to pass these laws.

What is amazing is that those who have historically been the Democratic Party's most abused victims, from slave times to modern abortions, are today its most loyal voters.

Bipartisan Progressives

In 1924 a second Progressive Party emerged, centered on another Republican, Robert LaFollette, the energetic reformist Senator of Wisconsin.

Where Teddy Roosevelt wanted to regulate giant corporations, "Fighting Bob" LaFollette hated them and sought to stamp them out. He had also been an outspoken critic of America's involvement in World War I.

This second wave of Progressivism came after the Russian Revolution. Many Progressives felt energized by the revolutionary idea that old social orders, including capitalism, could be swept aside and replaced with something that claimed to be better. Most would later become deeply disillusioned as they recognized the real nature of the Soviet Union.

Where Teddy Roosevelt's Progressive Party was largely made up of White Anglo-Saxon Protestant (WASP) social reformers and was critical of those who considered themselves "hyphenated Americans," LaFollette's Progressive Party was much more oriented to blue-collar organized labor, and to racial and ethnic minorities as well as recent immigrant groups who very much still thought of themselves as hyphenated.

Part of LaFollette's vision of something better was a future that put academic social planners in control. To this end, he encouraged the University of Wisconsin-Madison to play a significant role advising the state government.

In the 1924 campaign, the charismatic, emotional LaFollette was endorsed by the American Federation of Labor (AFL) and the Socialist Party of America.

He got 17 percent of the popular vote nationwide, yet won only the 13 Electoral Votes of Wisconsin, where his sons would later create a small dynasty of state officeholders. LaFollette finished second in 11 Western states. After this election his Progressive Party was finished and disbanded.

Third Wave Progressives

Following World War II, in 1948 a third Progressive Party arose to challenge President Harry Truman. This party's standard-bearer was Henry Wallace, who had been FDR's Vice President before Truman.

Less than six months after FDR replaced Wallace with Truman, President Roosevelt died. Truman became President.

Henry Wallace was by most accounts not a Communist, yet he demonstrated affection and admiration for Josef Stalin's Soviet Union, which had been America's ally during World War II. For four years, this Soviet sympathizer was a heartbeat away from becoming President while FDR's health was in steep decline.

The 1948 Progressive Party, however, by most accounts was heavily infiltrated and influenced by Communist Party apparatchiks and ideologues. Socialist Norman Thomas and several other prominent leftists resigned from the party over what they called undue Communist influence on Wallace.

Nearly every page of the 1948 Progressive Party Platform blames the United States for the dawning Cold War, and urges friendly relations with the Soviet Union, whose army was then occupying Eastern Europe and setting up puppet regimes.

The problems in America, this 1948 platform said, were caused by "Big Business control of our economy and government.... Today that private power has constituted itself an invisible government which pulls the strings of its puppet Republican and Democratic parties."

These "old parties," the Progressive Platform said, "refuse to negotiate a settlement of differences with the Soviet Union.... They use the Marshall Plan to rebuild Nazi Germany as a war base and to subjugate the economies of other European countries to American Big Business.... They move to outlaw the Communist Party as a decisive step in their assault on the democratic rights of labor, of national, racial, and political minorities, and of all those who oppose their drive to war.... We denounce anti-Soviet hysteria as a mask for monopoly, militarism, and reaction...."

The 1948 Progressive Party platform goes on like this for more than 30 pages, calling for the government to seize ownership of the means of production from private corporations, denouncing all anti-Communist investigations by Congress, and so forth.

In the presidential election, Henry Wallace won 2.4 percent of the popular vote and zero Electoral Votes. Dixiecrat Strom Thurmond also won 2.4 percent of the national vote, but he carried South Carolina, Alabama, Mississippi and Louisiana plus one electoral voter in Tennessee for a total of 39 Electoral Votes.

The *Chicago Daily Tribune* ran its famous "Dewey Defeats Truman" headline claiming that Progressive Republican New York Governor Thomas Dewey and his running mate Progressive California Governor Earl Warren had won.

This headline was mistaken for several reasons. It was based on polling done by telephone in an era when only the successful could afford telephones. Incumbent Democratic President Harry Truman, who as a young man had been a member of the Ku Klux Klan in Missouri, won re-election with 49.6 percent of the vote.

(A dirty little secret of polling is that today younger voters are sometimes undercounted if they use only cell phones, and working Americans are sometimes undercounted because many are too busy, or refuse, to talk to callers who claim to be pollsters.)

Today's Progressives

Many of today's Fourth Wave Progressives developed their political ideas from the anti-Vietnam War, Civil Rights and New Left movements of the

1960s and 1970s. Their views resonate with the Social Democratic political parties of Europe, which describe themselves as democratic socialist in ideology.

The 76 members of the Congressional Progressive Caucus are almost all Democrats. In past years this caucus openly embraced the group Democratic Socialists of America (DSA), of which labor leaders such as recent AFL-CIO President John Sweeney were proud card-carrying members.

Beginning with President Ronald Reagan's run for re-election in 1984, the Communist Party USA has ceased running its own candidates and directed its followers to cast their vote for the Democratic Party candidate. The CPUSA does this to avoid splitting the coalition of the political left. The Democratic Party certainly does not seek CPUSA support, nor does such support suggest in any way that Democratic candidates share Communist views.

This might mean, however, that America's Communist Party is either terrified of the Republican Party since Ronald Reagan, or that today's Progressive-dominated Democratic Party has shifted far enough to the left that Communists find its policies at least minimally tolerable.

In 2007 then-Senator Hillary Clinton during a presidential debate was asked if she described herself as a liberal. "No," replied Ms. Clinton, "I consider myself a proud modern American progressive, and I think that's the kind of philosophy and practice that we need to bring back to American politics."

"Progressive" has again become a fashionable designer label to wear among Democrats nowadays, in part because it is remarkably vague.

Judging by its three previous waves of evolution, the label called Progressive suggests that its wearer's thinking might be at least one part Progress, one part anti-Big Business populism, one part democratic socialism, one part class warfare, one part smug Nanny Statist "We Know Best" do-good-ism, one dollop of Goo-Goo ("Good Government") earnestness, and one small part old-fashioned liberalism.

Democrat or Socialist?

In 2015 two of the most popular Democrats on the 2016 presidential campaign trail have been former Secretary of State Hillary Clinton and independent Vermont Senator Bernie Sanders, a self-described socialist who favors imposing a 90 percent income tax rate on the rich and a 65 percent tax on their estates.

This inspired two Progressive journalists to ask the chair of the Democratic National Committee, Rep. Debbie Wasserman Schultz of Florida, what the difference was between a Democrat and a Socialist. In both cases, Schultz ducked giving any answer to the question.

So who are today's Progressives, and what do they believe? The chief political values of traditional Americans have always been liberty, rugged individualism, and taking responsibility for one's own life, family and values.

The foremost ideological values of Progressives in some ways seem to come more from the French Revolution than the American Revolution.

Progressives primarily desire equality and fraternity, i.e., a belief that the collective, the group however defined at any given moment, matters more than the individual.

In a Progressive world, everyone is equally special – which means that nobody is special. Exceptional qualities, ideas and achievements are weeds in the Progressive garden of Egalitarian Eden, where individuality is to be torn out by the roots and removed.

By equality, Progressives a century ago and today do not primarily mean equal treatment and rights under the law. They seek to use government power to end the inequality of rich and poor, man and woman, gay and straight, black and white, and much more.

Yet, paradoxically, Progressives have always been eager to use government to treat people unequally in order to impose their egalitarianism. They are delighted to confiscate wealth from the successful so government, which itself makes nothing (except war), can redistribute other peoples' money.

If the rich tomorrow were to create a fund to provide the poor with free food, housing, health care, and every other basic human necessity, would this satisfy Progressives? No. Equality can only be achieved by tearing the rich down because no one (except the ruling elite) should be permitted to stand taller than anyone else. Off with their heads!

Progressives likewise fight racism by using reverse racism – laws and government policies that discriminate in favor of members of one race over others in matters of preferential college admissions, hiring quotas and other opportunities.

To achieve egalitarian "leveling" of society, Progressives have always been eager to make government heavier and heavier in order to hammer down whatever individualistic nails stand out from the masses.

To fight business "monopolies," for example, Teddy Roosevelt and Wood-row Wilson were happy to expand the power of the biggest monopoly of all, the government.

Progressives claim to support the ideal that all people are equal. However, at the same time Progressives regard themselves as morally and mentally superior to those who hold different values. And in many instances, Progressives prefer to silence rather than debate those who disagree with them.

[The natural reality, of course, is that people are not equal in talent, beauty and other factors. We are waiting for the government to make us the quarterbacks of two NFL teams, and to make Hollywood hire us to star in two major motion pictures. This makes as much sense as the ways Progressives now enforce their notions of equality.]

As we have learned during the past 100 years, were it not for their double standards, Progressives would have no standards at all.

Donkey Drag

If you were an investor, how much of your capital – the lifeblood of capitalism – would you put at risk in a society where one of the two ruling political parties buys its votes by promising to confiscate ever more of what you have?

Never let Progressives tell you they do not believe in "capital" punishment. The divide-and-conquer politics of envy, hatred, plunder and redistribution are their bread and butter.

So long as such a political party has a credible chance to gain more government power in every next election, its mere existence acts as a huge deterrent to investment in businesses and jobs.

We have called this effect "Donkey Drag" in honor of the jackass symbol of America's keep-making-government-bigger party.

Since their President Franklin Delano Roosevelt, this party's successful motto has been "Tax and tax, spend and spend, elect and elect."

We estimate that just the fact that such an anti-business, anti-wealth party exists has become enough of a risk to reduce America's private sector investment, growth, jobs and paychecks each year by at least 25 percent.

This is the harm the Bigger Government Party does, even when it loses, simply by being a huge risk that companies, investors and entrepreneurs know they must hedge against.

When this party actually holds power, as it does in the White House of Progressive President Barack Obama, the damage Donkey Drag does to the American economy and working people becomes many times greater than this.

If anti-establishment early candidates fall away, voters by election time 2016 may find themselves stuck again with the usual unappetizing choice between the Stupid Party and the Evil Party.

The Progressive mainstream media will never tell them how prosperous America might have become if Donkey Drag did not constantly hang over our economy and society like a threatening, ever-enlarging storm cloud.

Do Progressives feel guilty about dragging down the economy, harming the poor, and depriving people of jobs, joy and opportunity? Of course not.

Many see this in Darwinian terms. Whatever they do that makes it harder for capitalism to succeed also makes it more likely to fail. If capitalism fails and the economy weakens, then more people will turn for help to the government.

Many Progressives see high taxes and burdensome regulation in the same way. The more things they can do to impede capitalism's success or push it towards the brink of failure, the happier they appear to be.

The Beehive

In 1912 Woodrow Wilson, a founding father of today's Progressive State, delivered a speech titled "What Is Progress?" that reveals much about the mindset and values of his ideological comrades. [27]

He described how inside the "house" of America he and other Progressives were fashioning a new and superior structure that would replace it.

"[A] generation or two from now," said Wilson, "the scaffolding will be taken away, and there will be the family in a great building whose noble architecture will at last be disclosed, where men can live as a single community, co-operative as in a perfected, coordinated beehive...."

Yes, a beehive, the perfect embodiment of a collectivist society. We admire bees for their industriousness. However, in nature the hive is a place where almost all the workers are nominally female, yet only the Queen Bee has offspring. Perhaps Plato would call her the "Philosopher Queen."

It is a place with almost no males except a few drones, whose job is to mate with the Queen once during her courting flight. Thereafter, these drones are prevented from re-entering the hive and, deprived of honey, quickly die.

Bees have been around since the time of the dinosaurs, scientists tell us. Their society is durable.

The bee, however, has scarcely changed during all that time. Most bees are collectivist species that make no progress, as we use the term.

They are thus a fitting symbol for back-to-feudal-serfdom reactionary "Progressives" such as Woodrow Wilson and Barack Obama.

Four Battlefields

A war is underway between the American Dream and the Progressive Dream, and places like Baltimore are battlefields in this war, as noted in this book's Introduction.

Our next four chapters look at other battlefields where Progressives are attacking, undermining and debasing key pillars of the American Dream.

Implicit in Woodrow Wilson's story of the beehive is a deep reality:

Progressives hate the U.S. Constitution and want it replaced.

Why? Because America's Framers wanted government to remain small, so they deliberately wrote a Constitution with checks and balances that make it hard to expand government.

The "new and superior structure" Wilson and other Progressives dream of would be a new Constitution with no limits whatsoever on government's size and power.

After all, Progressives believe, if you have a superior elite of philosopher kings in power, why tie their hands? Why limit in any way their power to make our nation and world better?

Judge for yourself whether Progressive changes are deliberately undermining these four cornerstones of the American Dream.

"Liberalism is just
Communism sold by the drink."

– P.J. O'Rourke
Educated in Baltimore

Chapter Four

Dream Home

*"Our Constitution places
the ownership of private property
at the very heart of our system of liberty."*

– Barack Obama
The Audacity of Hope [28]

*"The theory of the Communists
may be summed up in the single sentence:
Abolish all private property."*

– Karl Marx & Friedrich Engels
The Communist Manifesto (1848)

In June 2015, millions of Americans were shocked to learn of President Barack Obama's latest plan to "fundamentally transform" America. He proposed a far-ranging new rule, "Affirmatively Furthering Fair Housing" (AFFH).

This new rule, writes investigative reporter Stanley Kurtz, "would override local zoning authority and expand federal control over where and how Americans live." [29]

Cities and towns targeted under AFFH could, at least initially, refuse to comply with demands from Washington that they provide far more integration of poor and minority people. Those that resist, however, will find that tax dollars they send to Washington that used to return as federal assistance and grants suddenly no longer come back home. [30]

If these communities continue their noncompliance with federal dictates, bad things will happen. A swarm of other bureaucrats, radical activists, demonstrators, and lawyers – governmental and non-governmental – will arrive to harass the local government. If they still refuse to bend their knees to Washington, then via lawsuits and media attention that destroy the local business climate, the city or town will be bankrupted into submission.

Submission, however, might cause a plunge in local property values, huge changes in the traditional culture of communities, and even a tipping of voting (and hence officeholders) from Republicans and conservatives to Democrats.

Mr. Obama's aim appears to be a redistribution not only of property and wealth, but also of political power.

Progressive Social Engineering

Those who read our 2014 book *Don't Bank On It! The Unsafe World of 21st Century Banking* [31] know precisely what President Obama is doing. Progressives for more than a century have been paving an anti-capitalist path to move America away from the U.S. Constitution.

In 2014, Mr. Obama took Progressive social engineering to troubling new levels with this Housing and Urban Development (HUD) effort to enforce AFFH.

"The Orwellian-sounding regulation...would force some 1,200 municipalities to redraw zoning maps to racially diversify suburban neighborhoods," wrote *Investor's Business Daily* in June 2014.

"Under the scheme, HUD plans to map every U.S. neighborhood by race and publish 'geospatial data' pinpointing racial imbalances," writes *IBD*. "Areas deemed overly segregated will be forced to change their zoning laws to allow construction of subsidized and other affordable housing to bring more low-income minorities into 'white suburbs.'"

"The crusade has already started in New York's Westchester County, where HUD is withholding millions of dollars in community development block grants until the area relaxes zoning rules and builds 750 affordable housing units," says *IBD*. "Aurora, Ill., is under order to build 100 such units. Suburban counties in California, Texas and Iowa are under similar HUD order. And they're just the tip of the iceberg." [32]

Ritzy Westchester County, of course, is where Hillary and Bill Clinton own a multimillion-dollar home in Chappaqua. [33] This Obama measure appears timed to make Republicans who oppose it look like friends of the rich and foes of poor minorities going into the 2016 elections. Whether and how to impose such property manipulation will be left to Mr. Obama's successor, either a Republican or perhaps America's second President Clinton.

We recommend that Mrs. Clinton during the 2016 presidential campaign demonstrate the sincerity of her Progressivism by giving her Chappaqua mansion, with no strings attached, to the poor and minorities. Progressives are usually eager to give away other people's wealth and property – but almost never their own.

This has zero to do with housing discrimination, which has been illegal since 1968. As *Investor's Business Daily* noted: "This is about redistribution of resources. It's also about political redistricting, a backdoor attempt by Democrats to gerrymander voting districts." [34]

Progressives, we must never forget, hate the suburbs. America has long been divided into two political values – pro-city like Alexander Hamilton, who saw cities as dynamic productive places, or pro-country-side and anti-city like Thomas Jefferson, who saw cities as places of corruption and immorality.

In America today the biggest cities mostly have Democratic mayors who stay in power by buying support with the goodies of a welfare state. Big cities tend to impose high taxes on local businesses and successful residents.

As we explained, the Progressive impulse to think of themselves as the lords of all the land, of all property, goes back to at least Karl Marx and Friedrich Engels in the *Communist Manifesto*. Again, the collectivist, elitist nanny statism that became Progressivism in the U.S. metastasized in Europe into socialism, Marxism, Stalinism, fascism, Nazism and today's welfare-state "democratic" socialism, also known as economic or social democracy.

In recent decades, this anti-American alien ideology has hijacked the once-great, once-freedom-loving Democratic Party. As we wrote:

> *Like so much that now threatens and bedevils the United States, the seeds of today's Great Recession were planted by President Jimmy Carter. Mr. Carter won the presidency in 1976 because the political and gold-abandoning economic problems caused by President Richard Nixon weakened his successor Gerald Ford.*

CRAshing The American Dream

In 1977 Mr. Carter signed into law the Community Reinvestment Act (CRA), which would weaken banks and ultimately lead to the housing value meltdown and economic near-collapse of 2008.

President Jimmy Carter signed this law that gave government the means to strong-arm banks into making billions of dollars of loans to un-creditworthy individuals who were in politically-favored groups. These coerced bank loans, which have been a kind of expropriation from bank shareholders and short-changed, fee-bitten depositors, precipitated the Great Recession whose effects continue to drag down the U.S. economy.

This Community Reinvestment Act was a Progressive ideological effort to make banks absorb much of the cost of providing housing for low income Democratic Party voters. It worked so well that today, after the continuing crisis it set in motion, home ownership is at a 30+ year low.

Originally sold as only a law to gather data on bank lending to minorities, CRA immediately became a hammer whose data was used to accuse banks of racism and discrimination in their lending policies.

The liberal media accused banks of "redlining," making few loans in certain neighborhoods. The media almost never mentioned that Franklin Delano Roosevelt's very "Progressive" Federal Housing Administration (FHA) is what first imposed "redlining" during the 1930s, mapping and discouraging loans in deteriorating neighborhoods where property values were declining.

The FHA pushed banks to adopt this government guideline.

Making loans on the basis of politicized social engineering rather than credit worthiness is never a sound business decision, and it always creates unintended consequences.

Those who took out what came to be called "liar loans" – in which buyers, not required to provide documentation, simply claimed to make far more income than was true – ought to bear more responsibility than the government-coerced banks for what has happened.

If the government were scrupulous about financial propriety and law, it would now be checking whether borrowers committed fraud by making false income claims. What does it tell us that left-liberal politicians have never lifted a finger to do this?

Bank-Bashing

By the late 1970s the CRA was already being used by both government and radical activists to intimidate banks into lowering their lending standards so that more poor and minority borrowers could qualify for mortgages.

In 1993 new President Bill Clinton, backed by a Democrat-dominated Congress, greatly expanded this power. Banks were now given a so-called "CRA rating" of their minority lending policies and practices, a measure that involved any of four government bureaucracies.

Banks given a "poor" CRA rating could be refused permission to expand as their competitors did, or to add new branches.

"Banks that got poor reviews were punished," wrote University of Texas economics Professor Stan Liebowitz. "Some saw their merger plans frustrated; others faced direct legal challenges by the Justice Department."

"The pressure to comply with CRA was astounding," recalled former bank manager Noel Sheppard, "especially at Great Western as it was expanding throughout the country. Its ability to acquire other institutions was directly related to its CRA rating."

"When legislation was pending in 1999 during the Clinton Administration to permit banks to diversify into selling investment securities," writes economist Thomas Sowell of Stanford University's Hoover Institution in his 2009 book *The Housing Boom and Bust*, "the White House urged 'that banks given unsatisfactory ratings under the 1977 Community Reinvestment Act be prohibited from enjoying the new diversification privileges' of this legislation." [35]

Either implicitly or explicitly, banks were expected to meet an arbitrary quota for loans to poor and racial minority borrowers to get a CRA rating. At the high point of this policy, one key mortgage institution was directed to have 55 percent of its mortgages helping these minorities.

ARMing Ninjas

What followed, wrote *Investor's Business Daily's* Terry Jones in 2008, was that "in the name of diversity, banks began making huge numbers of loans that they previously would not have. They opened branches in poor areas to lift their CRA ratings...."

A large percentage of these were what the bankers nicknamed "Ninja" loans, given mostly to minority applicants who had No Income, No Job nor Assets.

In 2010 former Republican Speaker of the House Newt Gingrich described what the Clinton Administration strong-armed bankers into offering: "If you can't afford to buy a house, we'll waive your credit. If you can't afford to buy a house, we'll let you come in without a down payment. If you can't afford to buy a house, we'll let you have three years without paying any principal. If you can't afford to buy a house, we'll give it to you below interest rate. And guess what: None of it worked."

"That's how the contagion began," wrote Jones. "With those changes, the sub-prime market took off. From a mere $35 billion in loans in 1994, it soared to $1 trillion by 2008."

Many of the loans given were ARMs, Adjustable Rate Mortgages, often with low initial teaser rates to qualify a borrower for a home. When the teaser rate ended or loan interest rates adjusted upwards, many borrowers were no longer able, or willing, to keep making the higher mortgage payments.

Knowing that potentially millions of mortgages were going bad, some banks bundled this unreliable paper, acquired insurance and rating agencies' blessing for it, and sold the shoddy bundles to as many gullible entities here and abroad as they could. This was hardly ethical, but neither was government forcing banks at regulatory gunpoint to issue millions of such mortgages to un-creditworthy borrowers.

As these chickens began coming home to roost, parts of our banking system teetered on the brink of collapse. We plunged into the economic malaise that $8 Trillion in stimulus, mostly with paper dollars printed out of thin air, has been unable to fix. Truth be told, we remain in recession eight years later. And the more our Progressive politicians blame and threaten capitalists, defame local police, and practice class warfare, the more investors feel reluctant to invest and hire.

And again today, as *Washington Post* columnist Marc Thiessen observed: "This is what happens when a community organizer is president."

Cronyism and ideological favoritism replace meritocracy. As in primitive ancient times, success comes to those who do the king's bidding. Honesty, hard work and achievement no longer count for anything.

Imposing "Equality"

President Obama in 2013 had resumed strong-arming banks to do such lending. By mid-2014 banks were, indeed, giving away subprime mortgages again in growing numbers. Government simply has too much power to reward or ruin banks. The President's wish is their command. Welcome to CRA 2.0.

Mr. Obama's AFFH policy is simply the latest tactic to impose a Progressive utopian version of equality by taking from the productive and redistributing the fruits of their labor to the less productive.

As we show in *Don't Bank On It!*, banks have become the intersection, the nexus, where the Progressive efforts to confiscate property, cash, freedom and independence from Americans converge. Our book shows 20 major risks your banked assets now face, the near-zero interest banks pay savers for taking such risks, and how people can secure their assets in far safer ways outside of banks.

Welcome to the modern Progressive city, which as architect Frank Lloyd Wright said has "banks and prostitution and not much else."

Mr. Obama has added a few things: The modern city, like Baltimore, now has violent mobs and Political Correctness, which are to civilization as anti-matter is to matter, an absolute force of destruction.

As Congresswoman Mia Love (R.-Utah) says, Mr. Obama has used people as racial pawns in his federalized zoning scheme to increase collectivist power and government dependency.

The president's leftist legacy is that he has made America "progressively" worse.

And where does this lead? His new policy will drastically reduce property values, which will reduce property tax revenues, which will make cities and towns unable to provide as many benefits for the poor and minorities. Surely Mr. Obama can see this – so what is the real game he is playing with millions of American lives?

Progressive War on the Suburbs

The suburbs, beginning after World War II, were where city dwellers moved to escape urban crime and decay. This infuriated Progressives, who saw suburbs as tax havens just beyond the greedy grasp of city tax collectors. Without such taxes, it has been difficult to fund their welfare city-states of many takers and few makers.

President Obama has waged relentless war against a largely-Caucasian suburban America that he and his Progressive party do not control, as journalist Stanley Kurtz explored in his 2012 book *Spreading the Wealth: How Obama is Robbing the Suburbs to Pay for the Cities.* [36]

We should see Mr. Obama's use of HUD to attack the suburban communities around cities as part of this ongoing ideological assault on those who vote with their feet to flee high-tax welfare states, whether national or local. We should also see this motive behind President Obama's encouragement of mass youth migration from Latin America, and his 2014 busing and flying of these tens of thousands of Latinos without warning into targeted towns and suburbs throughout the nation. [37]

Progressives have long felt frustrated because America lacked an essential ingredient in Marxist class warfare – a Proletariat, a working class that felt it had nothing to lose and a world to win by overthrowing the capitalist business class. In socially-mobile America, workers have aspired not to overthrow the rich but to join them. How can Progressive class warfare activists like Mr. Obama create their desired socialist-Marxist "Dictatorship of the Proletariat" without a Proletariat?

Mr. Obama appears to have found an answer. If such people will not grow naturally in the traditional thriving soil of America, he will import them from Honduras and El Salvador as shock troops in his Progressive class war.

The more than 50,000 Latino youngsters who came flooding into America in mid-2014 are not refugees. They are Mr. Obama's class warfare recruits.

Obamamander

President Obama spread these new immigrants nationwide, and may have done so with an eye to where they might be able to tip political balances in favor of Progressive Democrats. When last we checked, the Obama Administration was still refusing to disclose precisely where, from Alaska to Florida, each immigrant had been sent.

This is what we have called the "Obamamander," changing the political balance in America by effectively re-drawing our national boundaries to take in vast numbers of people from Mexico and Central America. This is one of the most cynical and dishonest acts by any president in U.S. history.

The trouble with history, of course, is that it is written by the winners. This is why Progressives have always been willing to do anything to win. If you win, people with your values will write the history books. We wrote about the great Clinton precedent for Mr. Obama's new policies.

Behind the Clinton Administration policies of housing for the poor was a radical leftist ideal of equality that it was not enough to provide shelter for the poor. The unfortunate poor, Mr. Clinton believed, should be given housing as good as that owned by the rich, the fortunate who are merely "the winners of life's lottery."

In the name of radical egalitarianism, for example, the Clinton Administration used taxpayer money to give poor people homes in San Diego County's wealthiest beachfront California Riviera suburb La Jolla (Spanish for "The Jewel"), a community almost as pricey as Beverly Hills or the movie star beach colony at Malibu.

As part of its new Progressive-Left vision of "mixed-income communities" that include the poor, the Clinton Administration also established halfway houses for felons and drug addicts in homes located in well-to-do neighborhoods, thereby endangering and driving down the property values of those next door who had worked hard to earn their dream homes in what until then had been safe upscale communities.

Under President Bill Clinton, the Secretary of Housing and Urban Development (HUD) was Henry Cisneros, the former Mayor of San

Antonio, Texas. After a scandal, Cisneros became President and COO of Univision, one of the two largest Spanish-Language television networks in America.

Under President Barack Obama, the HUD Secretary who will implement AFFH is Julian Castro, another former Mayor of San Antonio, Texas, who is being carefully groomed to be the Democratic Party's youthful Latino running mate in 2016 to counter the possibility of Republicans running youthful Florida Latino Senator Marco Rubio. Castro's identical twin brother is Congressman Joaquin Castro (D.-Texas).

The Clintons have been ideologically close to longtime Cuban Marxist dictator Fidel Castro, as evidenced by their illegal Florida seizure of Elian Gonzalez and his return to Communist Cuba in defiance of the United Nations International Convention on the Rights of the Child that most Progressives pretend to support. Nothing could be more symbolic in 2016 than if Democrats offer American voters a Clinton-Castro presidential ticket. This is where Progressive ideology has always been headed.

Homeland

Ground down by the killing power of high taxes and heavy regulation, many Americans feel they are being driven not only out of their homes but also out of their homeland.

Like their ancestors, who pulled up stakes and came to America seeking freedom and opportunity, millions of Americans have begun looking for a better place in the world to move.

"There is all the difference in the world
between treating people equally
and attempting to make them equal."

– Friedrich Hayek
Nobel Laureate Economist

"When you consider socialism,
do not fool yourself about its nature.
Remember that there is no such dichotomy
as 'human rights' versus 'property rights.'
No human rights can exist
without property rights."

– Ayn Rand

"All socialism involves slavery."

– Herbert Spencer
British Philosopher

Chapter Five

Farther Than Your Father

*"Each generation goes further than the generation
preceding it because it stands on the shoulders
of that generation. You will have opportunities
beyond anything we've ever known."*

– Ronald Reagan

Americans now owe roughly $1.3 Trillion in student loan debt, more than
the total debt Americans owe on all consumer credit cards combined. The
average college loan debt is more than $27,000 per student. [38-39]

Going to college used to be the path to higher-income jobs, yet in today's
economy many experts are questioning whether this is an investment worth
going so deep into debt for.

One third of recent graduates in a recent Wells Fargo study said they regret
going to college. [40]

College used to be the path to a better and richer life. It was an opportunity not only to prepare for your life's chosen work, but also to explore the world of ideas and to acquire a larger understanding of many things.

College was a chance to fulfill one part of the American Dream: that with the key of a college degree, you could unlock opportunities to go even farther in life than your parents did.

This used to be absolutely true. A solid college degree had real value because it was perceived as increasing your knowledge and ability to think. A degree was a lifelong investment in having access to better and higher paying work, as well as to a more fulfilling breadth and depth of understanding.

Is this still true today?

Sheepskin

Alas, not necessarily. Some college and university degrees today are not worth the sheepskin – no, the artificial parchment so that no innocent animal is injured in the production of your degree – they are printed on.

First, we live in an America where more people have college degrees than ever before. On the campaign trail in 2015, Progressive Hillary Clinton is hinting that she wants taxpayers to provide essentially free college – or at least Community College – education for everyone.

The bigger the percentage of job applicants with such degrees, the lower the value of such sheepskins. What it amounts to is that a basic college degree from anything less than a top university is becoming what a high school diploma used to be.

The Ken Burns documentary series on the Civil War includes readings of many letters written in the 1860s. What stuns the listener hearing them read is how clear, concise and intelligent these letters from ordinary soldiers are, even though they had at most a high school education.

People then lacked the Internet, Google searches, and the astonishing variety of information at our fingertips – but what they knew, they knew well. They knew how to organize their thoughts into solid prose better than most college graduates can today.

As we have noted in earlier books, back then their three "R"s were Readin', 'Ritin' and 'Rithmetic, yet students acquired important individual skills and knowledge. Today's students from Kindergarten through college are taught a different three Rs – racism, recycling, and reproduction.

Truth be told, in these institutions largely controlled by Progressives, college degrees are becoming a currency as debased as they have made the U.S. Dollar.

As employers will tell you, it is not unusual to have job applicants with a college degree who are unable to do simple arithmetic or write a sure-footed, clear sentence in the English language.

What such graduates can do, however, is tell you why America is evil, capitalism is a crime against humanity, and global warming skeptics should be silenced.

If some college degrees are devalued today, it is because Progressive professors at many campuses no longer teach students how to think – but what to think.

The Foundation for Individual Rights in Education (FIRE) surveyed several hundred American college and university campuses and found that more than half – 55 percent – "maintain severely restrictive 'red light' speech codes – policies that clearly and substantially prohibit protected speech."

Did you think college was a place where a variety of ideas could be freely debated, or embarrassing questions could be put to Progressive professors who are members of favored elite groups?

No, such speech is now choked off in many ways.

Learning to Shut Up

Remember Janet Napolitano, who headed President Obama's Department of Homeland Security early in his administration? This is the same Ms. Napolitano who sent a memo to police departments across America telling them to view as potential terrorists anyone who favored Second Amendment gun rights, or opposed abortion, or were military veterans, or even who made statements critical of President Obama.

Janet Napolitano now runs the University of California, which in 2015 put out a directive against what it calls micro-aggressive racist statements. What were its examples of statements that constitute verbal acts of aggression against minorities? Here are a few phrases to be banned:

(1) "America is the land of opportunity." This statement is Politically Incorrect and prohibited because it perpetuates the "myth of meritocracy."

(2) "There is only one race, the human race." This statement denies minorities their own collective racial or other identities.

(3) "I believe the most qualified person should get the job." This statement implies that "people of color are given extra unfair benefits because of their race."

The University of California list of examples goes on, but you get the idea. Progressives can win every time if others are charged with Orwellian thought crimes for merely saying something to the contrary.

In George Orwell's dystopian novel *1984*, in its totalitarian future Big Brother is watching you. At the University of California, it is Big Sister.

Such speech codes, or isolated free speech areas on campus, or a hundred other gimmicks have been designed by the Progressives in charge not to expand free speech and debate, but to stifle them.

Both Rutgers University and the University of Colorado-Boulder encourage students to report if they overhear someone making inappropriate statements. This can potentially result in the speaker being subjected to "sensitivity training" or even being thrown out of the school.

One standard used in today's universities is whether you have said anything that "offends" or causes emotional distress to anyone. Those who disagree with your views, of course, might be offended by you saying anything at all.

Depending on who and what you are, the school might join in stifling your speech, or let you silence others. If you are Caucasian and masculine, you nowadays will be accused of having a mentality of "white male privilege," which means that you will be blamed for every act of racism, imperialism and enslavement that has happened during the last 5,000 years on planet Earth.

Note that this is precisely the kind of collectivist racial accusation National Socialist racists made against Jews. Progressives are so steeped in their view that we are to be defined not as individuals but only as members of collective groups, that they do not even understand how their radical ideology blinds them to reality.

Progressive Diversity

Diversity of a kind does exist on today's college campuses. Ask about their faculties and you will discover that colleges are proud to have among their professors a black Marxist, a transsexual Marxist, a Latino Marxist, a feminist Marxist, and so forth. Progressives embrace diversity, just not diversity in thought or ideas.

The bad news is that today's colleges are stagnant swamps of conformity.

The good, if ironic, news is that even Progressive professors are beginning to feel pressure to conform from their students. "I'm a liberal Professor," wrote one scholar anonymously at the Progressive website *Vox*, "and My Liberal Students Terrify Me."

As the head of FIRE, Greg Lukianoff, and New York University-Stern School of Business ethicist, Jonathan Haidt, argue in the September 2015 issue of *The Atlantic*, today's college students want more and more protection from words and ideas they do not like.

Jerry Seinfeld and Chris Rock are two comics who reportedly no longer do stand-up comedy on most college campuses because students have lost their sense of humor and take offense at any provocative or controversial idea.

A newly-minted college degree today might no longer be evidence of mental sharpness, but of dullness, conformity, and a grim unimaginative view of the world. This is apparently what the collectivist dogma of Progressive brainwashing is doing to many of today's young minds.

What do these students want? They want strict rules against "micro-aggression" speech, and they are prepared to report to school administrators speech that offends them by any Professor.

Because these are the kids who take out the huge student loans to pay the soaring tuition costs that keep colleges rich, such student complaints about professors are taken very seriously, write Lukianoff and Haidt.

These students also want the latest form of speech control, "trigger warnings," in which speakers or professors are expected to warn in advance if they are about to say anything that might shock or traumatize a student. This puts pressure on teachers not to offend.

Campus trigger warnings were used at Progressive Oberlin College and Georgetown University against feminist author Christina Hoff Sommers, who argues against the currently fashionable notion that women now live in a violent, paternalistic rape culture.

The conformist trigger warnings against her, Sommers says, claimed that her "very presence on campus" was "a form of violence" that threatened the mental health of students.

The speech restrictions on perhaps more than half of American campuses of higher learning violate free speech rights in the First Amendment. By exposing and legally challenging some of the most outrageous examples of stifled speech, FIRE is expanding the range of speech on some campuses.

At the University of New Hampshire, for example, in 2015 its president Mark Huddleston withdrew university backing for its "Bias-Free Language Guide." Before he acted, this guide meant that a student or faculty member could face disciplinary action for uttering "biased" words such as "foreigners," "mothering," "fathering," or "American."

As we reveal in our Epilogue, one of the universities FIRE numbers among its "12 Worst Colleges for Free Speech" is in Baltimore.

America remains home to many fine colleges and universities that fulfill the ideals of the American Dream.

Others serve the Progressive Dream and its objectives, including the political aims of Progressive Democrats such as President Obama and Hillary Clinton.

The Politics of College

The unemployment rate for working-age Americans under 25 is officially around 16.2%, which the *Wall Street Journal* calculates is closer to 22.9%.

Today unemployment among the young is almost as high as in several recession-crippled European nations.

Roughly half of recent graduates have been unable to find full-time work commensurate with the college degree they worked hard for and borrowed heavily to get.

We have been pulled out of past recessions by sales of cars and homes, but the fat student loan debts and slim job prospects of recent graduates have limited their ability to buy cars and homes, and start families.

Politicians, by making it easy for students to borrow a total of more than $1 Trillion for college, have distorted our economy, just as government strong-arming banks into giving mortgages to almost everybody led to today's continuing worst recovery since the Great Depression.

Republicans already passed a bill to keep student loan rates low. It would make the cost of such loans variable by tying them to the interest rate on U.S. Treasury notes, which might make loans more expensive if the Federal Reserve raised interest rates.

President Obama, by contrast, has at various times said he wants much lower, even fixed, loan rates. President Obama has had several political motives for this:

Students in college are not counted as unemployed, so it makes the official numbers for the economy look better;

America's colleges and universities are major bastions of the ideological left, and government-insured or funded student loans have increased ten-fold to enrich these institutions since 2007;

Students in such colleges and universities are inculcated with Progressive, leftist and anti-capitalist views akin to Mr. Obama's own in an environment that largely excludes and attacks conservative or pro-free market ideas.

Radical Recruitment

President Obama has also proposed that student loan debt be forgiven *if* a college graduate goes to work for government or appropriate (read: Politically Correct) non-profit organizations. This effectively would turn the student loan program into a recruitment tool for ever-bigger government. [41]

Both President Obama and Democratic presidential candidate Hillary Clinton, former Secretary of State, are hinting that they might simply "forgive" – that is, stick us taxpayers with – more than a trillion dollars in student loan debt.

Even before Progressive politicians began such talk, student loans had a higher default rate – around 11.2% – than car loans, mortgages or credit card debt. Now, with the prospect that these debts might be cancelled, this default rate has risen sharply. [42-43]

Why risk paying off a loan, only to find that the loans of those who did not pay have been erased – and you now cannot get back the payoff you made?

Millions are now apparently betting on being rescued by a student loan bailout, and are willing to absorb any penalties or credit damage that non-payment might cost.

President Obama has already had the government take over 90% of student loans, and has encouraged borrowers to renege on the other 10% of loans from private lenders.

Many of the government student loans include generous provisions that let former college attendees pay very little back in principal and interest so long as they have low-paying jobs, are unemployed, or are on welfare. This, in effect, gives graduates a perverse incentive not to seek good-paying employment.

Mr. Obama apparently sees control of student loans as a way to advance his ideology and to increase dependence on government by redistributing wealth from taxpayers to America's colleges and universities.

It should not surprise us that President Obama wants to tax working-class blue collar Americans in order to give a free ride to an educated, radicalized and privileged white collar elite of future government workers and community organizers like himself.

The long-term effect of what President Obama wants, of course, would be to raise taxes, further damage America's economy, and shift much more of the nation's capital from the productive private sector to unproductive ever-more-obese government.

A better education than this would come from parents and grandparents teaching their children about real-world economics.

In today's colleges and universities, students learn very different lessons, because these campuses are now bastions of Progressive ideology. The "free speech" leftist student radicals of the 1960s in many cases never left school.

They went on to become the professors at such institutions. But once they achieved the protected status of tenure, any notion of "free speech" quickly vanished unless it involved speech by those who share their ideology.

*"Liberals love to say things like
'We're just asking everyone
to pay their fair share.'*

*But government is not about asking.
It is about telling.
The difference is fundamental.
It is the difference
between making love and being raped,
between working for a living
and being a slave.*

*The Internal Revenue Service
is not asking anybody to do anything.*

*It confiscates your assets
and puts you behind bars
if you don't pay."*

– Dr. Thomas Sowell

Chapter Six

A Future That Doesn't Work

"Socialism only works in two places:
Heaven where they don't need it
and hell where they already have it."

— **Ronald Reagan**

"Labor Costs Rise at Slowest Pace in 33 Years," read a *New York Times* headline on July 31, 2015, as this newspaper spun the news frantically to paint lipstick on the pig that is President Barack Obama's wallowing economy. [44]

If the President were a Republican, this same *Times* story from Reuters would have carried a very different headline: "Wage Growth at Slowest Pace in 33 Years."

The Department of Commerce announced that in the Second Quarter of 2015 America's economy grew at an annualized rate of 2.3 percent, which other countries that do not engage in our data manipulations would see as equivalent to less than a 0.6 percent growth rate quarter-on-quarter.

The Commerce Department also said it has revised what began as Minus 0.2 percent growth during the First Quarter up to 0.6 percent growth...anemic growth, but better than much of the rest of the world where meager growth rates are now in decline.

But then came stunning news: the 2.3 percent growth Mr. Obama's bureaucrats calculated during the 2012 and 2014 elections were revised sharply downward. Our economy's growth from 2011 through 2014 had grown by an unlucky 13 percent less than claimed – averaging a miserably weak 2.0 percent growth.

This embarrassingly-low growth, remember, happened in an era where the U.S. Treasury and Federal Reserve were injecting more than $6 Trillion of stimulus into the economy – and this astronomically-large expenditure that added $8 Trillion to America's debt for gimmicky programs like Cash for Clunkers, much of which must be repaid by our children and grandchildren, produced only 2.0 percent growth.

We might have done better by simply sending a check for more than $20,000 to every American.

In several of our books, including 2014's *Don't Bank On It! The Unsafe World of 21ˢᵗ Century Banking*, we expanded our prediction and analysis of why all this Keynesian stimulus would in reality become an "anti-stimulus."

As we predicted, this huge expenditure terrified business owners. They expected it to cause huge economic distortions and, ultimately, high inflation – so they cut back sharply on investment and hiring. This wrecked the middle class. In 2015 the Census Bureau reported that average household income is 6.5 percent lower than it was in 2007.

British economist John Maynard Keynes taught that the "multiplier" from such stimulus spending would increase the velocity of money in the economy and encourage growth. After almost a century of analysis, this appears to be true – but mostly in primitive economies with a static money supply. In advanced nations such stimulus can enrich high-rollers in the Wall Street casino roller-coaster, but can make the economy far worse for companies and those in need of jobs. Today the "velocity" of money in our economy is close to its lowest rate in 50 years.

In this, the weakest economic recovery since World War II, government claims of adding 200,000 jobs per month ring hollow – especially when the bulk of these are low-wage, hamburger-flipper jobs with static wages that are killing America's middle class.

Sadly, in today's stagnant economy the traditional American Dream of home ownership is also dying. This is especially true for those 34 years of age or younger who cannot buy a first home or new car with their low credit, average $27,000 in college loan debt to repay, and low incomes.

Many Millennials have postponed starting a family, and for the first time in history America's fertility rate has fallen below the needed 2.1 babies per couple replacement rate. At 1.84 babies per couple, we have now joined the downward death spiral to demographic doom seen in Western Europe and Japan.

Cut through the deception of not counting those who no longer look for a full-time job and we discover that 94 million working-age Americans lack the full-time job they need. Another 101 million have full-time jobs, but they are taxed to pay for the 108 million receiving means-tested welfare of some kind. In 49.5 percent of American households, at least one person now receives means-tested government benefits.

Among these benefits are Social Security Disability Insurance, now collected by more than 10 million Americans. The Obama Administration greatly eased standards to qualify for SSDI, so now SSDI will run out of funds in 2016. We have almost as many on SSDI as have full-time jobs in all of manufacturing.

The Federal Reserve is happy that inflation, even without counting rising food and fuel costs, has apparently "risen" to 1.8 percent – but, Baby Boomers, do not count on this to cause an upward Cost-of-Living Adjustment (COLA) to your Social Security.

Our economy is supposedly growing by 2.3 percent but is being eaten up by 1.8 percent inflation not fully factored into the government's books. This might mean that our real annual "growth" could be 0.5 percent.

Welcome to the New Normal.

Why Work?

In 35 of America's 50 states, the most attractive choice for many is not to work at all. These are the states where welfare pays more than the minimum wage, even after accounting for the Earned Income Tax Credit.

Once upon a time, collecting welfare came with social stigma and shame because it was understood that welfare recipients were not earning their way and were using money taken at gunpoint as taxes from their neighbors.

The government has waged a long propaganda war to eliminate this stigma and shame. What used to be Food Stamps or other welfare-related coupons have now been put on credit cards so the user looks like every other customer at the supermarket.

Did we say supermarket? These welfare cards have also routinely been used at gambling casinos and liquor stores….your tax dollars at work.

It used to be that America's Scots-Irish settlers in the mountains just west of Baltimore and other Atlantic Coast cities had what was called "Appalachian Pride," a spirit of self-reliant independence and dignity that deterred them from going on the dole.

One federal bureaucrat won an award for spearheading ways to eradicate Appalachian Pride, which the Progressive welfare state sees as an old-fashioned, backwards impediment to bringing the blessings of welfare addiction and dependency on government to all Americans.

Perversely, this propaganda effort to hook people on welfare has also used shame – telling people that they are hurting their families by not letting the welfare state provide food, healthcare and a thousand other benefits for them.

Entitled

These Progressives also argue that even if you have never paid a dollar in taxes or done a day's work in your life, the unpaid or underpaid labor of your ancestors means that you are entitled to tons of cradle-to-grave taxpayer-funded benefits at other folks' expense.

Please forget that the biggest beneficiary of Progressive Ponzi schemes such as President Lyndon Johnson's Great Society spending programs is not the poor. The poor on average by some estimates have been getting less than 19 pennies of every government dollar spent to help the poor.

The biggest beneficiaries obviously are not middle-class or upper-class Americans, who are heavily taxed to pay for these programs. And with social spending such as welfare, plus interest on the national debt, now devouring 71 cents of every tax dollar, the welfare state is a significant factor in rapidly crowding out all other spending. The higher the welfare spending, the less is left for "non-mandatory" spending for national defense, highways or space exploration.

Every dollar taxed away from a hard-working middle-class family is a dollar they could have spent on their own children, or an earlier retirement, or starting their own business, or paying off their mortgage sooner.

The biggest beneficiary of such social spending is, of course, the government itself – the bureaucrats, social workers, highly-paid political appointees and others who raked off 81 cents of every dollar before it could reach the poor.

So how much is government spending on the poor? Answer: More than $1 Trillion annually from the Federal Government alone, and yet more from state and local governments.

Taken together, the CATO Institute think tank calculated that total government spending even back in 2012 was, on average, $20,610 for every poor person, or $61,830 for every poor family of three. [45]

Welfare for the Government

How can we designate people bringing in this much money as poor? If we simply gave this amount of money to each poor person or family, would not poverty disappear completely?

This question clearly shows that you do not understand. The purpose of poverty spending is not to help the poor. It is to fund a huge part of the government that justifies its existence by claiming to help the poor.

The one thing under Progressive government that must never be allowed to happen is that the poor whose existence justifies all this government spending get jobs or otherwise cease to be poor. This is why so many have said that when they tried to leave welfare programs, the social workers and bureaucrats whose paychecks and pensions depend on poverty programs tried to talk them out of quitting welfare.

"The welfare system, at its best, is a system that gives people a way to live when they can't find work for themselves, when they're down on their luck," say CATO Institute analysts Michael Tanner and Charles Hughes.

But "at its worst," they say, "the welfare rewards people for not working, and incentivizes people to develop habits that make it harder for them to find work in the future, miring them in permanent poverty." [46]

And a welfare addict's permanent poverty becomes permanent, well-paid jobs for those in the huge government poverty sector.

How much could you get on welfare? Tanner and Hughes measured this in hourly income in a recent CATO study. The more Progressive the state, the fatter your take from choosing not to work. [47]

If you live in New York, in 2013 you could have pocketed more than $21 an hour, or $43,700 annually.

In Connecticut a single welfare recipient's take could be more than $21 per hour...an annual income of $44,370.

In Massachusetts, welfare could bring in $24.30 per hour, or $50,540 for avoiding work all year.

In Washington, D.C., the lone welfare beneficiary could rake in $24.43 per hour, an annual income of $50,820.

Lotusland Aloha

Their national welfare champion, however, far outpaces these other places. Hawaii, where President Obama's birth certificate was issued, gives its welfare recipients up to $29.13 an hour for spending their time surfing or lying on its warm tropical beaches. That is an annual welfare income of $60,590.

With such lucrative Progressive incentives for sloth, why work?

In 2015 America, 49.5 percent of households have one or more persons living there receiving some kind of government benefit. So do 51 percent of immigrants. [48] In Illinois almost twice as many are signing up for Food Stamps as new jobs are being created. [49]

President Obama did make one major modification in America's welfare policies. In mid-2012, months before facing re-election, Mr. Obama used his executive authority to eliminate President Bill Clinton's 1996 "workfare" reform that had required welfare recipients to at least show they had applied for jobs in order to get their next welfare payment.

Mr. Obama's apparent intention, as we wrote at the time, was to gimmick the unemployment numbers to make his economic policies look like less of a failure just before people went out to vote.

If someone applies for work but finds no job, he is officially counted as unemployed. If he does not apply for work at all, he vanishes from the unemployment count, which makes the official rate of unemployment fall, even though he got no job.

President Obama cynically eliminated this job-application requirement for welfare recipients not to help them, but to create deceptively better unemployment numbers to conjure the illusion that his economy was improving.

In doing so, Mr. Obama incidentally eliminated the only tiny monthly task that had been required of those receiving welfare. This freed *all* their time for what they wanted to do.

The Progressive Arts

In 2012, Baltimore-born Congresswoman Nancy Pelosi said that Obamacare allows people to quit their jobs to become a "photographer," a "writer," a "musician," or "whatever." This is "a liberation," said Pelosi. "This is what our founders had in mind – ever-expanding opportunity for people." [50] No, America's Framers wanted you to have such freedom with your own money, not with a subsidy stolen at government gunpoint from taxpayers. Progressives like Pelosi have a warped understanding of the American Dream.

The Netherlands' welfare state decades ago had a similar idea. If you fancied yourself a painter, the government would spend taxpayer money to buy and warehouse your paintings, no matter how bad they were. After Morley Safer mocked this on CBS' "60 Minutes," the Dutch ended this waste of money and eventually gave its thousands of paintings away. [51]

In the unreal thinking of American Progressives, the redistribution of wealth via welfare is an idea with many permutations. As a famous Progressive once told one of us, "Don't you understand, Lowell? Welfare is the price we pay for keeping the poor *in their place!*"

Other Progressives recognize that welfare is a tricky name, that when the Framers wrote about providing for the "general welfare" in the Constitution, they used that term to make sure government money was to be used for the benefit of everybody, e.g., by building a new road or courthouse; they meant "general welfare" to exclude government from giving welfare money to specific individuals. Yet Progressives have built their political power precisely by dispensing such *de facto* bribes to voters.

Doomsaying Progressives would be happy to eliminate the word "welfare," if not its wealth redistribution. They simply want every American to be provided a "guaranteed basic income," no matter how much or little they work. This, they believe, could eliminate any residue of the old stigma that came with taking welfare. [52]

Why have such a "guaranteed basic income," a kind of universal welfare for all? Because they believe a day is fast approaching when robots will take over more than half of our jobs, and there will no longer be enough good-paying jobs for more than half of America's humans to do. [53]

In a pre-Progressive age, they believe, this would have been a disaster – leaving millions without the income to survive. But in our Progressive-ruled future, robots will do the work for companies. These companies will be heavily taxed. The tax will be redistributed to provide a "guaranteed basic income" for hundreds of millions of unnecessary Americans – at least those who are not aborted or are born despite sterilants in our drinking water or food supply.

In this Progressive vision of the future, the average person may not have much – perhaps a government-provided 10-foot by 15-foot apartment in Baltimore. But that apartment will look bigger with its mirrored walls, and it will have an amazing video and sound system that allows viewers to live vicariously through the sensory experiences it provides. Life can become one big video game, an art form that even in 2015 was earning more money than all of Hollywood's movies.

After all the states legalize mind-altering drugs, most Americans will be hypnotized by this artificial Progressive future.

We prefer a future in which people are left free, allowed to keep what they earn, and to safeguard it without the inherent risk of unreliable government paper money. Free people are entrepreneurial, imaginative, and able to create amazing solutions to challenges.

This is certainly better than using a dubious crisis to panic people into accepting a paternalistic Progressive state that confiscates the resources of a population infantilized into thumb-sucking, drug-addled helplessness, a kind of assisted suicide for Western Civilization, a *Brave New World* dystopia to suffocate the American Dream.

The Sharing Economy

A popular new distorted form of capitalism, "the sharing economy," is emerging in America, and those on the left are fighting among themselves over whether to embrace or attack it.

One such enterprise is Uber, which facilitates entrepreneurs using their own vehicles to provide transportation for money.

New York City's Democratic Mayor Bill de Blasio wants to restrict Uber from competing with crony taxi cab companies that pay huge medallion fees, taxes, and campaign contributions to have a lucrative monopoly.

However, in job-hungry New York State, Democratic Gov. Andrew Cuomo is an Uber booster.

"Uber is one of these great inventions, startups, of this new economy," says Cuomo. "It's offering a great service for people and it's giving people jobs."

"How do you really say to a company you can't grow here…and in the case of Uber they will move next door," Cuomo continued. "I hope they wouldn't move to New Jersey."

When driverless cars are perfected, a car will drive itself to your front door each morning from a cheap parking lot miles away. Uber will still be there, but its "gig work" drivers might be among the millions put out of work by robots.

New York City is cracking down on another sharing economy company, Airbnb, that matches up visitors with one of 25,000 local families willing to rent out spare bedrooms by the night.

This, too, reduces revenues from steep hotel room taxes on customers who do not live or vote locally.

Sharing economy services must compete without having government monopolies and therefore are more responsive and reliable than the taxis and hotels of government crony businesses that take customers for granted.

Those suffering with low and stagnant incomes under the Obama economy are happy to save by using Uber and Airbnb.

But for many on the left, such "collaborative consumption" elicits fury. As Nancy Cook wrote in the Aug. 1, 2015 issue of *The Atlantic*, the original utopian idea behind the sharing economy that began in 2008 was to coordinate the sharing of tools and other assets without anyone making any profit.

Baltimore was home to one of the first sharing economy libraries that lent out any of 150,000 books without the same constraints as public libraries.

Yerdle, a rival Web-based enterprise Cook describes as founded in 2012 to help people give things away, was launched "on the day after Thanksgiving, the traditional start of the Christmas shopping season, with the goal of reducing by 25 percent the amount of stuff that people buy to promote, as the company calls it, 'unshopping.'"

We could call "unshopping" other things, like an anti-capitalist effort by a former Sierra Club president to undermine capitalism, industry, profits, and jobs in the U.S. economy.

The loony left webzine *Salon.com* wrote: "You're not fooling us, Uber!... the 'Sharing Economy' is all about corporate greed" by making "money for Silicon Valley venture capitalists while pretending to espouse progressive ideals."

"Companies like Uber and Airbnb may seem to lean left," wrote *Salon. com*, but are merely using "the language of 'sharing'...to conceal ambitions far more libertarian."

Yes, for these lefties, the fundamental libertarian notions of capitalism, free markets, competition, investment and profit are obscenities. Leftists are collectivists who believe that individualism and private property must be expunged.

In "The Case Against Sharing" in the political cartoon webzine *TheNib. com*, Susie Cagle wrote: "For the past few years, the 'sharing economy' has characterized itself as a revolution: Renting a room on Airbnb or catching an Uber is an act of civil disobedience in the service of a righteous return to human society's true nature of trust and village-building that will save the planet and our souls. A higher form of enlightened capitalism."

Instead, she writes, the "sharing economy" could drag people back into the precarious work of the early 20th Century, with few rights for workers or consumers.

Radicals conveniently forget that socialism and Marxism have failed to deliver on their utopian promises.

As Cook observes, there may be "another limit to these purer forms of the sharing economy: human nature. Anyone who has reared children knows that sharing isn't a natural behavior — that it often requires incentives or threats."

This is the choice: Incentives so we work voluntarily, or threats, coercion and involuntary servitude. As Nobel laureate economist Milton Friedman said, "There ain't no such thing as a free lunch." Somebody — free market capitalist or unmotivated socialist slave — must produce the goods we want and need. The new capitalism produces more goods and more freedom.

Un-Man-ing America

When Progressives decide to play God by re-engineering society, they often create unintended consequences. Or are these huge earthquake faults splitting American society apart being created by collectivist design?

President Obama's anti-free market economic policies have caused fear, uncertainty, and economic stagnation in the real economy – if not in the stock market casino buoyed by more than $1 Trillion each year in paper stimulus money.

These Progressive policies have caused devastatingly high and long-term unemployment in America. One aspect of this that few analysts have noted is that the Obama unemployment is highly asymmetrical by gender.

"In the worst economic times of the 1950s and '60s, about 9 percent of men in the prime of their working lives (25 to 54 years old) were not working," wrote *New York Times* Economix reporter David Leonhardt in April 2011. "At the depth of the severe recession in the early 1980s, about 15 percent of prime-age men were not working." [54]

"More than 18 percent of such men aren't working," writes Leonhardt. "That's a depressing statistic: nearly one out of every 5 men between 25 and 54 is not employed."

Two years later male unemployment had grown even worse, according to Nicholas Eberstadt of the American Enterprise Institute. In an analysis titled "The Astonishing Collapse of Work in America," Eberstadt in July 2013 found that 30 percent of adult American men – nearly one in three – is neither working nor seeking work. In 1953 this number was only 14 percent. [55]

Over the past 60 years, the labor force participation rate for adult men has fallen by about 16 percentage points, Eberstadt wrote, to 62.6 percent. Seventy-six million men are working, but at Eisenhower-era levels this would have been 96 million men employed.

The "great bulk of the change is due to an exodus out of the labor force – that is to say, to a massive long-term rise in the number of adult men who are neither working nor seeking work," writes Eberstadt, author of the 2012 book *A Nation of Takers: America's Entitlement Epidemic.* [56]

Men on Strike?

Why is this tectonic shift in male employment happening? Eberstadt offers little explanation, noting that "America's leadership has not yet paid serious attention to the collapse of work in modern America."

We know this: the rise of the Progressive welfare state, especially since the Great Society entitlement programs of the 1960s, has redefined the role of the man in American society.

Men used to be the family breadwinner, the provider, the person who went to work and brought home the bacon. Government has all too often taken over this role of the male spouse, thereby coming between men and women. Women with small children were in many cases able to obtain more government benefits *without* a husband than with one, and to that extent a man could be an "anti-provider" who reduced family income.

In today's hard times caused by Obamanomics, many men have given up on finding jobs that pay well. In up to 40 percent of American households, working women have become the primary breadwinner.

In her 2013 book *Men On Strike: Why Men Are Boycotting Marriage, Fatherhood, and the American Dream – and Why It Matters*, practicing psychologist Helen Smith writes that many men have soured on marriage and work because "[T]he new world order is a place where men are discriminated against, forced into a hostile environment in school and later in college, and held in contempt by society." [57]

"Maybe there is no incentive [for men] to grow up anymore," writes Smith. "It used to be that being a grown up, responsible man was rewarded with respect, power and deference. Now, not so much."

Backing Away

The "new world order" Smith refers to is the Progressive world order that, indeed, polarizes the relationship between men and women and favors feminism over old-fashioned masculinity. With government reducing the value of their traditional role as provider, many men are left to seek other ways to become valuable.

This male withdrawal from work, marriage and other traditional male roles is clearly redefining America's society and economy. What would the ancient Greek playwright Aristophanes, who came from conservative island culture and saw Athens decaying, see in today's America?

Aristophanes twenty-four centuries ago in his play "Lysistrada" depicted the women of Athens going on a sex strike to make their men stop making war. What would he make of today's America where, according to Smith, millions of men are going on a different kind of sex and work strike, and are being infantilized by the Progressive State?

As sociologist Charles Murray reported in his 2012 book *Coming Apart: The State of White America 1960-2010*, upper and upper-middle-class whites are becoming more traditional in their behavior, even if they espouse Progressive ideas. Their divorce rate and recreational drug use is falling. [58]

The lower class and lower-middle class, by contrast, have lost much of their work ethic and traditional values. The middle class in general has, in inflation-adjusted dollars, been stuck at roughly the same income for the last 30 years. The old pride in being a man is waning.

From Murray's data, it appears that the bottom third of White America is becoming a slacker nation. Without decent job prospects or education, millions of men no longer see much wrong with living off government checks that in 35 states pay as much or more than minimum wage, or off the paychecks of their wives or girlfriends.

More than 50 years of Progressive propaganda designed to undermine whatever stigma these people used to feel about taking welfare has succeeded.

Nearly 100 years of Progressives teaching class warfare has taught slackers to believe they are entitled to money taxed from the rich and the middle class who somehow cheated them out of a better life.

The work ethic of working-class whites was the foundation on which America's industrial success was built, writes Murray. The erosion of working-class morality, and today's 40 percent rate of white out-of-wed-lock births, may be destroying this bridge back to the old ethics that were essential to manufacturing in an earlier era.

The new era for the higher end of the white spectrum will mean private schools, gated communities, and jobs in finance and high tech and consulting. These people will do very well, at least until the economy crashes.

Most whites, says Murray, used to think of themselves as middle class in an America of widely-shared values, morals and work ethic. He sees a widening fault line as perhaps 20 million working-class mostly-white males have become slackers and stopped working, or now work "off the books" in America's underground economy. Many of them increasingly have more in common with the culture and status of minorities, Murray suggests, than with upper-middle-class whites.

At both ends of the white spectrum birth rates are falling. By unmanning working-class white males, the Progressives have reduced their desirability as mates and fathers. This may be a new kind of "birth control" imposed economically by the Progressives, an echo of eugenics inherent in their collectivist, control-freak ideology.

Upper-middle-class whites, by contrast, are graduating from grad schools with student loan debt and intense competitive pressure to establish their careers. These driven people, male and female, are now postponing marriage, first-home buying, and starting a family. This will reduce total fertility, leaving them with fewer – yet very well cared for – children. This, too, could be seen as a Progressive way of reducing the white birthrate in America.

They Blinded Us With Science

As we began discussing in Chapter Three, the Progressivism of Margaret Sanger lives on in Planned Parenthood. Since the 1973 Supreme Court ruling *Roe v. Wade*, an estimated 57 million lives have been ended by abortion in the United States, roughly the same number of additional productive citizens we need today to keep our collapsing social programs solvent. President Obama is a strong supporter of Planned Parenthood.

President Obama as an Illinois State Senator supported making legal what might be called "post-natal abortion" – the killing of a baby that had slipped outside its mother's body, and therefore been born, before an abortionist could kill it inside his or her mother.

Those on the cutting edge of Progressivism go even farther. Princeton University ethicist Peter Singer has written an entire book to urge a merger of the political left with Darwinian thought to advance their shared dehumanized view of humankind. [59]

Professor Singer and other Progressive intellectuals have proposed giving parents six months or so *after* a baby is born to decide whether its continued survival is in their, and its, best interests. The dictionary has a word for this. That word is infanticide. [60]

When you hear Progressives demanding that we give vast new regulatory powers that would largely erase the very concept of private property, along with another $100 Trillion in environmental taxes and penalties collected by Big Government to deal with purported planetary warming (which satellite measurements indicate may have ended 18 years ago) – all because some government-funded-and-therefore-biased scientists say so - remember who Progressives really are and what they really want.

When you learn that Progressive U.S. Senator Sheldon Whitehouse (D.-Rhode Island) and 20 prominent climate scientists have called for using the anti-racketeering (RICO) statutes to coerce the silence of global warming skeptics – literally to make free speech that is critical of Progressive views a crime punishable by crushing fines and perhaps even prison time, remember who and what Progressives really are. Touch the camouflage paint that disguises them and you will almost always find an authoritarian control-freak hidden beneath. [61]

When you hear Progressives promoting Obamacare and its "death panels" that have the government power to decide who lives and who dies, who gets treatment and who will be denied, remember who Progressives really are and what they really want. These are Progressive moral relativists to whom a dying snail darter or African lion are more important than a dying human being. How did such people take control of whether you can get a needed kidney transplant at age 89? How can this be happening?!

When you hear President Obama grabbing control over America's health care system, energy sector, auto industry, cable television industry, banking industry, student loans and, soon, your private retirement accounts – in the name of re-engineering American society into the kind of feudal monarchy America's Founders fought a revolution to escape, remember who Progressives really are and the total control over the rest of us that they really want.

"Every election is a sort of
advance auction sale of stolen goods."

– H.L. Mencken
Journalist "Sage of Baltimore"

*"The American people will never knowingly accept socialism.
But, under the name of 'liberalism,' they will
adopt every fragment of the socialist program,
until one day America will be a socialist nation,
without knowing how it happened....
I no longer need to run as a
presidential candidate for the Socialist Party.
The Democrat Party has adopted our platform."*

— Norman Thomas
Six-time Socialist Party candidate
Attributed to Thomas by Ronald Reagan & others

*"A society that puts equality...ahead of freedom
will end up with neither equality nor freedom."*

— Milton Friedman
Nobel Laureate economist

Chapter Seven

Retirement's End

"The American dream is not that every man
must be level with every other man.
The American dream is that every man
must be free to become whatever
God intends he should become."

– Ronald Reagan

Progressive President Franklin Delano Roosevelt signed Social Security into law on August 14, 1935. In 2015, this huge government program celebrated its 80th birthday.

Social Security and its related benefit programs Medicare and Medicaid are being depleted – and may soon be in real trouble.

Social Security Disability Insurance (SSDI) is expected to run out of money in 2016. The reason is that President Barack Obama's administration so eased its qualifications that those collecting SSDI benefits have increased by roughly 50 percent, to more than 10 million.

This is almost the total number of Americans with full-time jobs in all of manufacturing.

Social Security may not be there for a large share of today's workers – but could soon demand that they pay 25 percent or more of their income in taxes to keep Social Security benefits coming for Baby Boomers and Generation Xers.

Our ruling politicians looted the Social Security Trust Fund, and current economic policies have destroyed Social Security's promise of a secure retirement for millions of Americans.

Here are 12 troubling facts about Social Security and Medicare:

1. Social Security was supposed to keep Americans safe from old-age poverty – but Social Security, Medicaid and Medicare are rapidly running out of money. Ironically, its taxes on younger workers might soon drive *them* into poverty and an after-tax income so low that many will be unable to retire.

2. No matter how much you pay into Social Security, the high courts have ruled that no money is set aside in your name. Social Security has no legal obligation to pay you anything – although you will have an obligation to pay into this system.

Progressive IOUs

3. Social Security on paper has a trust fund of at least $2.8 Trillion that, along with taxes, was supposed to keep the system solvent until the early 2030s. But as *Washington Post* columnist Charles Krauthammer has reported, the Office of Management and Budget has described this fund "balance" as a mere "bookkeeping" device that does "not consist of real economic assets that can be drawn down in the future to fund benefits."

"In other words," wrote Krauthammer, "the Social Security trust fund contains – nothing." The politicians looted it of $2.66 Trillion over the years, leaving only IOUs that will require citizens to be taxed all over again to pay for the IOUs.

4. Medicare, signed into law by Democratic President Lyndon B. Johnson as an expansion of Social Security, in mid-2015 celebrated its 50th birthday. In order to fund Obamacare, President Obama and a Democrat-controlled Congress looted approximately $735 Billion – nearly three-quarters of a trillion dollars – from Medicare's trust fund.

5. Social Security was supposed to be a better way to save for retirement than private pensions because, its creators promised, the government would provide COLAs, cost-of-living adjustments in its benefit payments to offset the purchasing power stolen by inflation. The cost of living skyrocketed during President Obama's administration, but he refused to grant any COLA increases for Social Security beneficiaries in 2009, 2010 and 2011, before providing some relief in 2012, a re-election year.

Mr. Obama thus permanently lowered recipient baselines for all future COLAs, which forever robs all present and future Social Security beneficiaries via inflation. And no COLA is coming in 2016.

6. When created 80 years ago, Social Security benefits were not taxed. During Democratic President Bill and Hillary Clinton's administration, however, the law was changed so that up to 85 percent of a recipient's Social Security income can be taxed at his or her highest marginal tax rate…in effect, taxing again what had originally been collected as taxes to create security in that person's old age.

This cynical tax "claw back" of money by the government affects mostly those who continue to work into old age while collecting Social Security. But the enormous damage that Mr. Obama's anti-business policies have done to our economy has so reduced incomes and net worth that millions are forced to keep working. The Greatest Generation is required to pay again.

This greedy grab by government to take back a large part of their Social Security benefits is doubtless making many work until they die "in harness" like an old mule, after a life of forced labor for the taxman and no retirement. What this reveals is that Social Security has always just been a tax, more important as revenue for the government than security for you.

Changing the Rules

7. Social Security's original retirement age set by Democrats was 65 -- which just happened to be beyond the then-lifespan of the average African-American male, millions of whom would never live to collect benefits. So much for Progressive claims to be for "equality." If "Black Lives Matter" to Democrats, why did they build racial discrimination into Social Security?

Today the retirement age for full-benefits Social Security has been raised to 66 for those born 1943 to 1954, and to 67 for those born in 1960 or thereafter. The rationalization for this is that people on average now live longer than their parents – a pretext that may soon be used to raise the Social Security full retirement age to 70, 75 or 80 so that government can renege on paying the same benefits it provided to earlier generations.

This is raw discrimination by birth date and generation, age discrimination that would not be tolerated if imposed instead by race or gender – even though women on average outlive men and those of certain races on average live longer than those of other races.

8. Politicians such as Republican Governor of New Jersey Chris Christie have called for changing Social Security's rules in a variety of discriminatory ways to increase or preserve its assets. In addition to raising the age of eligibility for full benefits and reducing COLAs, planners have proposed reducing benefits either for everybody, or for retirees born after a certain year.

9. Planners talk of increasing Social Security taxes, especially by eliminating the current ceiling on taxing beyond a certain level of income. President Obama's allies have spoken of breaking the tax ceiling beyond its recent level of $113,700 and imposing this tax on every dollar earned, even on those who make billions. This would create a total disconnect between how much some will pay and the relatively small benefits they could collect.

Mean Testing

10. Many Progressives now argue that Social Security benefits ought to be means tested, like welfare payments, and denied to those rich enough that they "do not need" Social Security. This used to be resisted by liberals on the grounds that the political security of this program depended on all paying in and receiving benefits out.

Social Security has been expanded into a welfare, not merely retirement, program. Means testing, however, could start with the rich and soon be denying benefits to the middle class.

An ugly cynicism lurks behind such unequal standards. People who were taught to work hard and save their money in a 401(k) or IRA would be punished for their thrift if savings disqualified them for Social Security benefits they had been forced to pay into their entire working lives.

11. Even many of Social Security's supporters admit that it strongly resembles a Ponzi scheme that depends on today's worker taxes to pay today's retirees. Despite President Obama's mass importation of Latin Americans, America's fertility rate has recently fallen to a non-replacement level of 1.84 children per woman. Meanwhile, the huge Baby Boom generation is retiring, and nearly 94 million working-age Americans do not have full-time jobs. This likely means that benefits must soon be cut or Social Security taxes raised, which would reduce the working capital companies have left to hire more workers. If the economy sinks further, Social Security might sink with it.

12. Although the federal budget largely conceals this, Social Security and its related programs devour a larger hunk of total government revenues every year. If present trends continue, they will soon be eating up 25 percent or more of America's entire annual Gross Domestic Product. The entire federal budget is around $4 Trillion. Social Security alone each year creates another off-the-books $5 Trillion in long-term unfunded liabilities.

To paraphrase the Little Red Hen of the story, if you someday want to retire with money you will have to do this yourself, not rely on a geriatric Social Security's politicized financial gimmicks.

You also might want a portion of your savings in something more reliable than paper dollars that the government's printing presses could devalue overnight merely by printing trillions more of them.

If you want real security, you should act decisively to build it yourself.

During President Obama's first term, the government massively expanded the welfare state, took over American healthcare, effectively expropriated several major banks and two of the nation's three biggest car companies, and nationalized 90 percent of a trillion dollars of student loans.

In President Obama's second term, his biggest takeover target is the more than $20 Trillion that Americans have saved in their personal Individual Retirement Accounts (IRAs), 401(k) plans and pension accounts.

These may be the biggest pools of private money left in America, and our spendaholic politicians would love to divvy them up. [62-64]

"Guaranteed Retirement Accounts"

How will the Progressives seize your retirement savings? The public got a glimpse of one of their plans in 2008 and again in 2010 when the then-Democrat-run House Education and Labor Subcommittee invited Economics Professor Teresa Ghilarducci of the New School for Social Research in New York City to discuss her proposed new "Guaranteed Retirement Account" (GRA).

The GRA she envisions would replace today's 401(k)s and their $80+ Billion in annual tax breaks, as well as your IRA, that she believes unequally benefit the upper-middle class and the rich. [65]

"The government would deposit $600 (inflation indexed) every year into the GRAs," explained American Enterprise Institute economist James Pethokoukis. "Each worker would also have to save 5 percent of pay into the accounts, to which the government would pay a measly 3 percent return." [66]

GRAs would pay less than half the average return of the stock market, but they would be "safe." Or perhaps not, because GRAs would invest worker "contributions," taken from their paychecks just like Social Security taxes, in government debt paper.

This is a good deal for government, because its Treasuries have become a hard sell on world markets. The Federal Reserve has had to step in and buy more than 80 percent of them in recent years. GRAs will compel the purchase of such government debt and its low returns by ordinary working Americans.

So here is what Professor Ghilarducci and her Progressive politician comrades want for you. Government will take the IRA or 401(k) you now own and control, and will convert it into a GRA effectively owned by the government.

The government will pay you a small but reliable annuity based on government debt paper, meaning that your GRA will be a kind of "Social Security 2.0," only smaller. Ms. Ghilarducci's program would, she proposes, even be administered by Social Security.

And like Social Security, if you die early your family will not get the money they would have gotten from your IRA or 401(k). The government would likely take at least half of it, maybe more. Social Security takes it all.

Ultimately, as Ghilarducci told Seattle radio host Kirby Wilbur, her plan favors "giving everybody a flat amount so that it's more equal....spreading the wealth." GRA's real aim, in other words, is the redistribution of society's wealth – especially away from private sector capitalists and towards Progressive government. It takes what you saved for retirement, often at great personal and family sacrifice, and redistributes it to pay for the retirement of others.

Making Others Pay

In 2013 California lawmakers considered their own "Secure Choice Retirement Savings Program" that would require private employers with five or more employees to squeeze 3 percent from every employee paycheck, then send it to be mingled in a state fund, CalPERS, the California Public Employees Retirement System. The purpose: to cover the huge shortfall caused by California not adequately funding public employee retirements.... and to become another slush fund politicians can loot. [67]

This new law is expected in its first year to add $6.6 Billion to the coffers of a California government retirement system already underfunded by as much as $500 Billion. This is one more way to tax private sector workers' earnings to bankroll fat pensions for the public employee unions that have run a once-golden State of California into the ground.

California, as we have written, has experienced a 'reverse gold rush' of successful people fleeing to keep from losing the gold they have earned to the sky-high taxes. By destroying this state's once-prosperous economy, politicians have made it appropriate that the animal on the California flag is a bear, not a bull.

Apparently no "lockbox" protects your involuntary GRA contributions in her plan. "If subsidies for 401(k)-style plans and IRAs can be relocated to Guaranteed Retirement Accounts, why not use this money to shore up and expand Social Security? This is certainly an option," writes Ghilarducci. [68]

In 2010 President Obama's Treasury and Labor Departments, as well as ruling Congressional Democrats, were openly discussing such ways to confiscate private retirement accounts and "replace" them with a government "annuity" backed by Treasury bonds.

This would force Americans to buy risky government debt, just as China, Japan and other nations are now less and less willing to do.

In effect, this scheme would seize peoples' private savings, which politicians would then spend immediately to expand the welfare state, making more voters dependent on government handouts.

The New Bondage

Retirees, in place of their savings, would be paid a government bond interest rate lower than the rate of inflation.

Or, instead of their savings, retirees would get inflated paper government dollars worth less than what they had saved. In effect, this would transfer to the government trillions of dollars that senior citizens had earned.

This confiscation of trillions of dollars from the savings of retirees would already be happening if voters in 2010 had not thrown out the Democratic majority in the House of Representatives.

Argentina in 2008 effectively expropriated the money in private pension funds, leaving debased government bonds worth only 29 cents of their face value in their place – much as our politicians looted and spent $2.66 Trillion from the Social Security Trust Fund, leaving paper I.O.U.s in its place.

Bulgaria likewise transferred approximately $60 Million in private retirement savings into a government pension scheme. Ireland levied money from the National Pension Reserve Fund to bail out banks.

In 2010 Hungary demanded that citizens give the government their private savings or forfeit all state pension money they had been promised.

President Obama is eager to "spread the wealth around" that belongs to achievers who have earned and saved it. But the more he takes from these savers, by "means testing" or a hundred other Progressive gimmicks, the more he will discourage people from saving for their own retirement – and the more he will make retirees dependent on an already-bankrupt government.

People need to wake up and see the bull's-eye, the red laser dot, where rapacious, money-hungry politicians are aiming for their IRAs, 401(k)s, and pensions.

Your retirement nest egg is being targeted for political confiscation. A prudent decision could be: "Move it or lose it." Move it where? Into something you can hold securely in your hands, but that is not paper dollars or anything denominated in dollars. You need something that makes your retirement independent of government.

Take at least a portion of your savings and convert it into something that will not be lost if the politicians suddenly confiscate your retirement accounts, or further debase the dollar's value to cover the stratospheric debts caused by out-of-control government spending. At some point, the only way politicians will be able to "pay" America's sky-high debt will be to "monetize" the debt by printing hundreds of trillions of new paper dollars that will instantly incinerate your saved dollars in a firestorm of hyperinflation.

The End of Inheritance

Progressives also hate inheritance, the traditional path by which successful and thrifty families are able to pass on and increase their wealth generation after generation.

Progressives hate inheritance for several reasons. It is anti-egalitarian, amplifying the visible difference between successful and unsuccessful families. It is unjust, Progressives believe, because it parlays the winnings of those who were merely "winners in life's lottery."

And, worst of all, wealth accumulated via inheritance creates families and individuals with enough wealth that they become islands of freedom that can protect those who defy Progressivism, much as the Left's hated Koch brothers were able for many years to fund the libertarian free market think tank the Cato Institute.

Nations work best with reliable rules and laws that apply equally to all. These give people the trust and confidence to plan, build, make decisions and invest, free from fear that some greedy ruler on a whim will expropriate their property or confiscate their savings.

Since ancient Rome this ideal was a "government of laws, not men," in which the same rules impartially applied to all. The problem, as the ancient Roman poet Juvenal wrote, is that governments are administered by human beings. What happens when the guardians, given vast powers to enforce the law fairly, become unfair and unjust?

What happens, for example, when a President intervenes in the bankruptcy proceedings of General Motors and Chrysler, slaps aside laws and legal precedents that for more than 200 years gave secured bondholders a significant share of remaining company value, and gives $26 Billion that should have gone to these bondholders and others instead to a labor union that has been a major campaign contributor to that President and his political party? [69]

MIT Economics Professor Jonathan Gruber, who was one of the major architects of the President's largest piece of legislation, the Affordable Care Act known as Obamacare, is seen on videotape boasting at various academic meetings about how the law was passed by deceiving and lying to the American people about what it would cost them. This was possible, he brags, because of the "stupidity" of most Americans. [70]

In our time such breaking of ethics, rules and laws has become commonplace. Immigration and other laws have been cast aside to benefit special interests. Politicians have used eminent domain laws to take the private property of some so it can be given to other private owners with better political connections. Tax laws are applied unequally to favor those of the ruling party and to punish its opponents. Environmental laws are used to advance ideological agendas and to crush private enterprises.

As we document in our 2014 book *Don't Bank On It! The Unsafe World of 21st Century Banking,* today banks are being shaken down for tens of billions of dollars in arbitrary fines and penalties, and much of this money has been transferred to radical activist organizations.

A Deficit of Trust

The President and Attorney General Eric Holder, when he was the nation's chief law enforcement officer, repeatedly defied congressional subpoenas and court orders by federal judges. The president continues to boast that if Congress refuses to give him the laws or funding he wants, he will impose his will via Executive Orders, regulatory rules and fines from agencies in his Executive Branch. He behaves as if he is a king, not a president with limited powers who swore to faithfully uphold the Constitution.

In less than seven years, this president's profligate spending has increased America's debt by more than $7.5 Trillion. America's total short-term debt is approaching $19 Trillion on its way to $20 Trillion.

The worst deficit the President has created, however, is a deficit of trust…a breach of trust and faith that for the first time in history has Americans doubting whether our future will be as successful as our past. Many wonder if they must now move elsewhere to regain the freedom and opportunity our ancestors once found by coming here.

As a presidential candidate, Mr. Obama said he was about to "fundamentally transform" the United States.

In his January 20, 2015 State of the Union address before Congress, the President recalled his campaign promise to "rebuild our economy on a new foundation," as if the limited government, free market economics, private property and individual liberty and responsibility set forth as America's foundation by our country's Framers is about to be repealed and replaced.

He would, the President said, begin putting forth specific plans for his brave new America two weeks after this speech.

"[W]e don't have the devilish details yet," wrote *Forbes* Magazine columnist and tax specialist Peter J. Reilly, evoking the old saying that in most such things "the devil is in the details." [71] But a January 17 document from the White House has well-informed Americans seeing red from what we already know.

"Close the Trust Fund Loophole"

Three days before the President's 2015 State of the Union speech, the office of the White House Press Secretary issued a "Fact Sheet" that described the President's ideas for "A Simpler, Fairer Tax Code...." [72]

The President's first objective in this paper was to "Close the trust fund loophole...to ensure that the wealthiest Americans pay their fair share on inherited assets....Hundreds of billions of dollars escape capital gains taxation each year because of the 'stepped up' basis loophole that lets the wealthy pass appreciated assets onto their heirs tax-free."

No, Mr. President, this is *not* a "loophole." It is a law duly enacted by Congress and signed into law. This is how things are *supposed* to work.

"The President's proposal would close the stepped-up basis loophole by treating bequests and gifts other than to charitable organizations as realization events, like other cases where assets change hands. It would also increase the total top capital gains and dividend rate to 28 percent...."

According to this vague White House document, "No tax would be due on inherited small, family-owned and operated businesses – unless and until the business was sold." It did not specify at what dollar value a "small" business would transform into "large enough to tax," or whether inflation would eventually make all businesses subject to this tax.

Married couples would be granted a combined $200,000 capital gains exemption plus a combined $500,000 exemption for personal residences. In a world of inflation, such dollar amounts could quickly become meaningless, as the people of Weimar, Germany discovered after World War I. Today, after more than a century of inflation, most of us are paying "Progressive" income tax rates that lawmakers once promised would hit only the wealthy.

What this White House document calls a "trust fund loophole" could therefore quickly become a noose for middle-class families trying to pass on their previously-taxed savings, investments and property to their children.

Making Death A Taxable Event

The White House Fact Sheet's proposed "loophole" closure "is so radical because....It makes death and gifting realization events" subject to potentially-immediate taxation, writes Peter J. Reilly in *Forbes*. [73]

"President Obama," writes Reilly, "would make death a taxable event."

In January 2015 the Obama White House left no doubt that it is targeting families and intergenerational wealth transfers of the kind found in trusts. It talked openly of imposing hefty taxes on 529 college savings plans, named for the section of the Internal Revenue Service code that allows a tax exemption for such savings.

Taxing these 529 accounts would break the promise politicians had made to savers to help educate their children. It would also break candidate Barack Obama's pledge that families earning less than $200,000 per year would not see their taxes increased "by even a nickel."

President Obama withdrew his plan to retroactively tax these tax-exempt 529 college accounts not because doing so was unethical and unfair, but only because prominent liberals in his own party, including former House Speaker Nancy Pelosi, warned that this would be "politically toxic." [74]

Other savings accounts are already being tapped by more stealthy means, as we documented in *The Inflation Deception* and other books. As those with bank savings accounts have painfully discovered, the U.S. Treasury and Federal Reserve are following a deliberate policy of "financial repression," holding the interest rate banks pay savers below the rate of real-world inflation.

This policy guarantees that savers are losing the value of their deposits faster than (taxable) bank interest payments increase them. They lose purchasing power every day they have their savings, denominated in paper dollars, in a bank account. And this creates an opening for government to profit by printing more paper dollars out of thin air, a government gain paid for in part by bank saver losses.

What Can You Trust?

Welcome to Progressiveland, where Americans face higher risk than reward by trusting their savings to bank accounts – especially when held in the form of inflating, debased U.S. dollars.

After the Chrysler and GM bankruptcy, how safe are secured corporate bonds? After the Detroit bankruptcy gave a "haircut" to its once-trusting bondholders, how safe are tax-free municipal bonds?

Note that in H.L. Mencken's quote on the page opposite this book's Introduction, the great Baltimore journalist in 1925 warned that leftists were in favor of seizing the property of bondholders.

With the stock market yo-yoing wildly from being drunk on Federal Reserve stimulus and artificially-low interest rates, what sober person wants to risk his or her future in this casino of speculators and high-frequency traders who hold stock for only milliseconds while economies around the world, especially in Europe and China, are skidding sideways towards possible recession or worse? [75]

And now, if you have been hardworking, thrifty and lucky enough to have a home and savings and a successful self-made business (oh, wait, the President says "you didn't build that"...that somehow the government, not your family, deserves the profits), our government of cash-starved spendaholic politicians wants to impose yet more death taxes of various kinds on what you leave your children.

In 2008 the two final Democratic presidential candidates, Mr. Obama and Hillary Clinton, met in an ABC televised debate in Philadelphia. Co-anchor Charles Gibson asked now-President Barack Obama about the capital gains tax: Why did the Illinois Senator want to raise this tax, when experience showed that government made more revenue by lowering the tax and less revenue by raising it? (Apparently people take more steps to legally avoid a higher capital gains tax.) And why use a tax that could hit 100 million stock-owning Americans?

Mr. Obama replied that he "would look at raising the capital gains tax for purposes of fairness." [76]

"How To Tax The Rich"

This kind of ideological class warfare – waged not to lift up the poor but to tear down rich and average investors and free market job-creators, even if doing so costs the government revenue – suggests what we can expect from Mr. Obama's last year as President. Some analysts dread what he will feel free to do with executive powers in the weeks between the 2016 November election and the end of his term in late January 2017.

Where does President Obama get such class warfare ideas? One source is David Kamin, his former Special Assistant for Economic Policy in the White House.

Kamin, now an Assistant Professor at New York University School of Law, on January 5, 2015 published an article that should frighten every successful American. His article lays out some of the same ideas that appeared later that month in the White House "Fact Sheet." Professor Kamin's article – utterly contrary to our Framers' belief in economic liberty; in equal treatment before the law, including tax law; and in small government – is titled "How to Tax the Rich." [77]

This is the kind of contempt today's Progressives hold for America's Framers and Constitution.

No wonder so many people – who used to trust the laws and rules that were supposed to keep their trust fund a safe haven for their children's inheritance

– are now feeling uncertainty and fear, and beginning to see that a different, safer haven may be urgently needed to secure their children's future.

"To tax the larger incomes at a higher percentage
than the smaller is to lay a tax on industry and economy;
to impose a penalty on people for having
worked harder and saved more than their neighbors."

– John Stuart Mill
British Philosopher

"The principle of spending money to be paid
by posterity, under the name of funding, is but
swindling futurity on a large scale."

– Thomas Jefferson

"Christmas is a time when kids tell Santa
what they want and adults pay for it.
Deficits are when adults tell the government
what they want and their kids pay for it."

– Richard Lamm
Former Colorado governor

Chapter Eight

The War On Cash

"The anonymity of paper money is liberating.
The bottom line is, you have to decide
how you want to run your society."

– Prof. Stephen Cecchetti
Brandeis International
Business School [78]

Denny Hastert is a casualty of war.

In 2015, the former Speaker of the House was caught in a legal trap [79], one weapon being used in a "war against cash" our government and others are now waging. This trap was set to catch those who have the old-fashioned notion that they are free to withdraw their cash money from their bank as they wish.

You, too, are a casualty of this war if you have a bank account – and probably do not even know it.

Cash is tangible money, bills and coins, and governments have always had at best a love-hate relationship with it.

Such money for thousands of years gave people a medium of exchange, a unit of account, and a store of value that governments could tax indirectly by debasing its coins with cheaper metals – or directly by confiscation.

But cash also gave people ways to buy, sell and enrich themselves without anyone knowing. Cash was anonymous money that often allowed people to move and carry away their earnings in complete privacy.

Progressives now characterize cash as the currency of the black market, drug dealers and other lawbreakers.

However in a young American Republic of low taxes, cash was also the currency of the free. It was the great equalizer where each person's hard-earned, gold-backed dollar was as good as anyone else's, almost regardless of the pedigree of their ancestors.

America's founding values began to disappear in a fundamental transformation in 1913, as we discuss in our 2014 book *Don't Bank On It! The Unsafe World of 21st Century Banking.* [80] In that year the new Democratic President Woodrow Wilson signed into law the "Progressive" income tax to tax previously-equal people very unequally in order to redistribute wealth in our society.

In practice, the largest redistribution has not been from rich to poor, but from the private sector to the government itself and its crony institutions such as giant banks.

Wilson also authorized the kind of European central bank opposed by many of America's Framers and dismantled almost a century earlier by Democratic President Andrew Jackson.

Wilson's Federal Reserve System was sold to the people as a way to protect the integrity of the U.S. Dollar by taking the politics out of monetary decisions. The Fed, however, was chartered to furnish an "elastic" currency.

Progressive politicians had been frustrated that the inelastic, hard money gold standard prevented them from printing endless quantities of dollars to expand the government. The Fed moved quickly to ease the golden handcuffs on politicians [81], and in 1933 another Progressive Democratic President, Franklin Delano Roosevelt, eliminated not only the gold standard but also the gold clauses that kept contracts honest -- and even the right of Americans to own gold bullion at all. To the delight of many, certain gold coins were exempted, and this remains in effect to this day.

The Fed has protected our currency so well that today's debased U.S. Dollar, no longer backed by anything except the "full faith and credit of the United States Government," has roughly two pennies of the purchasing power of the 1913 dollar.

The fix for this, a growing number of economists now argue, is to eliminate pennies and dollars. They want to outlaw cash and usher in a "cashless society," and to implement a totally digital facsimile.

Cashing In

Despite its apparent failure to protect the dollar's value, the Fed in 102 years has acquired enormous influence and power. Under another Democratic President, Jimmy Carter, the Fed acquired a second "mandate," to use monetary policy to maximize employment.

Critics have said that the Fed seems to have secret mandates as well – to "levitate" the stock market (Bernanke said as much in 2010), and even to help time the ups and downs in the market to benefit particular presidential candidates, incumbents or challengers.

In a November 4, 2010 *Washington Post* Op-Ed column, then-Fed Chairman Ben Bernanke nearly confessed. Of the Fed's Quantitative Easing II (QE II) commitment to inject another $600 Billion into the economy that had been announced a day earlier, Bernanke wrote:

"Stock prices rose and long-term interest rates fell when investors began to anticipate the most recent action.... And higher stock prices will boost consumer wealth and help increase confidence, which can also spur spending. Increased spending will lead to higher incomes and profits that, in a virtuous circle, will further support economic expansion." [82]

The Fed has certainly become a central planner in the U.S. economy, redirecting vast flows of energy by how the Fed Open Market Committee acts to adjust available money and credit.

Most Fed policymakers, like those of President Barack Obama, are Keynesians. The late British economist John Maynard Keynes believed that the ups and downs of the business cycle could be smoothed if national governments and central banks raised aggregate demand by injecting stimulus money into a down economy and increased taxes during up times.

A dollar taxed from the rich and then given (via government) to the poor should generate a "multiplier effect" of up to $1.50 or more worth of economic stimulus, Keynes believed, because the poor had to spend this money immediately, not save it. This is supposed to increase the "velocity" of dollars from one hand to the next, thereby boosting prosperity.

By this same logic, Keynes wrote of the "paradox of thrift," that it is bad when people save money because this slows its circulation in the economy.

Keynes was not necessarily a socialist for much of his life. He in fact came to dislike the Soviet Union and high deficit spending. And Keynes is that rare economist who actually invested in the market – made one fortune, lost it, and then made another as a practicing capitalist.

Yet because Keynes favored taxing the rich, high government spending (but only at times, not perpetually), and advocated redistributing money from rich to poor, he gave leftists the ability to pursue many of their Big Government policies while claiming to be Keynesians, not socialists.

Most of Keynes' theories have failed in practice. In the real world, as we noted earlier, stimulus works only in primitive economies. In advanced economies, government stimulus spending gets discounted – taken into everyone's investment calculations – instantly.

Since the start of the continuing bad U.S. economy in 2008, the Fed and Obama Administration have conjured roughly $8 Trillion of stimulus out of thin air. This should have been enough money to stimulate almost everyone into prosperity, according to Keynes.

Oddly, however, all this money proved to be an "anti-stimulus," as we predicted. Its potential to create high inflation and more taxes made investors afraid to invest and businesses afraid to hire. Today, after all this stimulus and debt heaped onto present and future taxpayers, the velocity of money in the U.S. economy is at its slowest in nearly 50 years. The job participation rate shows 94 million working-age Americans without a needed full-time job – the lowest this indicator has been since President Carter's "malaise" in 1978.

Cashing Out in Wonderland

The Fed has largely used up its bag of monetary tricks. Like an addictive drug, its fixes of money no longer stimulate. Its debt manipulations such as Quantitative Easing no longer work.

And the Fed now finds itself painted into a corner. It dealt with the crisis by adopting ZIRP, a Zero Interest Rate Policy, driving the interest rate at which government and the giant corporations can borrow to almost zero, no more than 0.25 percent.

This essentially-free money until recently kept the stock market casino open and above 18,000 – but this is mostly based on companies using the free money to buy back their own stock or other companies. The GDP during the first Quarter of 2015 was at minus 0.7 percent. Only the building of unsold inventories and oil fracking on private land, contrary to President Obama's policies, have narrowly kept the U.S. out of full-blown recession. The economy, simply put, is not really growing!

Even the Fed's economists know that ZIRP in the long run will destroy the economy for those needing interest income, such as elderly bank savers. The government, however, is addicted to borrowing at zero interest and lacks the revenue to cover its huge debts if interest rates rise more than a fraction of one percent in the near future.

The Fed and many other central banks around the world have an odd solution that brings us back to cash: let the interest rates fall *below* zero.

Fall through the looking glass with Alice in Wonderland, many neo-Keynesians now promise, and somehow even more negative interest rates will cause amazing new economic stimulus.

"Like chemotherapy, negative interest rates are a harsh medicine," writes *Bloomberg Business* reporter Peter Coy. "It's disorienting when people are paid to borrow and charged to save." [84]

Only one thing stands in the way of this Central Bank miracle solution, writes Coy, and that thing is cash.

"As long as paper money is available as an alternative for customers who want to withdraw their [bank] deposits, there's a limit to how low central banks can push rates," writes Coy. "At some point it becomes cost-effective to rent a warehouse for your billions in cash and hire armed guards to protect it." [85]

What zero or negative rates mean to bank savers is that they receive no interest for taking the 20 major banking risks we describe in *Don't Bank On It!* To add insult to injury, savers are now starting to be required to pay the bank a fee for the honor of lending it their money for free.

The War Against Cash

If people wish to withdraw their cash, why would the banks not just let them take their dollars and go? The answer is that doing this might unravel today's economic grand illusion and bring the whole game crashing down.

As one research firm put it, "Cash is a MAJOR problem for the central banks." Here, as they explained, is why:

"The total currency (actual cash in the form of bills and coins) in the U.S. financial system is a little over $1.36 trillion." [86]

Include digital money in short and long-term accounts and we have roughly $10 Trillion in "money" in the financial system, they write.

U.S. stock market equity is over $20 Trillion. The U.S. bond market, including various government bonds, is around $38 Trillion.

Total credit market instruments ("mortgages, collateralized debt obligations, junk bonds, commercial paper and other digitally-based 'money' that is based on debt"), they calculated, add up to $58.7 Trillion.

And atop it all, as we've discussed in our books, "Unregulated over the counter derivatives traded between the big banks and corporations [are] north of $220 trillion." [87]

"[A]ctual physical money or cash (as in bills or coins you can hold in your hand)," they write, "comprises less than 1% of the 'money' in the financial system.... [I]f investors/depositors were ever to try and convert even a small portion of this 'wealth' into actual physical bills, the system would implode. (There is simply not enough actual cash.)" [88]

"[W]hen the 2008 Crisis hit, one of the biggest problems for the Central Banks was to stop investors from fleeing digital wealth for the comfort of physical cash," they note. "Indeed, the actual 'thing' that almost caused the financial system to collapse was when depositors attempted to pull $500 billion out of money market funds." [89]

In *Don't Bank On It!* we analyzed this threat in the context of Money Market Mutual Funds (not to be confused with what some banks call Money Market Funds), where in 2008 frightened customers withdrew $300 Billion in one week. The SEC has endeavored to put withdrawal delays in place to prevent a recurrence, but could these prompt some simply to withdraw even sooner? [90]

The "War Against Cash" is happening because cash has become intolerably dangerous to the giant illusion built mostly out of debt paper. See the paper moon? See the cardboard sea? It's all make-believe, Alice.

Our un-backed fiat currency itself is also an illusion. In 2015 the International Monetary Fund postponed that year's planned October meeting until September 2016 to consider taking away the U.S. Dollar's monopoly as the Global Reserve Currency and to give the Chinese Yuan/Renminbi a share of the dollar's once-exclusive status. You will not want to be wholly invested in dollars or anything denominated in dollars such as stocks and bonds if and when that day comes – unless you have taken prior defensive actions.

There are far more real and time-proven alternatives to paper money, as America's Framers knew and affirmed in the Constitution.

As Austrian economist Ludwig von Mises remembered watching during the Weimar hyperinflation of the early 1920s, the wise made a "flight into things," exchanging their evaporating German Marks for inherently valuable things such as gold that could not be run off a government printing press by the trillions and thereby debased, like fiat currency.

Even in its debased status, the physical dollar still commands more faith than most other faith-based currencies.

To use Thomas Jefferson's term, your bank account may be only "the ghost of money," mere flickering electrons in a computer memory bank somewhere waiting to be hacked or erased. Cash you can at least hold in your hand.

It is not hard to see a run on banks and digital funds, with millions of panicked people demanding dollars instead of the investment paper they already have.

This, say its critics, is why cash ultimately must be killed.

People must stop believing that they have the choice to flee into cash. That option must soon be diverted, thwarted, blocked and ultimately eliminated forever. This is what the "War Against Cash" means.

Stigmatizing Cash

Who is behind the "War on Cash?"

The United States Government is fighting against cash on many fronts, including its apprehension of former Republican Speaker of the House Dennis J. Hastert. Since 1970 the government has required banks to report any cash withdrawal or deposit of $10,000 or more.

In recent years a secondary crime was created called "structuring," which means withdrawing or depositing some amount less than $10,000 with the intent of avoiding the transaction being reported to the government. As we noted in a research paper, this is almost Orwellian, the sort of thought crime one finds in George Orwell's dystopian novel *1984*. Hastert was indicted for "structuring," for the crime of withdrawing less than the amount that must be reported to the government. [91]

Your bank actually is now required to report to the government any financial behavior on your part it deems "suspicious" or "unusual." If you withdraw $500 over several weeks for big weekend yard sales, your bank might report this as "unusual," flagging you for government surveillance.

Your bank is under threat of regulatory punishment if it does not spy on you for the government. The government, so far as we know, gives only vague guidelines, not exacting standards, as to what in your finances might be unusual or suspicious.

It is clear, however, that withdrawals and deposits in cash will arouse more suspicion than doing your banking by check, credit card or electronic transfer.

The government justifies such scrutiny by invoking the RICO anti-racketeering statues and 2001 Patriot Act, claiming to need to monitor your once-private transactions to fight organized crime and terrorism. (This is ironic in Hastert's case, because he has been indicted via a law he helped enact.) Does anyone seriously believe, however, that 73-year-old Denny Hastert is either a terrorist or a racketeer?

Black Market Money

A larger, logical government motive in going after cash is tax evasion. We analyzed this in our 2012 book *The Great Debasement: The 100-Year Dying of the Dollar and How to Get America's Money Back*:

> A 2011 study by Edgar Feige of the University of Wisconsin-Madison and Richard Cebula of Jacksonville University in Florida concluded that between 18 and 19 percent of total reportable income in the United States is effectively off the books, hidden from the government.
>
> This income – from drugs, prostitution, private gambling, home repairs, and a thousand other things paid in cash – could, Feige

and Cebula estimate, have harvested half a trillion dollars in tax revenue for the government.

Cash makes it easy for criminals to thrive in an economic underworld of untraceable illicit transactions. A cashless society, say advocates, would drag this underworld out of the shadows and into disinfecting sunlight. In a cashless society, they say, crime would not pay as well as it does today.

Civil libertarians, however, are troubled that cashless crusaders now seem to be demonizing cash.

"We're trying to use industrial age money to support commerce in a post-industrial age. It just doesn't work," David Birch, a director of Consult Hyperion, a firm that specializes in electronic payments, told *Slate* Magazine.

"Sooner or later," Birch continued, "the tectonic plates shift and then, very quickly, you'll find yourself in this new environment where if you ask somebody to pay you in cash, you'll just assume that they're a prostitute or a Somali pirate."

"Do you see what is happening?" libertarian journalist Lew Rockwell wrote in April 2012. "Simply using cash is enough to get you branded as a potential criminal these days."

The Federal Government now tightly limits how much cash citizens are allowed to carry through border checkpoints into or out of the United States. When you withdraw or deposit $10,000 in cash, your bank reportedly is to notify the government of this transaction, thereby marking you for potential surveillance. [92]

Denny Hastert was initially flagged by his bank for withdrawing cash – reportedly as hush money for a blackmailer – in increments of $50,000. He might be a free man today if he had read our books. We continued:

Merely doing transactions with $100 bills, the standard currency of illicit drug dealers, can attract government attention. The law has authorized the asset forfeiture of objects carrying detectable traces of cocaine, however small, which reportedly is the case with as much as 90 percent of U.S. currency notes in circulation. This law has been used to confiscate currency on those grounds. [93]

Cases of Forfeiture

Our federal, state and local governments have also made it more risky to carry cash because of their growing use of civil asset forfeiture laws. Many have had sizeable amounts of cash in their possession confiscated by law enforcement officials.

In many cases, the person whose cash has been taken is not charged with any crime. Instead, his or her cash is declared to be an accessory to criminal activity, and the burden of proof is put on the owners to prove that the cash is legitimately theirs. In some cases, the targets of such asset forfeiture are told they will get back a third or half of their cash if they sign an agreement that the government is entitled to the rest. Your money, which it took a piece of your lifetime to earn, is now guilty until proven innocent.

Consider a few examples of how the government now confiscates cash from what used to be regarded as law-abiding citizens:

In Arlington, Virginia, Army Sergeant Jeff Cortazzo had been saving from his paychecks for his daughter's education since around the time of the financial crisis in 2008. After several years, he decided to redeposit this cash in a bank but was afraid it might be taxed again, so the bank teller told him to make deposits of less than $10,000. After he had done this, the government seized his $66,000 college fund, then after his long and costly legal battle it returned only $45,000. This innocent man who committed no crime lost $21,000. [94]

Virginia State Police stopped Victor Luis Guzman for speeding, then confiscated $28,500 in his car. A Pentecostal Church secretary, he was carrying parishioners' donations. The police refused to return this money until an attorney who served in the Justice Department's Asset Forfeiture Office during the Reagan Administration took the case pro bono. [95]

In Athens, Georgia Andrew Clyde, a Navy veteran, saw the government seize nearly a million dollars from the bank account of his small firearms store. Like Hastert, he was accused of "structuring." His "crime": having an insurance policy capped at $10,000, so he and his staff never carried that much in cash when going to the bank to make deposits. It cost Clyde more than $150,000 in legal and other expenses, plus a fine of $50,000 to get the rest of his money back.

"I did not serve three combat tours in Iraq only to come home and be extorted" by his government, Clyde told a congressional hearing in February 2015. [96]

In Fairmont, North Carolina, country store owner Lyndon McLellan saw the IRS seize $107,000 from his bank account. The IRS then offered to return half his money if he signed an agreement to let them keep the other half. He refused, and faced with growing publicity about his case on Fox News and elsewhere, it finally returned his money without explanation. [97]

During legal battles, McLellan noticed an affidavit from a state official. The Department of Justice has an Equitable Sharing Program that gives state and local law enforcement agencies a share of the proceeds of forfeiture opportunities they give to the Feds.

In Helper, Utah, the city offered an even more ominous incentive. It gave one-quarter of the value of anything forfeited to the police officer who made the asset forfeiture bust. [98]

Even at best, this gives police an unbalanced motive to spend their time looking for forfeitures, not violent criminals. At worst, it could become a temptation for police to become criminals themselves. An officer sees a $100,000 convertible sports car, or a $1 Million home – and all this policeman needs to do to pocket 25 percent of their value is to toss a bit of an illegal substance into the car or through an open house window, then seize the property.

Such potentially self-serving power seems dangerous to our civil liberties, but the way most governments now use civil asset forfeiture is little better. An individual officer might not profit, but his department does – and so do city or state governments where asset forfeiture becomes the new "speed trap" as a rich source of revenue.

One of the most famous early abuses of asset forfeiture happened in 1992 when a California drug task force raided a man's home in Malibu and shot to death the reclusive millionaire owner when he tried to resist the strangers invading his home. [99]

No drugs were found there, but lawyers looking into the case found police documents with margin notes fantasizing about all they could do with his 200-acre property.

The government will never give up any power as lucrative as asset forfeiture, but veteran Judge Jim Gray recommends reforming it by requiring that anything forfeited go into a neutral fund – a charity or the like. Forfeitures should not directly profit individuals or agencies that carry out the forfeitures. This would reduce their incentive to abuse this frightful government power. [100]

Choking Off Cash

The Obama Administration Justice Department implemented what it calls "Operation Choke Point." Banks have been given a list of approximately 30 types of business it associates with "high-risk." Bankers are then asked to divulge detailed information about the finances of any customers who fit the list and to close the bank accounts of any the banker deems to be engaged in "suspicious" activities.

Here, too, the Obama Administration offers only vague notions of what might cost a business its bank account. As we reported in *Don't Bank On It!*:

> "Operation Choke Point" throws a very wide net. It requires banks to impose government policy in ways that may be ideological, unethical or even illegal against people and legal businesses that have been convicted of no crime whatsoever. [101]

The Obama Administration, for example, seems obsessed with restricting the constitutional rights of gun owners, and two of the businesses targeted by Operation Choke Point are firearms and ammunition sellers.

When such government pressure on banks takes away a small company's ability to have bank accounts, the business to survive may start operating in cash. But if it deals in cash, it might then become a target for asset forfeiture by government.

The message sent by such government policies is that cash is risky. People have known for thousands of years that carrying cash might make you a target for thieves. During today's "War Against Cash" it can also make you a target for law enforcement officers.

The Anti-Cash Ideology

The "War on Cash" is also an ideological war. According to longtime Pace University economist Joseph T. Salerno, it should be seen as nothing less than "a despotic attack by the ruling elites on the personal privacy and liberties of their citizens."

A central combatant in this push towards a "Cashless Society" is "The Better Than Cash Alliance," which Professor Salerno describes as "initiated and funded by the left-leaning Ford Foundation in 2012." [102]

Among its "partners," writes Salerno, are "the U.S. Agency for International Development (USAID); the Bill and Melinda Gates Foundation; and (surprise, surprise) the failed and bailed-out Citi [bank] as well as credit card companies MasterCard and Visa."

"The United Nations is also involved," writes Professor Salerno, "with the UN Capital Development Fund serving as the alliance's secretariat…. One of the key initiatives promoted by the Alliance is to induce governments of developing countries to deliver welfare electronically."

The positive spin of The Better Than Cash Alliance depicts a Third World with young female entrepreneurs in isolated rural farming villages able to have a business by using a cell phone as their bank and credit card link.

Because they use only the phone, not cash, the Alliance contends that such business people are far less likely to get robbed or shaken down by government officials for bribes.

In such a cashless future, it probably will be harder for an ordinary petty thief to rob you, but it will be much easier for the government to rob you. When every transaction must go through a government-monitored digital financial link via a cell phone, all financial privacy will vanish. As we speculated about a "cashless" future in *The Great Debasement:*

> To make such a system work, its advocates quietly add, all transactions must be equal and each one must be a taxable event. Give your son $100 for high school graduation? The 20 percent tax is automatically deducted. Buy an old lamp at a neighbor's yard sale? Pay 20 percent. Lose a sports bet with a co-worker? Pay 20 percent. Give to a hungry poor family? Or to your church or synagogue? Or to the politician demanding a bribe to approve your building permit? Pay 20 percent. No exceptions....

> Much as gold was replaced by inflation-plagued paper fiat money, the cashless society envisioned by such advocates could replace paper fiat money with magical digital money that is always connected to the government – and that loses another 20 percent of its value to the government every time you use it.

> In such a Brave New World, of course, there will be no place to hide. You cannot purchase food or fuel without the transaction being monitored. Your cell phone, by government mandate, contains a locator chip that makes you easy to find (unless you remove its battery).

> Could the American Revolution have been won if our Founders lived in such a cashless society? If every transaction must be cleared by a central computer, then whoever controls that computer can monitor or block any transaction a targeted individual attempts to make.

> The George Washingtons and Thomas Jeffersons of a future cashless America could easily be neutralized by Progressive redcoats. [103]

Cash allows individual autonomy. What does a cashless society allow?

Cash and Carry Tax

In a future cashless society, as we wrote in *Don't Bank On It!*, everything will be hackable, trackable and taxable. [104] If a government official wishes, he can know within seconds your whereabouts and everything you have recently bought or sold. Indeed, he can probably turn off your ability to buy and sell. As we wrote in *The Great Debasement:*

> *Anyone, whether Christian or not, might find it disquieting that the Bible (Book of Revelation 13:17) foresaw a coming day when only those who carry the mark of the ruler's number on their bodies will be able to "buy and sell." [105]*

This much seems likely: the face on the invisible coin of the cashless society will be that of Caesar.

Cashless advocates such as the Alliance will try to persuade you to voluntarily abandon cash for the greater convenience of a cashless future. But make no mistake: cash will eventually be outlawed or restricted, with capital controls already coming down hard in Sweden, Denmark, France, Greece, and many other places. Eventually those caught carrying cash might be subject to its forfeiture….or even imprisonment. Call it "CashCrime."

And understand that what has happened to Speaker Hastert is merely a variant of this…withdrawing his own cash contrary to government surveillance laws.

Cash can be killed or made impractical in other ways, of course. In his *General Theory*, John Maynard Keynes toyed with issuing paper money that included a device so that this cash kept losing value. Because the worth of such cash was evaporating, the holder had a huge incentive to spend it immediately, not save it.

Keynes liked the idea of money that could not be saved, that was being depleted by a built-in "carry tax." With the technology available at the time, however, Keynes saw the idea as impractical.

In 1999, another version of such a "Carry Tax" on cash was set forth by Marvin Goodfriend, a Senior Vice President of the Federal Reserve Bank of Richmond, Virginia. Such a tax, he wrote, "would serve as a powerful deterrent to hoarding currency." He argued that such a tax was feasible. [106]

Goodfriend understood full well that our money already has a time-bomb tax ticking away inside it and lowering its value. That tax is the inflation deliberately created by the Federal Reserve by printing money in excess of our nation's productivity.

Today, to punish savers, the Federal Reserve compounds the punishment of savers with "financial repression," the technical economics term for deliberately holding the rate of interest banks pay below the rate of inflation. This guarantees that savers in America today lose part of the value of their savings every day they keep their cash in the bank.

Most investors now painfully understand that the Fed is punishing nearly every traditional safe haven for savers – who are now losing value by having a savings account, by keeping their money in dollars, and who hoped to have a pleasant retirement by investing their earnings into a home.

Most now recognize that Americans are being systematically herded, like sheep, into higher risk investments full of moral hazard – especially the stock market.

Perhaps everything is going through Alice's looking glass and being reversed. We used to save, but saving is now by design a path to financial punishment.

The new game appears to be to get us away from cash and into the equivalent of casino chips – which we will spend digitally with no recognition that they actually are a kind of money. This, after all, is what credit cards are – casino cash.

And we, whose ancestors knew the value of saving, are now expected via student loans and other offerings, to spend our lives not accumulating cash but accumulating credit, which we convert into debt. As Tennessee Ernie Ford used to sing: "St. Peter, don't you call me 'cause I can't go. I owe my soul to the company store."

Your Social Security card and number are now your ear tag in this herd of sheep. Welcome to the new "cashless" feudalism that Friedrich Hayek warned was at the end of our road to serfdom.

Hayek, of course, wanted us free to use whatever currency, cash or money we wish – to end the dollar monopoly and make these denationalized moneys compete with each other, as we explained in our 2011 book *The Inflation Deception: Six Ways Government Tricks Us...And Seven Ways to Stop It!* [107]

Instead, even cash will soon be banished....and we will live in a world haunted by the digital ghosts of money.

We would do much better by cashing in our chips, and then investing in real assets. We need to understand that the "War Against Cash" is actually a war against all of us.

Texas Bullion Depository

A new kind of "bank" is being born that might break the money monopoly of the Federal Reserve, thwart President Barack Obama's takeover of our banks, and restore honest money in America.

In this new bank your hard-earned savings are secured not in ever-inflating dollars, but in gold, silver or other precious metals. Your bills can be paid by electronically transferring not dollars but quantities of gold with others who have accounts there.

"Bank runs" and panics should not happen because this is a 100 percent-reserve "bank," not today's fractional-reserve banks with less than 10 percent of their accounts in cash on hand if worried depositors demand their money back.

And if President Obama attempts the government's new "bail-ins" like those in Cyprus and Greece confiscating deposits to pay bank debts, the State of Texas promises to block any federal attempt to seize your account. [108]

On June 12, 2015, Governor Greg Abbott signed into law a bill to create a Texas Bullion Depository. This measure passed the state legislature with strong bipartisan support – 140-4 in the Texas House, 27-4 in the Senate.

This new law would create something akin to Ft. Knox under the protection of the Texas state government where companies, foreign governments, state citizens and Texas agencies could for a small fee securely store their gold.

Among the first deposits here reportedly will be 6,643 gold bars that the University of Texas Investment Management Company (UTIMC) began acquiring in 2009. Today, this physical gold is worth a sizable fraction of $1 Billion and is between 2.5 and 5 percent of the second largest university endowment (after Harvard's) in the United States.

Texas until now has stored its gold in a New York City vault of Hong Kong and Shanghai Banking Corporation, a London-headquartered bank that by some measures is the world's largest. HSBC was the first bank named in our 2014 book *Don't Bank On It! The Unsafe World of 21st Century Banking* because it had begun resisting depositor requests to withdraw their own money.

When Germany tried in 2012 to withdraw a fraction of its gold reserves from the Federal Reserve Bank in New York City, we documented, it was told that this would require at least 7 years. German officials were not allowed to audit, or even to see, their gold deposits, and eventually gave up. The government has refused all requests, even from Congressman Ron Paul when he chaired the subcommittee overseeing it, to audit how much gold remains in Ft. Knox.

No wonder Texas was eager to "repatriate" its gold and make it difficult to confiscate.

The other half of this new Texas law has the potential to subvert President Obama's push to impose a cashless society of digital transactions that are all trackable and taxable, a road to serfdom, surveillance and income redistribution.

The "bank" side of this Texas Bullion Depository, by laying the foundation for a 21st Century restoration of the gold standard of America's Framers, might halt the unchecked growth of a "Progressive" welfare state fattened on limitless printing of fiat paper money.

According to Rick Cunningham of the Texas Center for Economics, Law and Policy, who drafted the original version of this law, the depository could be "a wholly unique solution" to the 2008 financial near-collapse.

Competing Monies

Cunningham has said that "an advanced, state-owned system of electronic payments and settlements, denominated in ounces of precious metals, barred from engaging in lending, leasing, speculating or derivative transactions, and always maintaining a 100% ratio of bullion reserves to account balances…not only could it sustain state and local government operations, it could potentially sustain large swaths of the Texas economy, even in the face of a national financial or currency crisis."

"[W]ith this depository," said Texas State Representative Giovani Capriglione (R-Southlake), the law's co-author, "private individuals and entities will be able to purchase goods, and will be able to use assets in the vault the same way you'd be able to use cash."

What Rep. Capriglione is saying, according to the liberal-left *Texas Observer*, is that by using this depository like a bank, people will "be able to conduct transactions backed by the gold stored in the bank, circumventing the Fed."

"[U]nless Texas is anticipating withdrawing from the union, which I suspect is some peoples' want, I don't see what advantage [the bullion depository] has," said Edwin Truman of the Peterson Institute for International Economics. Building such a secure depository will cost more than the $605,000 Texas pays HSBC each year to store its gold now.

"When we came in the union in 1845, one of the issues was that we would be able to leave if we decided to do that," said then-Governor Rick Perry, another depository supporter, in 2009. "It's codified, anytime Texas wants to pull out of the union it can instantly," Gov. Perry has said. "That's the treaty, it's on record."

Texas seceded to join the Confederacy and was brought back into the Union. We need to remember, however, that from 1836 until 1845, Texas was its own country and had diplomatic or trade relations with Belgium, Denmark, France, Great Britain, the Netherlands, the Russian Empire, the short-lived Federated Republic of Central America and Republic of Yucatan....*and* the United States.

If Texas became a nation again, it today would be the 10th largest economy in the world, bigger than Canada, with a Gross Domestic Product of approximately $1.648 Trillion. With its Republican-run, pro-free enterprise government, Texas has produced one-third of all the new American jobs for which President Obama claims credit. Texas continues to be a powerful magnet, drawing in overtaxed businesses from more liberal states.

If the Texas Bullion Depository creates an independent sound money and sound banking system that cannot be dragged down by debased Fed dollars or the Federal Government, this would expand Texas' opportunities for secession – which in 2014, according to Reuters polling, roughly one in four Americans approved – or for increased success and prosperity.

Could it be Texas will lead the charge to restore financial freedom – by liberating us from the tyranny of the Federal Government's and Federal Reserve's monopoly fiat paper money system?

"When the state of Maryland raised its tax rate
on people with incomes of a million dollars...
the number of such people living in Maryland fell....
Rich people do not simply stand still
to be sheared like sheep."

-- Dr. Thomas Sowell

*"Collectivism doesn't work because
it's based on a faulty economic premise.*

*"There is no such thing
as a person's 'fair share' of wealth.*

*"The gross national product
is not a pizza that must be
carefully divided because
if I get too many slices,
you have to eat the box.*

*"The economy is expandable and,
in any practical sense, limitless."*

– P.J. O'Rourke
Schooled in Baltimore

*"Liberty is not collective, it is personal.
All liberty is individual liberty."*

– Calvin Coolidge
President

*"I don't believe in quotas.
America was founded on a philosophy
of individual rights, not group rights."*

– Justice Clarence Thomas
U.S. Supreme Court

Part Three

The Choice

Chapter Nine

Unreal Economics

"The chief value of money
lies in the fact that one lives in
a world in which it is overestimated."

– H.L. Mencken
Journalist "Sage of Baltimore"

The Federal Reserve's Zero Interest Rate Policy, known as ZIRP, began on December 16, 2008 amidst the uncertainty and fear of the worst financial crisis since the Great Depression.

With one of America's largest banks in ruins and several others at risk of collapse, the Fed Open Market Committee (FOMC) ended almost a century of tinkering up and down with interest rates and simply slammed its economic accelerator pedal to the floor – driving the short-term Fed Funds Rate at which banks could borrow money from each other and from the Fed as low as it then could go – to between Zero and 0.25 percent. [109]

In essence, the Fed offered the big banks and certain other entities virtually free money, a policy that continues almost seven years later.

ZIRP began, we are told, as an effort to provide the liquidity to stave off economic freeze-ups, meltdowns and burn-downs of "Too Big To Fail" financial institutions during a crisis. It continues because, although it hurts many, ZIRP greatly benefits government and other key powerful entities.

But by imposing wildly unreal low interest rates, it has created a distorted, unnatural economic system that also dislocates asset values.

What the Fed did in 2008 was no mere adjustment. Imagine those episodes of "Star Trek" where the Starship Enterprise escapes danger by going into warp drive, only to find itself in a whole different galaxy where the old familiar laws of economics and star charts that point the way home no longer work.

The former Vice Chairman of the Fed, Alan Blinder, in his 2013 book *After the Music Stopped* wrote of ZIRP: "To call such a low interest rate abnormal is an understatement."

"Many of the Fed's actions were previously unimaginable," wrote Blinder, now a Princeton economist, of ZIRP and other drastic measures that the Federal Reserve put in place during this crisis. [110]

The Fed's massive injection of liquidity and easy money arguably helped relieve a moment of crisis for several "Too Big To Fail" banks.

Yet what the Fed did may have changed forever the American economy and the values shaped by our views of money, work and the role of government. The Fed certainly dislocates asset values in our economy and society.

From where the Fed's ZIRP drive has warped our economy and society, we might never be able to find our way back home to genuine free enterprise and honest money.

Having moved its key interest rate to zero, the Fed to deal with this liquidity trap turned to other tactics to influence the economy, including a series of Quantitative Easing (QE) and "Operation Twist" purchases which in 2015 have left the Fed with $4.5 Trillion in accumulated assets, which it expects to hold for a long time.

The Fed's "Reserve"

The Fed, in other words, has stockpiled in Treasury notes and other assets the equivalent of 26.25 percent of America's entire annual Gross Domestic

Product...up from only 6 percent of GDP in 2007, just before the financial crisis. [111] These astronomical Fed purchases have certainly altered market supply and demand, and we do not know what the Fed's privileged "Primary Dealers" might have purchased in the marketplace using fungible Fed-provided money and credit.

The Fed by law each year returns much of the profits from its activities and assets, minus operating expenses, to the U.S. Treasury. In January 2015 this central bank sent the government a record $98.7 Billion, much of it from low interest that taxpayers paid on U.S. debt purchased by the Fed. [112]

Bolstered by ZIRP, our biggest surviving banks have bulked up in today's easy money environment, growing on average more than 30 percent larger, and have increased their leverage by more than a third, than they were in 2008 – despite demands from critics that they be broken up for the public good.

Today, some Federal Reserve members say that ZIRP is no longer needed and that the Fed Funds Rate should gradually be raised back towards its historic average that lets banks lend at between five and six percent interest.

Truth be told, warns analyst Nicole Gelinas of the Manhattan Institute, "No one knows what will happen if the central bank raises interest rates." [113] The economy might move up or melt down.

"Zero is not the right number for this economy," says the President of the Federal Reserve Bank of St. Louis, James Bullard. "It is hard to rationalize a zero policy rate," says Bullard, 53, because America's economy has "a lot of momentum." [114] (Bullard will not again be a voting member of the FOMC until 2016.)

In 2015, however, the Fed repeatedly voted to postpone any such increase in this rate. [115]

In recent years some Fed economists have argued that this key interest rate should not be raised until at least 2017 to avoid the risk of harming a still-fragile economic recovery. [116]

ZIRP policy, according to the Board of Governors of the Federal Reserve System, is that FOMC "anticipates...that it likely will be appropriate to maintain the 0 to ¼ percent target range for the federal funds rate for a considerable time." [117]

Fed Transformation

From the inauguration of President Andrew Jackson in 1829 to that of President Woodrow Wilson in 1913, America's leaders and legislators generally resisted empowering a European-style central bank in the U.S. to control our money supply and interest rates.

That changed in December 1913 when Wilson signed a charter for a new Federal Reserve System that gave it the power to furnish "an elastic currency" for the United States. Wilson, like his fellow Progressives, hated our gold-backed dollar that politicians therefore could not print in limitless amounts to grow the government.

The Fed – a hybrid entity of 12 private banks, a ruling committee with quasi-governmental powers, and a Chair and Vice Chair appointed by the President of the United States – was originally chartered to protect the purchasing power of America's money and take monetary decisions out of politics.

Since the Fed began, the purchasing power of the dollar has fallen to only two pennies of its 1913 value. Private ownership of gold bullion and non-numismatic gold coins was outlawed in 1933 by another Progressive President, Franklin Delano Roosevelt. Then the last link anchoring foreign-held dollars to gold was severed in 1971 by President Richard Nixon.

The Fed has gradually evolved into a Fourth Branch of government, and its unelected Chair is the one person whose global power in important ways surpasses that of America's President. World stock markets rise and fall, and trillions of dollars can be gained or lost, based on a mere hint from a Fed Chair that America's central bank might raise or lower interest rates or adjust Fed economic stimulus by even a tiny amount.

Fed policies alter the quantity and hence the quality of our dollar, the world's global reserve currency. Decisions by the Fed Open Market Committee have the power to influence presidential elections, help shape America's and the world's economy, maximize employment, and "levitate" the stock market.

Some analysts argue that the Federal Reserve has been helping to rig the stock market in various ways. As David Santschi wrote in *TrimTabs Weekly Liquidity Review* in 2013, "The Fed is exchanging about $4 billion in newly created money every business day for various types of bonds. All else being equal, the Fed's bond buying puts more money in investors' hands to buy other assets, including stocks." [118]

"[T]he Fed has rigged interest rates and asset prices to the extent that investors can no longer distinguish reality from fiction....," wrote investment advisor Michael Pento in 2014.

"[K]eeping interest rates at record low levels directly re-inflated bond, real estate and equity market bubbles. This further boosted money supply growth and fueled greater consumption," writes Pento.

"Once the Fed stops buying banks' assets...these institutions will have no need to replace them," writes Pento. "Therefore, the money supply will shrink as asset prices tumble. It is then logical to conclude that the end of the Fed's manipulation of interest rates and money supply will lead to a collapse of this phony consumption-driven economy, as it also takes the stock market along for the ride down." [119]

Prosperity Mirage

In ZIRP World and the Quantitative Easing (QE) Fed policies that zero interest rates led the Fed to turn to, a vast hallucinatory mirage of stock market growth emerged. Since ZIRP began, the S&P 500 has soared by 200 percent.

Financial Times Assistant Editor Gillian Tett noted in 2013 that Fed easy money policies were increasing the U.S. monetary base about 100 times faster than the growth of the economy. This could open the way for banks to lend vastly more at low rates. [120]

Hearing her remarks in the context of what he already knew, financial journalist Bill Bonner concluded that "central banks' monetary policies had become a kind of financial doomsday device." [121]

Take a step back from this frenzy of the Wall Street casino, which we did in August 2015, near 18,000, and you can begin to see more clearly. Through ZIRP and its related QE policies, the Fed has flooded the stock market with easy money.

Companies since the financial crisis began have spent more than $2 Trillion of this easy money not to make their companies more innovative or efficient, but to buy back shares of company stock. Imagine that you are a company with 10 million shares of stock and you buy back half of them, instantly putting the issues of dividends and debt and executive stock options in a more favorable light. The value of your remaining shares greatly increases, even though the company may be bringing in no more customer dollars than before.

Yet because of the easy Fed money from ZIRP and QE, your company now appears to be growing and successful, and you look like a genius. This then lures more stock buyers, desperately seeking the income that the Fed's low interest policies have taken away from their bank accounts. [122]

This "wealth effect" that former Fed Chair Ben Bernanke intended to create to stimulate consumer spending and the economy is based on inflation and easy money conjured by the Fed out of thin air. It is at best a self-fulfilling prophecy, a shared hypnotically-induced mass illusion that stocks now have more value than they really do. It is at worst a con game, a Ponzi scheme, a trick used to rob the gullible. As *Forbes* columnist Charles Biderman put it, what the Fed is doing to achieve this levitation of the stock market through conjured money "would be a crime if anyone other than the Fed did this." [123]

Illusion of Value

How much of current market value has been created by Federal Reserve manipulation and the odd bookkeeping and policies companies have adopted in ZIRP World? BlackRock's 2015 *Investment Outlook* said this:

Corporate earnings are a key risk. Analysts predict double-digit growth in 2015, yet such high expectations will be tough to meet. Companies have picked the low-hanging fruit by slashing costs since the financial crisis. How do you generate 10% earnings-per-share growth when nominal GDP is just 4%?

It becomes tempting to take on too much leverage, use financial wizardry to reward shareholders or even stretch accounting principles. S&P 500 profits are 86% higher than they would be if accounting standards of the national accounts were used, Pelham Smithers Associates notes. And the gap between the two measures is widening, the research firm finds. [124]

If stock profits are in effect 86 percent overvalued, what happens if or when the Fed's easy money and zero interest rates that made this possible begin to go away?

What happens if or when today's ZIRP-distorted market is forced to return to real values even lower than BlackRock and Pelham Smithers foresee?

Truth be told, the Fed over the past quarter-century "has only really tightened policy three separate times," wrote *CNNMoney*'s Patrick Gillespie, and never before from the warped unreality of ZIRP World. Writes Gillespie: "Making money as the Fed raises rates won't be easy." [125]

Worldwide debt has risen since 2007 by more than $57 Trillion and now stands at almost $200 Trillion. The Fed raising the interest rate on borrowing U.S. dollars, the world reserve currency in perhaps 80 percent of all major trading, could bury many countries beneath mountains of hard-to-pay debt. This could make both economic and political earthquakes around the world more likely.

"Overall debt relative to gross domestic product is now higher in most nations than it was before the [2008-2009] crisis," warned consultants McKinsey & Co. in a February 2015 report. "Higher levels of debt pose questions about financial stability." [126]

ZIRP World helped create this over-leveraged situation, and in the winds that will soon blow as rates rise, our own economy built of overvalued paper stocks and easy paper money could be severely damaged.

Fed decisions and policies now arguably shape America's economy more than any free market factor, as we explore in our chapter "Dawn of the Fed" in our 2014 book *Don't Bank On It! The Unsafe World of 21st Century Banking*. [127]

The Fed's growing power has transformed and politicized the U.S. economy into a hybrid like itself, no longer truly free enterprise, but not yet fully collectivized as Progressives desire. Our money is now Federal Reserve Notes un-backed by the gold that America's Framers looked to for independent solid value.

Our society and values are at a tipping point of fundamental change. Few decisions may have more impact on our future than the Fed at least temporarily giving up its power to reduce interest rates by taking them to zero with ZIRP.

We have been taken far away from America's founding ideals of personal and economic freedom. The night sky is full of unfamiliar constellations. Are we trapped on this brave new world, or can we find our way home?

The ZIRP Trap

After a central bank such as the Fed launches a policy of zero interest rates, it soon finds it difficult to escape from "The ZIRP Trap."

The ZIRP Trap is a term coined in a 2015 study by Philipp Bagus, an Economics Professor at the Universidad Rey Juan Carlos in Madrid. His study shows the many ways that this policy transforms a nation's economy and social values into a very different matrix he calls "ZIRP World." [128]

"The exit from ZIRP is likely the most difficult and important policy issue for Western economies today," writes Bagus. [129]

Most economists recognize that ZIRP was intended to be a short-term measure used to deal with an economic emergency, but that it cannot sustain a healthy economic recovery or long-term prosperity.

In the long run, ZIRP will turn America's economy into a stagnant, fetid swamp where we are neck deep in a stinking, unnatural liquidity that stunts growth and is too toxic to quench anyone's thirst.

In the long run, ZIRP World is a dead world.

It eventually conjures the kind of artificial, unnatural economics concocted by a ruling Progressive elite that workers in the former Soviet Union grimly joked about by saying: "They pretend to pay us, and we pretend to work."

Exiting this doomed economic policy is urgently necessary if we are to regain genuine health and prosperity in America.

In the short run, the political and economic cost of exiting and escaping this ZIRP Trap can be high and painful.

"Like a drug one can't stop taking, artificially low interest rates initially seem harmless," writes business journalist Gregory Bresiger. "Cheap money even seems to produce good results in the early stages. However, later comes disaster, which, once again, is looming." [130]

Condemning the Fed's easy money schemes "is a little like condemning sugar," wrote Agora Financial's Eric Fry. "Everyone knows sugar tastes wonderful. But no one really knows how much is too much...and, more to the point, almost no one wants to know how much is too much."

"The delicious sensation is immediate; the adverse side effects are distant," Fry continues. "That's reason enough for most folks to make their double ice cream cone a triple...." But like Bresiger, Fry warns that long-term gorging on the sugar of easy Fed money will destroy the needed healthy balance between speculation and prudence, and between spending and thrift. This will cause "Financial Diabetes." [131]

How ZIRP Grows Government

"Governments are one of the great beneficiaries of ZIRP," writes Bagus. [132] This near-zero-cost money allows politicians to continue spending without having to cut government's fat. Indeed, this easy money lets inefficient government continue to grow, especially in welfare state social spending.

The result is an ever-enlarging number of government dependents who can be counted on to vote for incumbent politicians.

"A government which robs Peter to pay Paul can always depend on the support of Paul," wrote the Irish Fabian socialist playwright George Bernard Shaw.

As we noted earlier, America's only President elected four times, Franklin Delano Roosevelt said in the same vein: "Tax and tax, spend and spend, elect and elect." Politicians of his Democratic Party continue to follow his divide-redistribute-and-conquer class warfare.

ZIRP makes government spending easy, at least until the bills to repay the borrowed trillions come due during some future politicians' time in office. ZIRP thus seduces today's elected officials into letting deficits and government indebtedness soar into the stratosphere.

What happens if the Fed soon ends ZIRP, and future refinancing of government debt requires payment of several percent interest on money the government now borrows at near-zero interest? The historic average market interest rate for borrowed money is between 5 and 6 percent. Six percent of $18.6 Trillion would be more than $1.1 Trillion in yearly interest, an increase of roughly one-third to the annual tax burden Americans already carry....and that is already slowing our economy.

As ZIRP World Turns

The Federal Reserve has made sure that giant banks have ample liquidity, but it has also warned those banks to avoid making "risky loans" of the kind that liberal Presidents Jimmy Carter and Bill Clinton forced them to make under the Community Reinvestment Act. This law is a root cause of the 2008-2009 housing bubble collapse, the aftershocks of which continue to plague us today.

This avoidance of risk left the banks with only a few entities to which they could safely lend money – the government, which has the power to tax and print money and therefore can never go broke; the largest corporations; and the Federal Reserve itself.

Today at least 18 percent of bank money is now deposited – and earning low but very safe interest – with the government and/or Federal Reserve.

What is unseen in this, writes Bagus, are the small businesses and entrepreneurs who have been crowded out, unable to secure loans or assets because of this ZIRP policy that preserves giant corporations and keeps bloated government afloat, but refuses loans at near-zero interest to the rest of us. [133]

"In general, a ZIRP environment makes an economy more rigid and less dynamic because low interest rates favor large established companies versus small, newer ones and shield them from their competition.....," writes Bagus. "It becomes more difficult to start a new business in a ZIRP world where established companies have easy access to cheap loans...." [134]

Easy ZIRP money allows big companies to control more of the market via leveraged buy-outs, take-overs and stock buy-backs. The Fed's policy has made it easier for companies to buy new technologies, including robots, to replace human workers.

And ZIRP has let multinational companies move jobs and keep profits overseas, away from America's business taxes – the highest in the world: on average, a 46.3 percent combined federal, state and local tax burden on American businesses [135] – while running their United States offices and factories with tax-exempt, zero-interest borrowed money.

Apple, for example, has a "cash pile of $170 billion and counting," writes *Forbes* columnist Tim Worstall, yet it is borrowing $6.5 Billion, as it has borrowed more than $20 Billion over the past two years. Why? "The reason it's doing so is the tax system," writes Worstall. [136]

Meanwhile, money borrowed by the government to enlarge itself and its own "workforce" is money not available for the private sector to grow companies, innovate new products, or hire new employees who do real, productive work.

Welcome to BorroWorld

Another way to think of ZIRP World is what we call "BorroWorld," an unreal land where politicians and government planners assume we really can borrow our way back to prosperity.

Progressives may mock any religious belief in God, but they have their own dogmatic belief in Santa Claus – in the idea that Uncle Santa government has a bottomless bag of free goodies that can be given away, even if all the makers move overseas and only a slacker nation of Gimme Pig takers remains.

Prior to the economic crisis of 2008-2009, we were told that Americans had begun a 15-year period of "deleveraging," of ending our credit card binge, paying down our loans and other debts, and getting back to honest economic basics such as saving.

This claim was questionable. Millions of Americans during the early 21st Century turned their homes into ATM machines, borrowing against their rising equity as easy lending and politically-coerced lowered lending standards drove home prices into the stratosphere. We explain and document all this in our 2014 book *Don't Bank On It!* [137]

Thanks to the advent of ZIRP, the housing crash of 2008-2009 did not end BorroWorld. In some ways, the Progressive notion that we could tax, spend and borrow our way to prosperity expanded.

"ZIRP reduced the pressure to pay back debts for variable rate payments," writes Bagus. "Instead incentives were created to increase indebtedness even more at lower interest rates. Indeed, central banks wanted the private sector to start increasing its indebtedness." [138]

Many in the private sector reduced their indebtedness despite these incentives, but, "while private agents deleveraged, the public sector increased its leverage," going deeper into debt. [139]

ZIRP money quickly tilted market competition to favor borrowers over those using traditional equity. With ZIRP, writes Bagus, "leverage becomes extremely attractive, and companies that keep financing themselves with equity are at a disadvantage. Lower interest rate spreads also pressure banks to increase their leverage. The structure of the financial sector is weakened as the banks' equity ratio falls." [140]

The harm caused by near-zero interest rates thus metastasizes. When banks pay near-zero interest rates to savers, they discourage the capital formation that in an earlier era came from thrift – from people having the self-discipline to defer pleasure today and to save in order to earn greater rewards tomorrow.

Losing Interest

The Federal Reserve almost openly is practicing what economists call "financial repression," deliberately holding the rate of interest banks can pay savers below the rate of inflation. This guarantees that savers every day will lose more in purchasing power to inflation than they gain in interest paid on their bank accounts. [141]

Forget about accumulating a pleasant retirement nest egg safely through compound interest. ZIRP eliminates the cautious, prudent saver that uses traditional low-risk forms of savings. Like the 1923 hyperinflation in Weimar Germany, ZIRP erodes bedrock middle-class values on which genuine prosperity and free enterprise depend – thrift, prudence, independence, a work ethic and entrepreneurial virtues, among other things. [142]

Albert Einstein, it is said, was once asked what the most powerful and mysterious thing in the universe was. "Compound interest," the great nuclear physicist instantly replied.

The amazing power of compound interest used to empower ordinary families to safely bank small amounts of money during their working lives and then retire with a meaningful accumulation of savings. The ZIRP policy has robbed most Americans of this saving power.

This cynical ZIRP policy to benefit government has stolen more than the life savings of everyday Americans. It has stolen secure retirements and peace of mind from millions, and this Progressive-caused "ZIRP Stress" and anxiety has doubtless caused thousands of fatal heart attacks and other ills.

This financial repression, it appears, is intended to force savers to look elsewhere and face moral hazard in order to receive a reasonable rate of return on what they have earned. As we argue in *Don't Bank On It!,* the government and Fed appear to be systematically closing off the relatively safe havens for savings – and to be herding ordinary Americans into the high-risk casino of the stock market, where they can be sheared by market manipulators.

Savers are not the only victims of the decline in interest. "[D]efined benefit pension funds become troubled as they fail to earn sufficient returns with ZIRP," writes Bagus. "Similarly, life insurance companies that also invest in safe financial titles such as bonds incur difficulties to earn sufficient returns on their investments."

"In such a situation, we can expect insurance companies as well as money market funds to 'reach for yield,'" Bagus continues, "i.e. assume more risk in order to obtain higher yields." [143]

ZIRP thus pushes people who used to have relatively safe options for their retirement savings into more and more risky investments and malinvestments. The overall effect of this is to further destabilize the economy and peoples' lives.

And in the productive sector, ZIRP "makes early debt repayment less attractive and encourages companies to borrow even more."

"This reliance on debt affects business culture, especially if ZIRP prevails for a sustained period of time," he writes. "Highly indebted or leveraged companies tend to behave differently than companies that have no or few debts." [144]

In such a ZIRP World, the owners of highly-leveraged companies lose a measure of independence, often needing the approval of creditors for their decisions. Both owners and managers feel pressure to generate cash more quickly, to adopt policies that bring in maximum money this quarter for debt repayment, not wiser policies that will improve company profits over many years. [145]

In many such ways, ZIRP undermines the health of the body politic and the free market economy. It not only sucks away the lifeblood of capitalism – capital – but also destroys the morals, values, entrepreneurship, work ethic and thrift needed for successful free enterprise.

Less Than Zero

We may, however, soon look back longingly on ZIRP as the good old days. From Europe a new, even more extreme approach to central bank interest rates is now rapidly spreading – less-than-zero, sub-zero or as it is becoming fashionable to call them, "negative" interest rates.

Facing negative rates, someone opening a bank account of, say, $100 will expect to get back only $98 a year later....and, thanks to deliberate inflation, this might have only $96 of purchasing power compared to the original $100 a year earlier.

Instead of increasing their nest egg, such depositors in five years will lose roughly one fifth of the total purchasing power they put in their bank.

The European Central Bank (ECB) cut a key interest rate below zero in June 2014. Small central banks in Europe have occasionally used negative rates before, and in July Sweden again cut its deposit rate below zero. Denmark followed in September, and Switzerland in December. [146]

Why take the 20 major bank depositor risks we document in *Don't Bank On It!* if your bank is paying you less than nothing – is charging you money just for the honor of having a bank account?

Many are now closing their accounts if all the bank offers them is risk and guaranteed loss.

This is why commercial banks in Denmark have been paying for their depositors' negative rates, out of fear of losing customers.

As *Bloomberg*'s Jana Randow reports, "When banks absorb the costs themselves, it squeezes the profit margin between their lending and deposit rates, and might make them even less willing to lend." [147]

Today's central banks tend to follow the views of the late British economist John Maynard Keynes, whose "paradox of thrift" holds that saving money in the bank is bad because it reduces the quantity and velocity of money in the marketplace.

According to Keynesian macroeconomics, forcing savers to withdraw their money is good. The more and faster their money is spent, the more it stimulates economic growth. Both ZIRP and negative interest rates, in this view, are merely useful kinds of financial repression to force bank savings back into commerce.

Central banks are also trying to increase inflation, in part to help devalue their own currencies so that their nations' exports are less expensive and more competitive in foreign markets. Zero or Below-Zero central bank interest rates are becoming a standard tactic in today's currency wars.

Central banks also use deliberate inflation as an antidote to deflation, in which the currency increases in value. Inflation prompts people to hurry and spend their money, whose value keeps declining. Deflation encourages people to keep their money because it will be even more valuable tomorrow than it is today. (And governments eagerly use inflation as a hidden regressive tax, as we explored in our book *The Inflation Deception*.)[148].

Giant banks go along with central negative interest policies not only because they must, but also because they can. If depositors are willing to pay the banks for taking their money, instead of demanding interest on what are really customer loans to the bank, then banks will happily take their customers' money.

And this shearing of compliant sheep is spreading rapidly to other parts of the economy. Governments and giant corporations such as Nestle have begun issuing bonds that pay less than zero interest – and customers are snapping these up.

Unyielding

The fashionable new term among these investors is "ZYNY," which stands for "Zero-Yield to Negative-Yield," as they seek desperately for some place to put their savings that will create some kind of gain. They listen when JPMorgan Chase reported in January 2015 that 16 percent of its Global Bond Index – roughly $3.6 Trillion worth of developed market government bonds – was at negative yield. [149]

"Zero yields on safe government debt pushes the search for yield into hyperdrive, swamping local fundamentals," said JPMorgan. "Term Premia, liquidity premia, and volatility premia are all under pressure." This is how hyperdrive likewise takes us to a strange, troubled future on what CNBC calls "A ZYNY world." [150]

Perhaps such buyers are gullible and unthinking. Or perhaps they sense that economies are in trouble all over the world, that huge losses are coming, and they are content if some entity can preserve most of their money. They hope their profit will come if their paper money rises in value after the crisis begins.

Many seem unaware that today's fiat currency in a crisis might lose value faster than the promises of the politicians who printed it out of thin air. Never having lived under the stability of America's historic gold standard, many simply do not understand that far more reliable wealth preservers exist than paper money.

Up to a point, ZIRP and negative interest rates increase inflation in an economy. However, as current Fed Chair Janet Yellen testified during her 2013 confirmation hearing, the closer the deposit rate gets to zero, the bigger the risk of disruption to the money markets that help fund banks. [151]

"When rates fall beyond a certain point," warned the London-based *Financial Times* in February 2015, "hoarding physical cash becomes rational, as does sinking it into assets like gold or property...." [152]

With central banks boasting of their plans to debase national currencies via deliberately-created inflation – that is, to steal the value from those who trust their nation's money – today it makes urgent sense to diversify and convert a portion of one's savings from paper fiat money into solid, reliable stores of value such as gold.

"Life below zero interest must not become the new normal," says a *Financial Times* editorial. [153]

Yet for much of the world, this is becoming the latest giant step away from honest money and free markets – and towards the very unfree market of politicized, manipulated currency and economies.

Four ZIRP Future Scenarios

What is the future of ZIRP? Philipp Bagus sees four possible scenarios, which we expand as follows:

1. ZIRP continues and, at least in the short run, causes another artificial boom based on financial bubbles. The mass hallucination of hypnotized people continues. At some point these bubbles will burst.

2. ZIRP causes stagnation and an economy that "lingers in a recession-like, anemic state." The government has gone at least $7.5 Trillion deeper into debt since 2009, but the stimulus of all this money has produced a stagnant U.S. economy struggling to maintain 2 percent growth while America has the smallest percentage of working-age Americans with jobs since President Jimmy Carter's malaise in 1978. America today has almost as many people receiving Social Security Disability benefits as are employed full time in manufacturing, actually making things of value.

Fully 49.5 percent of American households have at least one person receiving a government benefit of some kind. Tax increases to fund the welfare state are devouring the capital seed corn that used to grow future private sector prosperity. Our future is being lost in this downward spiral.

3. ZIRP triggers financial collapse as governments and giant banks default on the huge, low-interest debts they have run up. The economic landslide that began in 2008 can no longer be held back and this time drags the whole economy down with it.

4. ZIRP is overcome by the American Dream's optimism and effort. The American people's hard work, faith and traditional values triumph over Progressive collectivism. We kick government-dependent addiction to Uncle Sugar's Progressive welfare state, and are cured of economic diabetes. Life again becomes naturally sweet, prosperous and free.

We would add that such a restoration of America depends on millions of us keeping traditional economic and ethical values alive in our own lives. [154] One way to preserve such values is to teach our children by example. For instance, the government took away the dollar gold standard, but we can each rebuild our own gold standard by converting a saving remnant of our nest egg. America's Framers made gold the Constitutional standard of our money because they had studied what the Bible says about honest, reliable money. Gold needs no central bank or government to give it value. It has been recognized worldwide as universal money for thousands of years.

Have you and your children ever held the kind of solid gold coin that George Washington and Thomas Jefferson carried? Just holding such a coin that needs no Fed behind it is a life-changing educational moment. It is a doorway back to the American Republic and values they established for future generations.

On the day that people have their own independent solid money again, the Federal Reserve and all its schemes like ZIRP can be bypassed on our road back home to America.

> *"Politicians never accuse you of 'greed'*
> *for wanting other people's money –*
> *only for wanting to keep your own money."*

– Joseph Sobran

> *"I want a government small enough*
> *to fit inside the Constitution."*

– Harry Browne

"In general, the art of government
consists in taking as much money as possible
from one party of the citizens
to give to the other."

– Voltaire

"A wise and frugal government,
which shall restrain men from injuring one another,
which shall then leave them otherwise free to regulate
their own pursuits of industry and improvement,
and shall not take from the mouth of labor
the bread it has earned.

This is the sum of good government,
and all that is necessary to close
the circle of our felicities."

– Thomas Jefferson
1801 Inaugural Address

Chapter Ten

A Third Dream?

"Government is the great fiction
through which everyone endeavors to live
at the expense of everybody else.
They forget that the State lives
at the expense of everyone."

– Friedrich Bastiat
French political philosopher

Could the American Dream and Progressive Dream be combined to create an even better Third Dream? Or do inherent contradictions between the two dreams make such a merger in the long run unwise or impossible?

European Social Democrats call the best known attempt at this "The Third Way" of Nordic countries such as Sweden, Finland, Norway, Denmark and Iceland, where "cuddly" capitalism is encouraged but hefty taxes near or above 50 percent of income fund generous social benefits for all.

Denmark, Norway and Sweden rank among the world's top five "happiest" nations, according to the United Nations-related *World Happiness Report 2013*. This report ranked nations by Gross Domestic Product per capita, perceived freedom to make life choices, freedom from corruption, generosity and other factors. [155]

The British magazine *The Economist* has called these Nordic nations "The next supermodel," now studied by nations from the People's Republic of China to Latin America to learn why they are so successful.

"They have avoided both southern Europe's economic sclerosis and America's extreme inequality," writes *The Economist*. "Development theorists have taken to calling successful modernization 'getting to Denmark.'" [156]

Is it desirable, or even possible, to reshape the American Dream along Scandinavian lines?

We believe it is not, and we shall explore why in the long run a combination of capitalism and Progressivism is almost certain to fail. We will also look at two recent examples of why this has failed in Greece and Puerto Rico, and at new scientific research that indicates how Progressivism poisons people and societies.

As to the rest of Western Europe and its quasi-Marxist shotgun wedding of socialism with capitalism, this is mostly a region where the "New Normal" is chronic double-digit unemployment, stagnant economies and below-replacement population fertility rates. Europe is already dying and demographically doomed, at least as a home of the Western Civilization that shaped America's history and culture. In the long run, Europe will become Eurabia.

British Fabian Socialists and continental Social Democrats tried for many decades to replace capitalism piecemeal with socialism in their countries via mostly-peaceful democratic means.

Many of them now acknowledge that capitalism is an engine of productivity far superior to socialism and should remain a vital part of the welfare states they have created, as it is in the "Third Way" Nordic nations.

Scandinavia's Secret Sauce

What do the Nordic nations have that makes their hybrid capitalism work for them?

Until recently, the Scandinavian countries were for the most part monocultures in which almost everyone had a shared Nordic Viking heritage of clinging together to help each other survive in lands with short summers and long, dark winters nearer the Arctic Circle than the rest of Western Europe. One could almost think of their culture more as an extended family than a diverse nation of many peoples like the United States.

The pagan mythology of these serious Norse held that someday even their heaven, Valhalla, was destined to be destroyed by the frost giants.

When Nordics converted to Christianity, they embraced the Protestant work ethic. Today the population of Sweden is 87 percent Lutheran, of Finland 82.5 percent Lutheran, of Norway 85.7 percent Lutheran/Church of Norway, and of Denmark 95 percent evangelical Lutheran. [157]

Within their national families, Nordics are happy to become successful and to assert their individuality, which one scholar has described as "statist individualism." The rich and successful are respected, not turned into political targets of envy and class warfare. Private property and contract rights are enforced, and free trade is encouraged.

Sweden's corporate tax rate, according to *The Economist*, in 2013 had been lowered to 22 percent, far lower than America's. Government's share of GDP was "lower than France's and could soon be lower than Britain's."

Pragmatism trumps ideology in Nordic lands, writes *The Economist*:

> *As long as public services work, they do not mind who provides them. Denmark and Norway allow private firms to run public hospitals. Sweden has a universal system of school vouchers, with private for-profit schools competing with public schools. Denmark also has vouchers – but ones that you can top up. When it comes to choice, [Nobel laureate free market economist] Milton Friedman would be more at home in Stockholm than in Washington, D.C.* [158]

Far From Paradise

These Nordic lands, however, are not the American Dream's idea of paradise. Typically 30 percent of employed people in these countries work for the government, double the average rate of the mostly-European OECD countries. [159] Most who live there are relatively happy with the system, but arguably the best and brightest of each generation depart for countries where opportunities are better and taxes lower.

At least the days are gone when Swedish filmmaker Ingmar Bergman and Swedish creator of the Pippi Longstocking tales, Astrid Lindgren, were required to pay *more than 100 percent* of their income in taxes.

Bergman closed his studio and went into foreign exile over his harassment by tax authorities, and this by one estimate cost the Swedish economy many millions in tax revenue and lost jobs. Lindgren stayed and continued to vote Social Democrat, but the controversy over her 102 percent tax bill forced the Social Democrat Prime Minister out of office.

Could the Nordic "Third Way" work in the United States or most other major modern economies? Probably not. To the extent that this economic hybrid has worked, it is because these Nordic nations have an almost family-like commonality of values, culture, ancestry, religious faith and work ethic.

In some ways this produces kinds of equality that Progressives elsewhere would hate. In the United States, welfare benefits are not taxed, largely because Progressives intend them to be a class warfare wedge dividing two collective groups, a massive vote-buying transfer of wealth from overtaxed rich to untaxed poor.

In Sweden, by contrast, welfare benefits *are* taxed like regular income. As a result, 85 percent of Swedes pay taxes, participate in paying the cost of government, and have less reason to avoid getting a job. This reduces the Progressive-promoted perception that some pay all the taxes while a large group of others pay nothing and get a free ride, thanks to leftist politicians. Most Swedes have a tax incentive to keep government efficient. [160]

In most modern Western nations, Progressive political parties play the old Roman Empire game of controlling people called "divide and conquer."

They propagandize people to think of themselves as members of collective groups, not individuals, and then pit those groups against one another, "us" against "them." The Nordic nations have relatively few such internal differences for Progressives to exploit.

This Nordic immunity to Progressivism's poisonous tactics, however, may soon start to vanish.

Islamic Invasion

With the current increase of Muslim populations, many European nations there are feeling the kind of internal social pressures America has long experienced.

What does a once-insular society like Sweden or Norway do when people of different cultures appear in their midst, many of whom are taking more in government benefits from these nations' Progressive welfare system than they are paying in taxes?

The 2015 flood tide of Muslim refugees pouring into Europe to escape war in and around Syria had reached safety when they entered Turkey, yet they kept moving to reach the richest European welfare states, especially Germany. Others are also riding in on this tide.

Germany at first welcomed many of these immigrants because its own fertility rate has recently fallen below that even of Japan. Without such a massive influx of new, young workers, Germany faces fast-approaching demographic doom and a population of retired seniors with far too few young workers to pay for them. The question now is whether these newcomers will become, on balance, net consumers or producers of European resources.

Saudi Arabia refused to take in fleeing Syrian refugees. The Saudis, however, offered to help by paying for the building of 200 new mosques across Europe for the 800,000 or more unexpected Muslim immigrants who in 2015 were surging across European borders. [161]

Muslim forces from largely-Islamic Spain attempted to invade France in 732 A.D. but were defeated by the armored knights of Charles Martel, "The Hammer," the Frankish king whose grandson would be Charlemagne. Today's new Muslim invasion may be more successful, conquering not only by immigration but also by making love, not war.

French couples currently have on average 1.4 children, far short of the 2.1 needed to maintain their population; Muslim couples in France have on average 3.4 children, more than enough to have a rapidly-growing population. Unless this changes soon, the Progressive peoples of Western European nations face demographic eclipse.

Emasculating Europe

After World War II, the United States decided that we would use socialism to inoculate Western Europe against Soviet Communism. Our Marshall Plan poured vast amounts of aid into Europe.

By securing the continent's national defense with our nuclear umbrella and the North Atlantic Treaty Organization (NATO), we made it easy for European nations to divert money they would have spent for weapons into building welfare states that became the envy of American Progressives.

A cynic might say that we thus neutered Germany, leaving it too weak to attempt a third conquest of Europe – but, as we shall see, this assumption might have been mistaken. Germany has nearly succeeded with its own third way of conquering and unifying Europe.

We were right to recognize that welfare states became siphons sucking money away from military spending in many of these nations, and this over time could emasculate nations addicted to welfare.

We should have remembered our clever tactic, because this same loss of strength is happening to us.

Our attempt to graft together socialism and free market capitalism in Europe is now failing, for reasons we shall explain.

America's Third Way

During the Cold War against Communism, problems were not as evident in the United States because our biggest spending program *was* military spending. Many billions of dollars' worth of weapons contracts moved wealth into the districts of the most powerful members of Congress. The prize was good-paying jobs, which fit well with the traditional American Dream of honorable work and earning one's way.

Because power in Congress was then largely determined by seniority, such military contracts tended to flow to districts with the longest-serving members of Congress, which often meant Southern Democrats who faced no viable Republican opposition since the end of Reconstruction after the Civil War.

America has from its beginning been a nation of immigrants, but most came seeking freedom and opportunity, not welfare from a rich social safety net that they could turn into a hammock.

The 1849 California gold rush lured some who dreamed of quick and easy riches, but this did not change the hard reality most discovered. As one immigrant recalled, he came to America expecting the streets to be paved with gold, but quickly discovered three things:

(1) The streets were not paved with gold.

(2) The streets were not even paved.

(3) He was the one expected to pave them.

A lavish welfare state, put in place by Progressive politicians as a way to buy votes, can vastly change the kinds of people a nation attracts...and fundamentally transform the character and values of that nation.

The Slippery Slope to Serfdom

Those who shaped and experienced the young American Republic understood and warned of the forces that are dragging us down.

"The natural progress of things is for liberty to yield and government to gain ground," wrote Thomas Jefferson in 1788.

The author of our Declaration of Independence believed that preserving our liberty required a new, but not necessarily violent, revolution every 20 years. Jefferson believed that each generation is its own "country," and that it is immoral for us to run up heavy debts to be paid by our children and grandchildren.

"Freedom is never more than one generation away from extinction," warned Ronald Reagan. "We didn't pass it to our children in the bloodstream. It must be fought for, protected, and handed on for them to do the same, or one day we will spend our sunset years telling our children and our children's children what it was once like in the United States where men were free."

"The American Republic will endure," observed a French traveller in our young nation, Alexis de Tocqueville, "until politicians realize they can bribe the people with their own money."

"When the people find they can vote themselves money," warned Benjamin Franklin, "that will herald the end of the republic."

America's Framers did not like political parties, which they called "faction" because they pitted people against one another as a divide-and-conquer way to gain power for politicians.

The U.S. Constitution never mentions political parties. Our Framers designed the first branch of government, the Congress, to be elected not by party ideology but by geography, by the voters of a particular district.

This idea has in our time been subverted. When, for example, Speaker of the House Tom Foley, a Progressive Democrat, lost re-election in his largely-farming district in far eastern Washington State in 1994, more than 99 percent of Foley's campaign contributions came from outside his district.

Who owns your member of Congress, local voters or those who provide his or her campaign money? We already know whose telephone call he or she would return faster.

(To deal with this, we find ourselves in rare agreement with Progressive Texas leftist Jim Hightower, who says that in public appearances all candidates should be required to wear coveralls like those of NASCAR drivers that promote sponsors such as Valvoline. The politicians would display badges showing whose money they take – the names of special interests, corporations, unions, or ideological groups that are funding them. This would help voters see at a glance who their Representatives actually represent.)

The Economic-Political Spectrum

The two ruling political parties in America no longer represent geographic districts or voters. They represent vested interests, including ideologies and ideals.

One party professes to represent the small government ideals of the self-reliant individualistic American Dream. As of October 2015, its most popular presidential candidates were business executives, and a third a famed pediatric neurosurgeon. None of the three had ever held high government office.

The other party preaches the collectivist utopian Progressive Dream of ever-bigger government and wealth redistribution. As of October 2015, one of its two most popular presidential candidates has called for "toppling" the wealthiest one percent of Americans. [162] The other is a self-described socialist who advocates increasing government social spending costs by $18 Trillion. This, obviously, is no longer a moderate or centrist political party. Since at least 2008, it has dragged America's Economic-Political Spectrum far, far to the Left.

To appreciate why Jefferson expected liberty to yield and government to grow bigger, we should look at how our position on this Economic-Political Spectrum has changed since the American Revolution – right versus left, capitalism versus socialism, small government versus big, individualism versus collectivism, and the American Dream versus the Progressive Dream.

Imagine a scale with 10 steps, with the number 1 representing aspects of the original American Dream and 10 representing the final stage of the tactical and strategic triumph of the Progressive Dream, its own totalitarian version of Plato's *Republic*.

STEP 1. In our beginning was free enterprise with little government interference or taxation. This is a place where most property is private, business exchanges are voluntary, government keeps its paws out of the economy and citizen lives, and the people this free market serves are consumers.

STEP 2. Government begins to impose some additional taxes and regulations to deal with temporary situations such as wars or other emergencies, which establishes precedents for its wider future use of such powers.

STEP 3. Governments begin to squeeze businesses for taxes, fees and bribes – but the main intent is to enrich government officials. Politicians remember that businesses are free to move into and out of their jurisdiction and are eager to keep and attract geese that lay golden eggs.

STEP 4. Governments begin to impose their own Progressive ideas of social engineering, breaking up companies and requiring them to accept labor unions that then kick back a fat slice of coerced union dues to politicians who empowered the unions. This plateau at least pretends to serve workers, even though it greatly increases the cost of everything workers want to buy.

STEP 5. Politicians begin to impose "public-private partnerships" in which government, with its monopoly on legal coercion, is always the senior partner. Government begins telling companies who or from what collectivist groups they must hire, what they must pay, who they must serve, and more. And for this "service," public servants begin to act like masters while taxes and regulations increase.

The Ratchet

These steps move inexorably towards big government because of what we call "the ratchet." Whenever the economy is good and tax revenues go up, government expands. But when the economy goes down, the government refuses to reduce its size; it instead increases the tax burden on citizens and companies so that government never needs to tighten its belt or limit its spending. This creates a flow that relentlessly makes the private sector smaller and the public sector larger.

As the old saying goes, ground occupied by government is seldom surrendered. "Nothing is more permanent," said Milton Friedman, "than a temporary government program."

STEP 6. Government elitists begin taking over entire sectors of the economy, either by direct nationalization or regulatory power. Politicians, using emergency powers as they wish even when no emergency exists, seize automobile companies, health care, energy creation and distribution, food production and distribution, the banking system, stock and bond trading, university funding, telecommunications and all information allowed thereon, transportation, all retirement accounts, all private property via environmental and other regulatory pretexts, and much more. To disguise what is happening, the government carries out this mass *de facto* seizure piecemeal, threatening some companies as a way to intimidate others into subservience.

STEP 7. Politicians implement a system of crony capitalism in which only companies with friendly ties to the government's ruling party are allowed to succeed. The solar company Solyndra was given $535 Million in taxpayer money, then promptly went out of business. More than 80 percent of more than $90 Billion given to environmental enterprises was channeled to companies involved in giving huge amounts of money to the ruling political party.

STEP 8. Private business endures but is crushingly taxed and regulated. More than $200 Billion is extracted in heavy fines and penalties from America's banks, and the ruling party diverts a juicy slice of the money it extorts without Congressional approval into the hands of left-wing activist groups. [163] This, of course, violates the fundamental constitutional requirement that Congress controls the purse strings of the Federal Government. So does the creation of a new Progressive government regulatory agency called the Consumer Financial Protection Bureau (CFPB) that gets its budget directly from the Federal Reserve – and therefore operates without the traditional checks-and-balances control of Congress.

STEP 9. Because, as we have written, "the power to regulate is the power to kill," the illusion that America still has private companies, private property, and a real economy begins to disintegrate. The central government effectively "owns" everything via regulation. Because we have become a "cashless society," government can now instantly extend vast credit to its cronies and cut off the ability to survive economically from its enemies.

STEP 10. The Progressive government declares a national emergency, then uses it to officially implement the 10 points to destroy capitalism that Karl Marx and Friedrich Engels called for in their *Communist Manifesto*. This mattered little because previous Progressive presidents and lawmakers had already turned nine of these 10 points into law. Elections are not cancelled because Progressives had already guaranteed their victory by packing the voter rolls with non-citizens and installing rigged electronic voting machines.

On this scale, America from its beginning in 1776 has moved from Step One, the dawn of freedom of the American Dream, to Step Eight, a nearly completed Progressive collectivization and government takeover of our society.

The Obama Administration is rushing to put Step Nine in place before he is supposed to leave office in January, 2017. The economic collapse that this might trigger could provide an emergency pretext for the wholesale replacement of the American Dream and U.S. Constitution with the Progressive Dream of total government ownership and control of our society.

Obama may yet achieve the Progressive collectivist dream of turning America into Woodrow Wilson's perfect beehive – with a Progressive elite in control as the philosopher Queen Bee.

Progressivism Abroad

To catch a glimpse of our own future, we can look at two examples of the Progressive Dream turning into a nightmare in Greece and Puerto Rico.

Continuing a turbulent 2015, on September 20 Greek voters returned Prime Minister Alexis Tsipras and his Syriza Party to power.

Syriza is an acronym for the Greek words *Synaspismos tis Rizospastikis Aristeras*, "Coalition of the Radical Left" – the Greek word for left having the same root as "aristocracy," because in antiquity the ruling elite was disproportionately left-handed, southpaws like Barack Obama, George H.W. Bush, Bill Clinton, Harry Truman and Progressive Herbert Hoover.

Mr. Tsipras in his youth had been a Communist but is now a "moderate" leftist. The September election saw the leftmost fringe activists from Syriza form their own party and lose by calling for immediate Greek withdrawal from the Euro currency and repudiating the nation's debts to Europe.

Tsipras and Syriza were first elected in January 2015 by promising to end the austerity that Europe and the International Monetary Fund (IMF) imposed on Greece to pay foreign debts. After months of negotiating, Tsipras reneged on his promises by agreeing to harsh new debt payment terms, austerity budget cuts and tax increases in exchange for a third national bailout worth $97.2 Billion.

Days before the popular vote in September, Tsipras was depicted in an editorial cartoon as awakening one night in a sweat and telling his wife: "I had a nightmare that I was re-elected."

Mr. Tsipras, 41, and his likely ruling coalition must pass dozens of new laws that raise taxes, cut benefits and otherwise inflict pain by year's end in order to secure bailout money, recapitalize the nation's banks and unwind capital controls that have choked Greece's economy.

"A misstep could send the country crashing out of the Eurozone," warned the *New York Times*. "Greece's relations with Europe are in a fragile state, and several of its leaders are showing impatience, unlikely to tolerate the foot-dragging of past administrations."

"On the horizon, too, is the growing refugee crisis....," the *Times* reports. "Thousands have used the country as a steppingstone toward other parts of Europe. But Greece does not have the resources to provide food and shelter and it is terrified that other countries will close their borders leaving waves of newcomers to back up on its shores," especially on the island of Lesbos, home of the ancient Greek poetess Sappho.

A Ticking Bomb

The time bomb from early 2015 thus keeps ticking in heavily-indebted Greece, despite European nations having agreed in 2015 to provide it a third economic bailout.

If this bomb goes off – with Greece repudiating its international debts and exiting the Euro currency in a "Grexit" -- the damage could be severe worldwide.

If this southern European nation of fewer than 11 million people ever halts its debt payments, the future of the Euro currency and even the global economy could be plunged into uncertainty.

If this occurs, no one can be sure whether nothing more will happen.... or Greece becomes, as many experts fear, the little snowflake that could trigger an economic avalanche and devastate the global economy.

The assassination of one Archduke set in motion the falling dominos that produced World War I, caused the deaths of between 15 million and 50 million people, and changed the political landscape of the entire world forever.

To an outsider, the issue in Greece might look simple – with Europe using pressure to collect debts run up by one small, free-spending deadbeat nation.

We will explain why many economists warn that trying to collect these Greek debts will almost certainly fail – and is not worth the terrible risk.

A secret lurks behind this new currency, the Euro, that has ensnared Greece and several other European nations – including, ironically, the powerful nation that conjured the Euro into existence.

This matters urgently to all of us because Greece is not the only nation that has gone hopelessly deep in debt by using this month's credit card to pay the minimum required on last month's credit card bill....to daisy chain itself into unpayable debt.

Nearly all the major world powers have done likewise, including the United States.

As a result, the entire global economy today is an economic illusion pasted together using trillions of faith-based fiat paper dollars, other currencies and magically-created paper instruments such as bonds and derivatives.

We are living in an economic mirage of wealth conjured out of thin air.

We are *all* Greeks looking for someone else bearing gifts to bail us out of the mess that now ensnares us.

The chaos in Greece could become the finger-snap, the "wake up" call that breaks this hypnotic spell, the pinprick that pops the balloon of our money itself and causes the entire global economic house of cards we have built since the era of World War I to collapse.

We can all feel the instability, the sense that the avalanche is coming soon, that things have been piled up to the breaking point and are about to give way.

We have seen Greeks frantically withdrawing what money they can from their bank accounts before the bank doors are locked, as they were during the bank seizures in Greek-speaking Cyprus in March 2013. We have seen Greeks fleeing before capital controls were imposed and collapse happens. Those in Greece's bank runs are doing what they can while their money is still accessible and has some value.

Your survival instinct should already be sounding alarms. You need to be taking precautions now, shedding high-risk paper investments and diversifying into assets that cannot be run by the trillions off a printing press or that are denominated in dollars.

Breaking Point

Greece reached the end of what it was willing – or able – to pay on its debt on June 5, 2015.

As the old joke goes, "If you think nobody cares about you, try missing a car payment."

Greece on that date did not make its scheduled, required payment to the International Monetary Fund (IMF) – invoking a little-used option to put off that payment and three others, totaling €1.6 Billion [$1.8 Billion], until the end of June.

Greece took this step, the *New York Times* reported, because its creditors refused to release €7.2 Billion ($8.06 Billion) from the international Greek bailout program until the Greek government signs a new deal to honor its debts. Greece for years has asked for debt relief and paid its due debts by asking for additional bailouts, concessions and loans.

The creditor-representing "Troika" – comprised of the European Central Bank (ECB), the IMF and the European Commission – finally told Greece, in effect, "Enough! Stop pretending to pay your debts to us with our own money while making your debts bigger!"

A run on Greek banks withdrew more than $2 Billion from accounts in only three days. While the European Central Bank rushed in billions to sustain liquidity, economists called it a coin flip whether Greece's banks would be able to open on Monday morning.

Experts suggested bookkeeping compromises to resolve the crisis. Milan's Bocconi University adjunct finance professor Marcello Minenna, for example, proposed a 16-year "bond" structured so that Greece would acknowledge its obligation and keep paying $8 Billion each year of its $352 Billion debt to creditors – but creditors would effectively agree in the end to write off at least half of this huge uncollectable debt. [164]

Greece has already been given huge gifts. In May 2010 the Eurozone and IMF gave Greece a "rescue package" worth €110 Billion ($148 Billion). In 2011 a second bailout was needed amounting to €130 Billion ($173 Billion) in a deal that included a 53% reduction in Greek debt to private creditors and a giveback to Greece of any Eurozone central bank profits on Greek debt.

Greece has had little hesitation in borrowing more and more. It has promised, and then mostly reneged on its pledges, to reform its financial policies and behavior in exchange for these previous rescue payments and debt reductions.

The Greek Death Spiral

Greece now owes more than a third of a trillion dollars. Without a major economic rebound or huge debt forgiveness, Greece will be burdened by crushing debt for at least the next 60 years. Even before this latest bailout, Greece has debt equal to 176 percent of its annual Gross Domestic Product.

The unemployment rate in Greece is currently around 27 percent for adult workers and around 53 percent for workers 24 and younger.

Greece's banks hemorrhaged money in late June 2015 at the rate of more than $2 Billion every three days as those who could were taking their Euros out of the country, even if this required paying Greece's special tax on cash.

Other Greeks, paradoxically, rushed to buy new cars while they still have money left in Euros. Many fear that the government will seize their Euros and replace them with new Drachmas, run off printing presses by the billions, that will be hyper-inflated and have no purchasing power. Greece could thus monetize at least part of its debts while expropriating citizen Euros to pay the rest. [165]

The ruling radical-leftist Syriza government enacted a law that empowers the government to confiscate citizen retirement accounts, among other things. Similar laws are being created in many other countries.

Greece, in the long run, appears to be a doomed country. Who will invest in a country with a ruling anti-capitalist radical political party still eager to expropriate any wealth that arrives? The best and brightest young Greeks are fleeing in search of jobs and opportunity, and so have been older citizens with their life savings in Euros.

As it has elsewhere in the world, socialism is literally destroying the vital life force that economist John Maynard Keynes described as "animal spirits," source of the optimism and self-confidence needed to succeed.

Greece's fertility rate – the average number of babies women give birth to in a nation – has plummeted to 1.34 and continues to fall. Like the rest of democratic socialist Europe, Greece faces demographic doom.

Even if Europe and Greece agree to kick the can a bit farther down the road, this will almost certainly involve compromises that leave Greece with a heavier, ultimately unpayable debt burden for many decades to come.

Greece will remain a basket case and potential trigger for economic chaos no matter what happens in 2015.

Greece, we need to understand, is not the exception. Among Progressive welfare states, it is the "New Normal," just a few steps farther down the road to serfdom than the others. Worldwide debt is at its highest level in 200 years, and most of that debt is simply too huge ever to be repaid.

Prudent investors should promptly diversify their assets to protect against the range of risks and dangers this could cause. With Greece acting as an explosive harbinger, a sign of risks and problems rapidly approaching in the heavily-indebted United States and worldwide, doing such diversification has become urgently important, and each of us needs to do it to protect what we have.

Playing Euro Poker

If Greece ever renounces its debts to other Eurozone nations and abandons the Euro, leftist political parties in other nations – such as Podemos ("We Are Able") in Spain – may demand that their countries do likewise.

If this first domino falls, no one knows how many other countries might fall away from the Euro and undermine the fragile unity of Europe, which accounts for roughly 25 percent of U.S. trade.

Germany and the EU now face a possible lose-lose situation. A few possibilities:

If Greece ever leaves the Eurozone, political pressure will build among the other remaining relatively poor PIIGS countries [Portugal, Italy, Ireland and Spain] that now use the Euro to follow Greece's departure.

As Germany and the EU bail Greece out by forgiving and covering even more of its debts, or with new loans, how long will it be before other PIIGS countries demand the same debt help that Greece received?

Germany, the richest and most powerful country in Western Europe, might lose face if it ever backs down in fear of what tiny, poor Greece might do. This could prompt many other nations to see Germany as a country that can be pushed around.

On the other hand, if the Troika and Germany ever crush and further impoverish Greece or force it out of the Eurozone, Germany may be blamed for setting in motion the forces that sink Europe's currency challenge to the global power of the U.S. Dollar and the Progressive dream of creating a rival United States of Europe.

An *Economic* Weapon of Mass Destruction?

Meanwhile, global struggles are now underway that involve not only terrorism but also a currency war.

The International Monetary Fund (IMF) had planned an October 2015 meeting to consider ending the U.S. Dollar's privileged monopoly status as the Global Reserve Currency by granting elevated status to the Chinese Yuan/Renminbi currency.

The IMF postponed and rescheduled this topic for September 2016, which makes the future of the dollar disturbingly uncertain as both a medium of exchange and a store of value.

Many have been frightened by President Barack Obama's seemingly weak stance in negotiating a multinational agreement to slow the development of nuclear weapons by Iran.

Why, many wondered, did Mr. Obama agree to nearly every concession the apocalyptic theocratic regime in Tehran demanded, including Iranian control over inspections and a transfer of more than $100 Billion to this, the world's largest funder of international terrorism?

Could it be that President Obama secretly is even more afraid of a different doomsday weapon, an "Economic Weapon of Mass Destruction" that Iran already controls?

On August 5, 2015, President Obama told students at American University that any attempt to re-impose multinational sanctions on Iran might "trigger severe disruptions in our own economy" and "raise questions internationally about the dollar's role as the world's reserve currency." [166]

On August 11, 2015, Secretary of State John Kerry amplified the President's remarks, warning that if Congress blocked the Iran deal and the U.S. tried to pressure our allies to re-impose sanctions on Tehran, that this would be "a recipe, very quickly…for the American dollar to cease to be the reserve currency of the world – which is already bubbling out there." [167]

This was an odd moment as the Obama Administration was trying to push both Republican and Democratic lawmakers into agreeing to what most saw as a weak, hard-to-defend deal.

Secretary of State Kerry was arguing about monetary concerns.

Treasury Secretary Jack Lew on July 14 had also been far from his expertise by discussing diplomatic matters – and reassuring America that "we retain the ability to snap back both U.S. and international sanctions if Iran does not abide by the agreement….[W]e have ensured through this deal that we will have the means to respond swiftly and powerfully." [168]

Yet Mr. Kerry suddenly seemed to be saying that the dollar would be devastated and lose its global reserve currency status if we pushed our allies to do precisely such a sanction snap-back.

Is there more here than America has been told? Does the deal with Iran include yet another secret agreement that the Obama Administration refuses to share with lawmakers or the press? What might such a secret be?

Oiling the Dollar

In 1971 President Richard Nixon severed the last anchor that allowed friendly central banks to exchange the U.S. Dollar for gold. As the value of the now-floating dollar sank, oil producers saw their profits plummet and launched the first OPEC (Organization of Petroleum Exporting Countries) oil embargo in 1973 to boost gas prices.

Nixon responded in 1973 by making an agreement with Saudi Arabia's King Faisal: if the Saudis would accept only U.S. Dollars as payment for their oil and invest any surplus profits in U.S. bills, notes and Treasury bonds, the United States would protect Saudi Arabia against invasion by the Soviet Union and other nations such as Iraq and Iran.

In effect, President Nixon had in some ways moved the dollar from a gold standard to an oil standard. By 1975 the other members of OPEC also agreed to sell their oil only for dollars. The well-greased age of the Petrodollar was born.

A French finance minister described our monopoly over the dollars others had to acquire to buy oil as America's "exorbitant privilege," and so it has been for more than 40 years. All other nations needing dollars have boosted the value of our currency. This is what it means to control the global reserve currency.

As America printed more than $6 Trillion paper dollars out of thin air since 2008, a growing number of nations have started to question how much longer the United States should have this monopoly.

The Saudis and others see President Obama withdrawing from the Middle East while clearing a path for Iran to acquire nuclear weapons. If America can no longer be relied on to defend our dollar's value or them, some nations are asking, then why not welcome more diverse allies and global reserve currencies? The Saudis reportedly have begun holding meetings with Russia and Israel while acquiring nuclear weapons of their own.

American sanctions against Iran "have cost businesses in other countries a lot of money," says Paul Craig Roberts, a former Assistant Treasury Secretary under President Ronald Reagan and former *Wall Street Journal* editor.

During those sanctions, Iran has accepted Yuan as payment for its oil from China. Iran also sold oil on credit to credit-strapped Greece. Tehran has entered into marketing discussions with Russia, and joined Moscow's and Beijing's movement towards "De-Dollarization" of world trade. [169] As long ago as 2007, Iran expressed willingness to sell its oil for Euros through an Iranian Oil Bourse.

"If the dollar lost the reserve currency status, U.S. power would decline," Roberts says. ".... Washington would no longer be able to pay its bills by printing money. Moreover, the loss of reserve currency status would mean a drop in the demand for dollars and a drop in willingness to hold them. Therefore, the dollar's exchange value would fall, and rising prices of imports would import inflation into the U.S. economy." [170]

Soon we might need to pay a premium for some other nation's global reserve currency to buy overseas the things we need.

Could it be that our real, still-secret deal with Iran involves some kind of mutual agreement to protect the global reserve status of the U.S. Dollar as the world medium for buying oil?

One investigative reporter who suspects this is Peter Koenig, who writes for Global Research in Canada and for several Russian media outlets. Opinionated and suspicious of Western media and banking, Koenig is not alone in asking why our overthrow of Iraq's Saddam Hussein came not long after he proposed selling oil for Euros instead of dollars. [171]

Koenig has also asked whether our toppling of Libya's Muammar Gadhafi had anything to do with his proposal to mint a new coin, the Gold Dinar, that would have been a new competitor for the dollar. Being gold, such a coin would, to many, seem preferable to America's debased paper currency.

The Euro's Secret

The Eurozone was intended to have a disciplined common currency that should give Germany an advantageous trading position with neighboring, Euro-using nations.

Some see this as Germany's third attempt to conquer Europe in the 20th Century, this time with economic power instead of tanks and bayonets. The Euro, launched in 1999, is Germany's Deutschmark in disguise. Through its position as the dominant economy in Europe Germany can largely control the Euro.

During the 20th Century, Germany in two World Wars came close to conquering Europe. Both times it was driven back in part by American might embodied in America's industrial centers like Detroit and Baltimore.

Germany's objective was to establish economic hegemony over the rest of Europe. Its aim was to turn the peoples of other nations there, who could not match Germany's wealth and productivity, into "Euro-peons." [172]

What German policy miscalculated was that some Eurozone nations, especially the PIIGS – Portugal, Italy, Ireland, Greece and Spain – would be offered large loans by banks that assumed Germany would ultimately pay any such debt to keep Euro nations from defaulting. The PIIGS were intoxicated by the multi-billion-dollar credit cards they were offered as Eurozone members, and they spent like drunken teenagers, running up huge debts that they could not pay when the global economy slid into recession.

From Germany's point of view, the result has been a nightmare of more than $600 Billion worth of bailouts, with never-ending pressure to do more. [173]

Short of total debt forgiveness, which is a precedent Germany is almost certainly afraid to establish (lest other nations conclude that the "Greeking" wheel got the grease and imitate its refusal to pay), the only way out of perpetual debt and decline for Greece would be to restore economic growth, more jobs, and prosperity.

The Germans and Troika find Greece's behavior especially troubling because the Greeks apparently have the ability to pay far more. Greece, for example, reportedly has gold reserves of 112.5 Tonnes of gold worth approximately $4.338 Billion. Unless its bullion has been rehypothecated and committed as collateral elsewhere, Greece could pay its immediate obligations without begging for more handouts merely by using gold, the perennially reliable asset. [174]

The Debt Trap

By the 1970s, the Arab oil embargo and the ascent of leftist politics put Greece on a downward spiral of debt, dependency and in some ways the culture of Boss Tweed and other city political bosses.

"Public employment grew by fivefold from 1970 through 2009 – at an annual growth rate of 4 percent," wrote Greek economist John Sfakianakis. "Over the same four decades, employment in the private sector increased by only 27 percent – an annual rate of less than 1 percent." [175]

This expansion of government patronage jobs has meant that roughly 28 percent of those still employed in Greece today are government employees in a system where, as Sfakianakis wrote, "[w]ages in the public sector were on average almost one and a half times higher than in the private sector." [176]

In some government agencies, wrote Sfakianakis, experts estimated that "overstaffing was considered to be around 50 percent," and employees were given pay increases based on tenure, not competence. Pensions for government employees are lavish and early retirement became commonplace. [177]

Such government employment in Europe's socialist welfare states is not unusual. Italy, France and even Germany have more than Greece's 28 percent of their workforce as government employees. [178]

In the private sector, consider just one example of how extreme the Progressive socialist Greek welfare state became: the government officially defined 12,000 different professions as "hazardous," and provided that workers in these professions were entitled to retire at age 50 with a government-secured pension worth 80 percent of their highest lifetime year of income.

These "hazardous" professions included being a beautician or hair stylist, because of the risk of inhaling hairspray; being a baker, because of the risk of inhaling flour dust; and being a radio announcer whose nose and mouth were perilously close to microphones into which other announcers had breathed and coughed their germs.

A London School of Economics and Political Science analysis by two Greek scholars concluded that as the Greek government employment bloated, the quality of services delivered to taxpayers went from bad to worse. One thing worse than a costly welfare state is a costly welfare state that does not even deliver the goods it promises. [179]

"The peculiarity of the Greek public sector is the large size and exorbitant public expenditure on wages," they wrote, "but also the low efficiency along with extremely low quality of services for citizens." [180]

Both of Greece's political parties that took power after the end of military rule in 1974 took turns expanding the government and the welfare state to create a way to reward cronies and entrench a constituency of government-dependent voters for themselves.

Onto the private sector, they "increased the taxes to unhealthy levels and risked a recession to protect their clientele in the state apparatus," acknowledged a former Greek finance minister, Stefanos Manos. [181]

"Government spending on public employees' salaries and social benefits rose by around 6.5 percentage points of G.D.P. [Gross Domestic Product] from 2000 to 2009, while revenue declined by 5 percentage points during the same period," wrote Sfakianakis. The government's solution to this, in addition to raising taxes, "was to borrow more." [182]

Thus Greece's debt grew and wealth was diverted from private workers to government ones, from the "makers" who created wealth to Greece's parasitic "takers" who devour it while producing far, far less.

"Our research has shown that an employee in the private sector contributes 17,000 Euros more per year to Greece's gross domestic product (GDP) than a public sector employee," says University of Athens economics Professor Giorgos Bitros.[183]

According to Professor Bitros, most Greek reforms have been implemented against the private sector, not the government sector, of the economy. [184]

After adopting the Euro as its currency in 2001, Greece found it easy to borrow huge amounts. The reason was that creditors assumed they were no longer lending to high-risk borrower Greece, but to a nation of the new Eurozone whose debts would be backed up if necessary by the richest and most creditworthy of all European nations, Germany, to protect the Euro.

Banks from Germany and elsewhere rushed to offer fat loans to PIIGS nations that never dreamed they would ever be lent so many billions just for the asking. As Germany soon learned, its unwitting mistake was to open the door to giving almost unlimited credit to profligate nations like Greece.

Those nations promptly followed the Progressive policy of trying to tax, spend and borrow their way to prosperity and happiness, and then to stick foreigners or future generations with the bill when this failed.

The West's Debt to Greece

Greece may have little future, but to understand today's events, it helps to remember Greece's large past.

Greece and its colonies ruled much of the Mediterranean 2,500 years ago. Ancient Athenians invented democracy, and Greece's great thinkers developed philosophy, mathematics, poetry and drama.

Perhaps the greatest ancient Greek achievement, however, was defeating huge invading Persian forces at Marathon in 490 B.C. and at the sea battle of Salamis in 480 B.C. These victories ushered in a Hellenic golden age.

Had the Greeks lost these battles – and had Greek-speaking Macedonian Alexander the Great (along with his tutor, the philosopher Aristotle) not conquered Persia – you might be reading this text in Iranian/Persian Farsi – and the history of the West would have become a Persian despotism.

Greece itself would be conquered by the rising empire of Rome, but the Western half of the Roman Empire would in turn fall half a millennium later.

The eastern half of the Roman Empire, however, from its capital Constantinople (now Istanbul in today's Turkey) survived and thrived as the Greek-speaking center of Orthodox Christianity until 1453, less than 40 years before Columbus discovered the New World. The Byzantine Empire survived so long, in part, by producing the world's most reliable gold money.

The Byzantine Empire sent missionaries into Russia, converting it to a variant of Greece's Cyrillic alphabet and to Orthodox Christianity. Today Russia's President Vladimir Putin reportedly travels in the company of Russian Orthodox clergy, just as centuries of Czars did before him.

In 1453, Muslim Ottoman Turks overthrew the Byzantine Empire and would rule Greece itself until 1829, after Westerners such as the British poet Lord Byron had died in the struggle to win Greek independence.

The Ottoman Empire and its caliphate ended in 1923, following its defeat in World War I. In 2001, Greece joined the Eurozone, replacing its own Drachma currency with the Euro.

A Muslim Connection?

One of the great mysteries historians and sociologists have considered is national greatness.

Why do some nations achieve great success, prosperity and happiness while others fail or forever remain mediocre? Why do some such as Italy have multiple periods of achievement, a Roman Empire and a Renaissance, while others have only one Golden Age that is never repeated?

Economists coined the term PIIGS to describe the European nations that in recent decades have seemed unable to achieve prosperity. While the culture and history of each PIIGS nation is unique, all have in recent decades fallen into debt and economic stagnation.

In three or more of the PIIGS nations, we noticed something that nobody else is discussing.

In Spain, Moorish Muslims from Morocco ruled much of its land for as long as 800 years before the 1492 Christian re-conquest, which Spaniards call the *"Reconquista."* (Some Hispanic activists use this same term for their immigration into the American Southwest, once part of Mexico. One Mexican city is named Matamoros, literally "Moor killer.")

A smaller Iberian nation bordering Spain is Portugal, which was likewise largely under Muslim rule for 500 years.

Greece was effectively under Muslim rule for 376 years, from the fall of Byzantium in 1453 until regaining its independence and culturally rejoining the West in 1829.

All three of these sunny "siesta" nations have been influenced by hundreds of years of Islamic governance and culture. Greece had its Golden Age long before this happened and was also shaped by another dominant culture, that of Rome. The Romans generally admired Greek culture, and many educated Romans spoke Greek. Many have compared the relationship between these two cultures to the admiration many Americans feel for British culture.

Spain and Portugal, by contrast, built impressive empires after winning their freedom from Muslim rule – Spain in the New World, enriched by capturing hoards of Native American gold and silver; Portugal in Brazil and by circumventing Muslim-controlled routes to India and other eastern lands that were treasure troves of spices nearly as valuable as gold or silver.

Several other European nations created colonial empires, but none were as lucky as Spain and Portugal in claiming lands where vast amounts of gold, silver or spices were simply there for easy taking.

Italy was a sunny land of competing city-states and regions, not a unified nation until the 1800s. Various parts of the nation had been under foreign rule, including Saracen Muslim rule.

The PIIGS nations are predominantly Roman Catholic, except Greek Orthodox Christian Greece. German sociologist Max Weber in *The Protestant Ethic and the Spirit of Capitalism* argued that Protestant Christianity, with its work ethic that views earning wealth as good, is conducive to prosperity, as we see in Lutheran Scandinavia.

During the 20th and 21st Centuries several Islamic nations have become among the wealthiest on Earth, almost by luck. An industrializing Western world suddenly needed huge quantities of a resource that in prior centuries had been a nuisance in the nomadic Middle East and Indonesia – oil.

In places like Saudi Arabia, where a ten-foot pipe stuck into sand dunes instantly became a gusher of black gold, riches were not manufactured with effort…but easily harvested like low-hanging fruit.

America's technological advances, driven by free market innovation, have helped expand and enhance a variety of sophisticated oil drilling techniques. A credential for work in this modern industry around the Persian Gulf has for decades been a degree in petroleum engineering from the University of Southern California.

If America's Progressive-driven economic death spiral continues, however, our once-golden republic may experience both a "brain drain" and financial drain, as successful Greeks have caused by taking their money and themselves out of Greece.

Even in September 2015, Greek capital controls have restricted to only 500 Euros (approximately $560) per month how much Greek citizens may send out of the country from their bank. (A Greek family with a student studying abroad, as of August 18, 2015, could also send up to 8,000 Euros per quarter to pay accommodation costs.) [185]

Bank account holders fear a government conversion to worthless Drachmas if Greece leaves the Eurozone, and also fear a European "bail-in" that might confiscate a big hunk of their bank account if Greece stays in the Eurozone.

Our future may be in a Greece-like leftist welfare state of chronic high unemployment and a purposeless life.

The "Rich Port" Becomes Poor

Closer to home, we have a Greece-like land with close ties to the United States in our own neighborhood that in some ways resembles Baltimore.

How did the Caribbean island that the Spanish named Puerto Rico, "rich port," become a money-short basket case? Here, too, Progressive good intentions and an addiction to welfare have brought the island close to ruin.

The United States government built Puerto Rico's current economy on exotic tax breaks, especially for drugs. The Pharmaceutical industry had such juicy tax incentives that, at one point, nine of America's 12 biggest drug companies had major facilities in Puerto Rico.

In 1996, however, the U.S. Government began a 10-year phase out of such tax breaks. Big companies fled, and by 2006 the island economy had sunk into something like a depression.

Rather than cut back, however, the Puerto Rican government tried to maintain its lifestyle and rather lavish welfare state by borrowing, much as Greece did.

Puerto Rico likewise was lent hundreds of billions by creditors who in part assumed that as a Commonwealth of the United States, Uncle Sam would not let this island collapse.

The U.S. had given Puerto Rico various breaks, including the power to issue bonds that were triple tax deductible – federal, state and local – across the United States. Because of this special nationwide advantage, most big funds acquired a supply of various Puerto Rican bonds.

But on August 3, 2015, Puerto Rico defaulted on a $58 Million payment, and its debt now seems a less desirable purchase. Puerto Rico now owes $72 Billion to creditors. This is a bigger debt than any of America's 50 states except New York and California, both of which have vastly more ability to pay than does tiny Puerto Rico.

Puerto Rico is about the size of Connecticut and has only 3.5 million residents. (Greece, by comparison, has more than 10 million.) Only 40 percent of its working-age population, however, works – a job participation rate more than 50 percent lower than the rest of the United States. Welfare benefits pay about as much as working, so Puerto Ricans have little incentive to seek jobs.

Sixty percent of residents are on Medicare or Medicaid. It's easy for a family of 3 to get $1,743 a month in Food Stamps, AFDC and other government benefits – which is more than Puerto Rico's median family income. Per capita income is only half that in Mississippi, our poorest state.

Some stay because most residents of Puerto Rico receive American-style social benefits but are not required to pay personal income tax...all the goodies of America with only local taxes. Even so, depending on the tax the rate of tax evasion can top 50 percent there.

This begets what Puerto Rico's Governor recently called a financial "death spiral." The most productive young workers can and do legally flee to the United States for jobs and opportunity, because they come from a U.S. Commonwealth. Those who remain are often on welfare.

The government keeps borrowing, but at ever-higher rates of interest needed to attract bond buyers – which creates an ever-increasing drain on government revenues to service this growing debt. With less revenue, government provides lousier and lousier public services along with favorable pay for government workers and welfare benefits to buy off voters. Yes, it looks like Greece.

Every attempt to raise taxes is met with more tax evasion and a growing outmigration of the hardest working, most talented workers to the U.S., so fewer remain to pay taxes. Fewer makers, more takers. An economic death spiral, indeed.

Under U.S. law, Puerto Rico cannot declare bankruptcy to clear its debts.

Puerto Rico could, in theory, withdraw from the U.S., much as Greece has threatened to withdraw from the Eurozone. The island could print, and debase, its own currency to pay off debtors for a fraction of what is owed.

And, indeed, 54 percent of Puerto Ricans want to end their island's Commonwealth status. In a recent plebiscite, however, more than 61 percent voted not to leave the United States – but to apply for statehood, something Democrats might like but Republicans would hate, because a majority of the Spanish-speaking residents of this island would probably vote Democratic…and send at least two more Democrats to the Senate.

Only 5.5 percent want outright independence from the U.S. – as you might expect from a financially-dependent, welfare-addicted population.

As long as Republicans control the House and Senate, Puerto Rican statehood is unlikely – and might not win on the island, because it would require Puerto Ricans there to pay personal income taxes. And absent some amazing charismatic leader or galvanizing new direction, Puerto Rico is likely to remain poor.

Cities on the Cliff Edge

Like Puerto Rico, many American cities cannot legally declare bankruptcy. Many other cities and legal entities can declare Chapter 9 bankruptcy, and are doing so.

We pointed with concern to Puerto Rican bonds and warned of "problems to come" in our 2013 book *The Great Withdrawal: How the Progressives' 100-Year Debasement of America and the Dollar Ends*, where we examined in detail Detroit's dire situation and more-than-$18.5 Billion debt, which pushed it to become the largest American city ever to file for bankruptcy. [186]

Faced with shrinking tax revenues and neglected funding for employment pensions and other benefits, more than a dozen cities and counties have in recent years gone over the edge of the cliff into bankruptcy to shed obligations that past politicians promised. Among these have been the

California cities of San Bernardino, Stockton and Vallejo; Central Falls, Rhode Island; and Jefferson County, Alabama, which alone was burdened by $4.15 Billion in debts. [187]

Other cities reportedly are also in economic trouble, including Washington, D.C., Cincinnati, Camden, Chicago, San Jose, Los Angeles, San Francisco, San Diego, and Baltimore. [188]

In 2013 a study by Public Financial Management, Inc., commissioned by Baltimore, found that the city, in the words of Associated Press, "is on a path to financial ruin and must enact major reforms to stave off bankruptcy." [189]

After more than half a century of Progressive rule, Baltimore's problems are seen in many big cities. As expenses outrun revenues, the PFM study found, Baltimore will accumulate at least $745 Million in budget deficits by 2022. It will also face $3.2 Billion in unfunded pension and other retiree liabilities. And at the same time the cities' roads, bridges, buildings and aging schools will need another $3.6 Billion in repairs and rebuilding. [190]

Baltimore, meanwhile, has the highest property and other taxes in the state. Taxes might have gone even higher, but the State of Maryland puts ceilings on some taxes. The economy is likely to remain stagnant for the next 10 years, despite tax and other concessions to some large-scale developers.

The 2015 riots frightened away even more tax-paying businesses, residents and investors, and the city's murder rate soared as police retreated. The steel and shipbuilding industries that used to provide good jobs are gone, and the city's population has fallen by a third. Many who did not leave are poor and live in the Heroin Capital of the United States. No wonder Baltimore's Progressive Mayor is not seeking re-election in 2016.

But as the *Baltimore Sun* newspaper has reminded readers, this city has an ace up its sleeve that makes Baltimore very different from Detroit. [191] We will reveal that ace in our Epilogue.

The Price of Progressivism

Why do some societies succeed while others fail? One clue may be found in recent psychological research done by Dan Ariely of Duke University's Fuqua School of Business and others. Pat Boone mentions their work in this book's Foreward.

This research tested people who had grown up in either free market West Germany or Communist East Germany before the post-World War II Communist Iron Curtain came down and Germany was reunified.

The study found that those whose values were shaped by "egalitarian," collectivist Progressive East Germany "cheated twice as much as Western Germans overall." Moreover, these researchers found, "The longer individuals were exposed to socialism, the more likely they were to cheat on our task." [192]

These researchers concluded that "the political regime of socialism has a lasting impact on citizens' basic morality." [193] This is logical, because socialism is one vast system of stealing at gunpoint from some in order to give the fruits of their labor to others who did not earn it.

Socialism is, in essence, slavery.

No wonder it damages the minds, hearts and souls of all who live under it.

"Socialism is damaging in many ways," an *Investor's Business Daily* editorial said in summarizing the study. "It wrecks economies and batters the quality of life. It corrupts, dehumanizes and makes people worse.... The researchers further remind us that socialist regimes suppress speech, engender social distrust, create economic scarcity and breed moral hypocrisy." [194]

Progressivism, this new evidence suggests, has consequences – and is hazardous to the health and well-being of human individuals and society.

Progressivism is a poison that a few societies can survive, but never thrive on or fulfill their highest potential while being forced to swallow. Why should anyone or any nation swallow this toxic ideology when we could instead be free, healthy and prosperous?

Combining the healthy American Dream with the inherently poisonous, honesty-destroying Progressive Dream is simply irrational.

Progressivism does worse than cause Donkey Drag in an economy. It also literally poisons and damages the moral integrity and humanity of individuals who would live far better in the American Dream.

Freedom frightens some people because it requires them to be responsible. They would rather be like children with a paternalistic government to care for them. They would rather live as ghosts in somebody else's Progressive dream, building some ruler's pyramid instead of their own individual dreams.

The ancient Greek storyteller Aesop told of the profligate grasshopper that was doomed and of the wise ants who knew that a terrible time was coming in which only those who had prepared would survive.

We all can feel the instability, the tremors from Progressive Greece, Progressive Puerto Rico and elsewhere, one more step farther along the road to serfdom than Baltimore.

We can sense the coming collapse and avalanche that will sweep away those who trusted mere paper to protect their families.

The wise know that the hour is late, and that safety urgently requires us to diversify into solid things that have stood time's hard test. If that test comes today, have you prepared?

"I predict future happiness for Americans
if they can prevent the government
from wasting the labors of the people
under the pretense of taking care of them."

– Thomas Jefferson

"What the people wanted was a government
which would provide a comfortable life for them,
and with this as the foremost object ideas of freedom
and self-reliance and service to the community were
obscured to the point of disappearing.

Athens was more and more looked on as a co-operative business
possessed of great wealth in which all citizens had a right to share.

Athens had reached the point of rejecting independence....

When the freedom they wished for most
was freedom from responsibility, then
Athens ceased to be free and was never free again."

– Edith Hamilton
Historian

Epilogue

Baltimorrow

"Don't you remember?
We built this city.
We built this city
On Rock and Roll."

– The [Jefferson] Starship
We Built this City [195]

In 1807, a 12-year-old boy watched as his parents, following their Quaker Society's decree, freed the slaves who had worked the family's 500-acre tobacco plantation Whitehall in Anne Arundel County, Maryland, just south of Baltimore.

Some of the newly-freed slaves left, while others accepted the family's offer to stay and be cared for.

The young man became an abolitionist, dedicated to freeing all slaves, and a committed supporter of Abraham Lincoln.

He also became the president of Merchants' Bank and several other institutions. He became a corporate director and later chairman of the Finance Committee of the Baltimore and Ohio Railroad. He was also a savvy investor, especially in the B&O, which he bailed out of debt in 1857 and 1873.

He died in 1873, never having had a wife or children as heirs. At his death, he was, according to a 1996 financial history, the 69th wealthiest person in all of American history.

He left roughly two-thirds of his fortune -- $7 Million in 1873 dollars, worth approximately $138 Million in our inflated dollars – to create three things: an orphanage for Black children, a hospital, and a research university, all of which would bear his name – Johns Hopkins.

Detroit was the central example of how a great city can fail in our book *The Great Withdrawal: How the Progressives' 100-Year Debasement of America and the Dollar Ends.* Detroit had been one of the greatest centers of industry, a mecca of jobs turning out automobiles that set a standard of excellence worldwide. Yet when we wrote this book in 2013, the biggest employer in Detroit was no longer a company; it was the government.

Baltimore, by contrast, despite its problems has not turned government into its biggest employer. The greatest creator of jobs here today is Johns Hopkins University, widely recognized as one of the world's best private research universities. It almost single-handedly has, in the words of the *Baltimore Sun*, turned this city into "one of the great hubs for health care and biomedical research." [196]

Johns Hopkins' investment in the future continues to pay enormous dividends for Baltimore, America and the future of humankind.

Consider a few of those minds who have studied or taught at Johns Hopkins: business giants such as cable mogul John C. Malone, business news giant Michael Bloomberg, and former IBM Chairman Samuel Palmisano; economists Thorstein Veblen, Robert Skidelsky, and former Treasury Secretary Timothy Geithner; cinematographer Caleb Deschanel and film director Wes Craven; historian Frederick Jackson Turner; physicist John Archibald Wheeler who coined the term "black hole" and environmentalist Rachel Carson; writers Gertrude Stein, John Barth and J.M. Coetzee; CNN broadcasters Terry Keenan and Wolf Blitzer, as well as Fox broadcasters Dr. Keith Ablow and James Rosen; many Progressives, including John Dewey, Jacques Derrida, Woodrow Wilson and Alger Hiss; and great defenders of the individual, writer P.J. O'Rourke and philosopher-novelist Ayn Rand.

As you might guess, Johns Hopkins University is genuinely diverse but also predominantly Progressive. The Foundation for Individual Rights in Education rates this Politically Correct school among its "12 Worst Colleges for Free Speech."

Among the Stars

Americans watched in horror in early 2015 as the smoke of burning cars and torched buildings rose above Baltimore in live televised newscasts.

That summer, however, America's eyes were riveted to a scene that reminded all of America's greatness. The NASA spacecraft New Horizons, after travelling three billion miles since its 2006 launch, on July 14 flew by the mysterious dwarf planet Pluto, so small and distant that astronomers discovered it only in 1930.

The images of Pluto stunned scientists. Here was a world with water ice mountains almost as tall as the Rockies. [197] And on its surface was a giant heart shape, a valentine from Pluto that touched the hearts and dreams of billions of Earthlings. [198]

What few Americans noticed was that this close encounter of the best kind came not from Cal Tech's JPL or NASA Houston or Florida's Kennedy Space Center. It came from near Laurel, Maryland, a suburb 22 miles from downtown Baltimore.

In 2015, Mission Control for New Horizons was the Johns Hopkins University Advanced Physics Laboratory (APL), where this next step into space for humankind had been conceived and planned, and where its baby grand piano-sized spacecraft had been designed and built.

This Johns Hopkins lab has often played key roles in America's space age. The first photograph of Earth from outer space was snapped in 1946 aboard a V-2 rocket 65 miles above New Mexico using a special camera created by Clyde Holliday of APL. His colleagues near Baltimore included James Van Allen, after whom the belts of radiation above Earth are named, and other great scientists. [199]

Pluto is so far away that from there our Sun can be only 150 times brighter than a full Moon, and solar panels produce little electricity. Powered in these frozen depths of space by plutonium, the New Horizons starship worked perfectly, sending back data it will take our scientists years to analyze. And for the next 20 years it might continue to work, carrying the American Flag almost another seven billion miles in our curious quest for new horizons among the stars.

New Horizons was funded by NASA, but the Johns Hopkins scientist in charge of it, Alan Stern, told *Wall Street Journal* reporter Kyle Peterson that he is a fan of private spaceflight. [200]

"I think that that's an important coming wave," said Stern. "And it's great because it means it's a new source of capital."

"Competition rocks," Stern continued. "When the private sector started putting communications satellites in earth orbit, there was one company, and now there's like literally 30 and it's a $50 billion a year market."

How remarkable this is. So many immigrants and pioneers set sail for Baltimore because it was a center of some of the finest new high technology of its time, including railroads, which in the words of a song were our fathers' "magic carpet made of steel."

American railroads and the telegraph, the instant-communications Internet of its time, both took root through the pioneering Baltimore and Ohio Railroad, which created most of the wealth of Johns Hopkins. And the university that this private wealth built would, more than a century later, create and fly a spacecraft past Pluto.

The cutting edge center of high technology so many immigrants sought in Baltimore is still here.

Nearly a quarter of the jobs in and around Baltimore are in science, technology, engineering and mathematics, the fields together called STEM, thanks largely to the area's two biggest employers – Johns Hopkins University and Johns Hopkins Hospital.

In September 2015 *Bloomberg News* numbered Baltimore among the "unlikely cities that will power the U.S. economy." Its founder, billionaire Michael Bloomberg, is a graduate of Johns Hopkins University. [201]

But Baltimore will regain its prosperity and historic greatness as a center of technology only if the Progressives trying to drag us back into serfdom get out of the way and let the starship called Free Enterprise fly.

A Place of Destiny?

Johns Hopkins also built a hospital, widely regarded as the best in the world. For many years the Director of Pediatric Neurosurgery at this hospital was a brilliant and innovative neurosurgeon named Benjamin Carson.

An African-American from a broken home, Ben was born in Detroit and raised by a mother with only a third-grade education. She was a remarkable person who, as Dr. Carson has shared, was one of 24 children and was wed at age 13. She insisted that he and his brother complete their homework before going out to play.

The key to his future, Carson has said, was the library card his mother insisted he get. She required her sons to read two new library books each month and write a report for her about them.

She refused welfare, working multiple jobs to support her family. From her Ben Carson learned that hard work, determination, self-reliance, religious faith and education could let him achieve the American Dream.

Carson became a doctor, and his gifted hands and innovative approaches turned him into one of the world's most successful surgeons. Had he stayed with medicine, his life would have continued to bring ever-greater personal and financial success as a healer.

His religious faith, however, one day led Doctor Carson to be a speaker at a National Day of Prayer gathering at which he shared the dais with President Obama.

Being politically naïve, Doctor Carson spoke simply what was in his heart that day. Much of it happened to disagree with President Obama's Progressive policies in Obamacare.

Many were stunned. Here was an African-American, and one of America's most highly-respected surgeons, criticizing Mr. Obama to his face.

In Republican circles talk began immediately about whether Dr. Ben Carson would consider running for President of the United States.

After prayerful consideration, Dr. Carson began a quiet campaign to seek harmony among people of all colors, and to look for ways we can come together to solve problems, not simply use them as wedges to drive people apart.

Carson has never held any political office, which in another race could have been a losing liability. In the 2016 presidential race, however, Americans of both major parties seem fed up with the old ruling politicians.

By October 2015, Carson found himself near the top of several polls, along with two other non-politician business leaders, Donald Trump and former Hewlitt-Packard head Carly Fiorina.

Doctor Carson is seen by many as a man of destiny, an anti-politician who embodies many of the small government ideals of individual freedom and responsibility, humility and nobility, integrity and faith that our Framers sought in our leaders.

Doctor Carson found and maintains the spiritual strength in his life as a Seventh-Day Adventist, a faith whose Sabbath is Saturday and whose members avoid eating meat. Is America ready for its first near-vegetarian president?

If it turns out that President Ben Carson is destined to restore the American Dream, then our nation will have been healed, and our brighter future will have come, via Baltimore.

Footnotes

[1] Proverbs 29:2 is from the 2012 Thomas Nelson Bible translation The Voice; Proverbs 29:4 is from the 2011 Common English Bible; Proverbs 29:16 is from the Tyndale House Foundation's 2013 New Living Translation.

[2] Dan Ariely and others, *The (True) Legacy of Two Really Existing Economic Systems* (Monograph). Munich, Germany: Department of Economics, University of Munich, March 19, 2015. May be downloaded in English at http://papers.ssrn.com/sol3/papers.cfm?abstract_id=2457000; "Socialism of Progressives Such As Obama Brings Out Worst in Us," *Investor's Business Daily*, August 5, 2015; Zenon Evans, "Socialists Are Cheaters, Says News Study," *Reason* Magazine, July 22, 2014; Mark J. Perry, "Who'd a-thunk It? Socialism Is Demoralizing, Socially Corrosive, and Promotes Individual Dishonesty and Cheating?" American Enterprise Institute, July 19, 2014.

[3] Excerpts from "Liberty and Democracy," Baltimore *Evening Sun*, April 13, 1925. This also appears in Terry Teachout (Ed।)., *A Second Mencken Chrestomathy: New Selections from the Writings of America's Legendary Editor, Critic, and Wit*. Baltimore: Johns Hopkins University Press, 2006. Page 35.

[4] Elizabeth Chuck and NBC News, "Baltimore Mayor Stephanie Rawlings-Blake Under Fire For 'Space' to Destroy Comment," NBC News, April 28, 2015. URL: http://www.nbcnews.com/storyline/baltimore-unrest/mayor-stephanie-rawlings-blake-under-fire-giving-space-destroy-baltimore-n349656 This web page includes video of the mayor's statement.

[5] Jordan Maltor, "Baltimore's Economy in Black and White," *Money/CNN*, April 29, 2015. URL: http://money.cnn.com/2015/04/29/news/economy/baltimore-economy/

[6] *Ibid.*

[7] *Ibid.*

[8] *Ibid.*

[9] *Ibid.*

[10] *Ibid.*

[11] *Ibid.*

[12] Van Smith, "Baltimore's Narcotic History Dates Back to the 19th-Century Shipping-Driven Boom, Quietly Aided by Bringing Turkish Opium to China, *Baltimore City Paper*, October 21, 2014. URL: http://www.citypaper.com/news/mobtownbeat/bcp-baltimores-narcotic-history-dates-back-to-the-19thcentury-shippingdriven-boom-quietly-aided-by-bring-20141021-story.html

[13] Associated Press, "Baltimore Mayor Supports Legalization of Illicit Drugs," *New York Times*, September 30, 1988. URL: http://www.nytimes.com/1988/09/30/us/baltimore-mayor-supports-legalization-of-illicit-drugs.html

[14] *Ibid.*

[15] Chuck Ross, "Marilyn Mosby Appeared on Stage With Prince During Ode to Freddie," *The Daily Caller*, May 11, 2015. URL: http://dailycaller.com/2015/05/11/marilyn-mosby-appeared-on-stage-with-prince-during-ode-to-freddie-gray/

[16] Abigail Pesta, "Marilyn Mosby: 'You Have to Be Guided by What Is Right," *Cosmopolitan*, June 23, 2015. URL: http://www.cosmopolitan.com/politics/news/a42402/marilyn-mosby/

[17] Heidi Mitchell, "Meet Marilyn Mosby: The Baltimore Prosecutor in the Eye of the Storm," *Vogue*, June 23, 2015. URL: http://www.vogue.com/13274162/marilyn-mosley-baltimore-prosecutor/

[18] Royka Hanna, "Former Baltimore Prosecutor: Maarilyn Mosby Has A Role in City's Violence Increase," *Baltimore Sun*, August 12, 2015. URL: http://www.baltimoresun.com/news/opinion/oped/bs-ed-mosby-role-20150812-story.html

[19] Ta-Nehisi Coats, *Between the World and Me*. New York: Spiegel & Grau / Random House, 2015; Ta-Nehisi Coates, *The Beautiful Struggle: A Memoir*. New York: Spiegel & Grau / Random House, 2009.

[20] Paul Rahe, "Progressive Racism," *National Review*, April 11, 2013. URL: http://www.nationalreview.com/node/345274/print

[21] "The Pill" [WGBH/PBS Documentary in the "American Experience" series] descriptor sheet: "People & Events: Eugenics and Birth Control." URL: http://www.pbs.org/wgbh/amex/pill/peopleevents/e_eugenics.html

[22] Peter C. Engelman, "Margaret Sanger," article in *Encyclopedia of Leadership*, Volume 4, George R. Goethals et al. (Editors), SAGE, 2004.

[23] Sanger in *The Pivot of Civilization*, page 181; quoted in Charles Valenza, "Was Margaret Sanger a Racist?" *Family Planning Perspectives*, January-February 1985, Page 44.

[24] Richard A. Epstein, *How Progressives Rewrote the Constitution*. Washington, D.C.: Cato Institute, 2006, page 107.

[25] *Ibid.*, page 108.

[26] Paul R. Ehrlich, John P. Holdren and Anne H. Ehrlich, *Ecoscience: Population, Resources, Environment*. San Francisco/New York: W.H. Freeman, 1978. See pages 786-788; Ben Johnson, "Obama's Biggest Radical," *FrontPage* Magazine, February 27, 2009. URL: http://archive.frontpagemag.com/Printable.aspx?Artid=34198

[27] "Woodrow Wilson Asks 'What Is Progress?'" (1912), Heritage Foundation. URL: http://www.heritage.org/initiatives/first-principles/primary-sources/woodrow-wilson-asks-what-is-progress

[28] Barack Obama, *The Audacity of Hope: Thoughts on Reclaiming the American Dream*. New York: Crown, 2006. Page 149.

[29] Stanley Kurtz, "Obama's Next Transformation: And How to Stop It," *National Review*, June 9, 2014. URL: http://www.nationalreview.com/corner/419525/obamas-next-transformation-and-how-stop-it-stanley-kurtz; Stanley Kurtz, "Affirmatively Furthering Fair Housing: Sleeper Presidential Campaign Issue," *National Review*, June 10, 2015. URL: http://www.nationalreview.com/corner/419560/affirmatively-furthering-fair-housing-sleeper-presidential-campaign-issue-stanley; Stanley Kurtz, *Spreading the Wealth: How Obama Is Robbing the Suburbs to Pay for the Cities*. New York: Sentinel / Penguin, 2012.

[30] Tom Devaney, "Obama Making Bid to Diversify Wealthy Neighborhoods," *The Hill*, June 11, 2015. URL: http://thehill.com/regulation/244620-obamas-bid-to-diversify-wealthy-neighborhoods; Terry Eastland, "HUID's Power Grab: The Obama Administration Plots a Wholesale Federal Intrusion Into Local Housing Policy," *The Weekly Standard*, October 14, 2013. URL: http://www.weeklystandard.com/print/articles/hud-s-power-grab_759151.html; Tyler Durden, "How Obama Will Centrally-Plan Your Neighborhood: Here Comes the 'Affirmatively Furthering Fair Housing' Rule," *ZeroHedge*, June 11, 2015. URL: http://www.zerohedge.

com/news/2015-06-11/here-comes-affirmatively-furthering-fair-housing-rule-how-obama-will-centrally-plan-

[31] Craig R. Smith and Lowell Ponte, *Don't Bank On It! The Unsafe World of 21ˢᵗ Century Banking*. Phoenix: Idea Factory Press, 2014. Pages 108-110, 130-133.

[32] "Senate Republicans Must Defund Obama's Racial Housing Quotas (Editorial)," *Investor's Business Daily*, June 20, 2014. URL: http://news.investors.com/ibd-editorials/062014-705688- senate-republicans-must-defund-hud-racial-housing-quotas.htm; "Westchester USA: A Case of Racial Engineering that Obama Wants to Take Nationwide," *Wall Street Journal* (Editorial), July 7, 2014. URL: http://online.wsj.com/articles/westchester-usa-1404771358; see also Paul Sperry, "Obama OK's Subprime Borrowers for Prime Loans," *Investor's Business Daily*, January 14, 2013. URL: http://www.amren.com/news/2013/01/obama-oks-subprime- borrowers-for-prime-loans/

[33] Full disclosure: co-author Lowell Ponte worked as a Roving Editor for 15 years when its world headquarters was in Chappaqua, New York, a few blocks from what later became the Clinton mansion. He has been told when there that "Chappaqua" comes from a Native American term that roughly means "stinking swamp."

[34] "Senate Republicans Must Defund Obama's Racial Housing Quotas (Editorial)," *Investor's Business Daily*, June 20, 2014. URL: http://news.investors.com/ibd-editorials/062014-705688- senate-republicans-must-defund-hud-racial-housing-quotas.htm; "Westchester USA: A Case of Racial Engineering that Obama Wants to Take Nationwide," *Wall Street Journal* (Editorial), July 7, 2014. URL: http://online.wsj.com/articles/westchester-usa-1404771358; see also Paul Sperry, "Obama OK's Subprime Borrowers for Prime Loans," *Investor's Business Daily*, January 14, 2013. URL: http://www.amren.com/news/2013/01/obama-oks-subprime- borrowers-for-prime-loans/

[35] Thomas Sowell, *The Housing Boom and Bust*. Revised Edition. New York: Basic Books, 2010.

[36] Stanley Kurtz, *Spreading the Wealth: How Obama Is Robbing the Suburbs to Pay for the Cities*. New York: Sentinel / Penguin, 2012.

[37] Jim Geraghty, "'We're All Becoming Border States Now,'" *National Review*, July 15, 2014. URL: http://www.nationalreview.com/node/382748/print

[38] "Obama's Student-Loan Props," *Wall Street Journal*, May 30, 2013. URL: http://online.wsj.com/article/SB10001424127887323728204578515100635368008.html

[39] Alex Altman, "A Student-Loan Fix?" *Time*, June 10, 2013.

[40] Halah Touryalai, "Student Loan Problems: One Third of Millennials Regret Going to College," *Forbes*, May 22, 2013. URL: http://www.forbes.com/fdc/welcome_mjx.shtml

[41] "Obama's Student-Loan Props," *Wall Street Journal*, May 30, 2013. URL: http://online.wsj.com/article/SB10001424127887323728204578515100635368008.html

[42] Christina Medici Scolaro, "Student Debt Will Punish US for Years: Strategist," *Yahoo Finance*, May 16, 2013. URL: http://finance.yahoo.com/blogs/big-data-download/student-debt-punish-us-years-strategist-170547657.html

[43] Annie Lowrey, "Student Debt Slows Growth as Young Spend Less," *New York Times*, May 10, 2013. URL: http://www.nytimes.com/2013/05/11/business/economy/student-loan-debt-weighing-down-younger-us-workers.html?pagewanted=all&_r=0

[44] Reuters, "Labor Costs Rise At Slowest Pace in 33 Years," New York Times, July 31, 2015. URL: http://www.nytimes.com/2015/08/01/business/economy/labor-costs-rise-at-slowest-pace-in-33-years.html

[45] Michael Tanner, *The American Welfare State*. Washington, D.C.: Policy Analysis/CATO Institute, April 11, 2012.

[46] Avik Roy, "On Labor Day 2013, Welfare Pays More Than Minimum-Wage Work In 35 States," *Forbes*, September 2, 2013. URL: http://www.forbes.com/sites/theapothecary/2013/09/02/on-labor-day-2013-welfare-pays-more-than-minimum-wage-work-in-35-states/

[47] *Ibid.*

[48] Alan Gomez, "Report: More Than Half of Immigrants on Welfare," *USA Today*, September 2, 2015.

[49] Warner Todd Huston,"Food Stamp Sign-Ups Outnumber Jobs Created in Obama's Illinois," *Breitbart*, September 16, 2014.

[50] Elizabeth Harrington, "Pelosi: Obamacare Allows You to Quit Your Job and Become 'Whatever,'" *CNS News*, March 22, 2012.

[51] Marlise Simons, "Out of Space, Dutch State Dumps Its Non-Masters," *New York Times*, September 14, 1992.

[52] David R. Wheeler, "What If Everybody Didn't Have to Work to Get Paid?" *The Atlantic*, May 18, 2015.

[53] Derek Thompson, "AS World Without Work," *The Atlantic*, July-August 2015.

[54] David Leonhardt, "Men, Unemployment and Disability," *New York Times*, April 8, 2011. URL: http://economix.blogs.nytimes.com/2011/04/08/men-unemployment-and-disability/?_r=0

[55] Nicholas Eberstadt, "The Astonishing Collapse of Work in America," Washington, D.C.: American Enterprise Institute, July 10, 2013. URL: http://www.aei.org/article/economics/the-astonishing-collapse- of-work-in-america/ ; for a critique of Eberstadt's analysis, see Richard S. Salsman, "What's So Bad About Women Replacing Men In The Workforce?" *Forbes*, July 30, 2013. URL: http://www.forbes.com/ sites/richardsalsman/2013/07/30/whats-so-bad-about-women-replacing-men-in-the-workforce/

[56] Nicholas Eberstadt, *A Nation of Takers: America's Entitlement Epidemic*. West Conshohocken, Pennsylvania: Templeton Press, 2012.

[57] Helen Smith, *Men on Strike: Why Men Are Boycotting Marriage, Fatherhood, and the American Dream – and Why It Matters*. New York: Encounter Books, 2012.

[58] Charles Murray, *Coming Apart: The State of White America, 1960-2010*. New York: Crown Forum, 2012.

[59] Peter Singer, *A Darwinian Left: Politics, Evolution and Cooperation*. London: Weidenfeld & Nicolson / Orion, 1999.

[60] Peter Singer, "FAQ," Princeton University (undated monograph). URL: http://www.princeton.edu/~psinger/faq.html; _____, "Taking Life: Humans." Excerpt from his book *Practical Ethics*, Second Edition. Cambridge: Cambridge University Press, 1993. Pages 175-217. URL: http://www.utilitarian.net/singer/by/1993----.htm; Scott Klusendorf, "Peter Singer's Bold Defense of Infanticide," *Christian Research Journal*, Volume 23 Number 3 / Christian Research Institute, April 16, 2009. URL: http://www.equip.org/article/peter-singers-bold-defense-of-infanticide/; William Saletan, "After-Birth Abortion: The Pro-Choice Case for Infanticide," *Slate.com*, March 12, 2012. URL: http://www.slate.com/articles/health_and_science/human_nature/2012/03/after_birth_abortion_the_pro_choice_case_for_infanticide_.html; Alberto Giubilini and Francesca Minerva, "After-birth Abortion: Why Should the Baby Live?" *Journal of Medical Ethics*, February 23, 2012. URL: http://jme.bmj.com/content/early/2012/03/01/medethics-2011-100411.full

[61] Sheldon Whitehouse, "The Fossil-fuel Industry's Campaign to Mislead the American People," *Washington Post*, May 29, 2015. URL: https://www.washingtonpost.com/opinions/the-fossil-fuel-industrys-campaign-to-mislead-the-american-people/2015/05/29/04a2c448-0574-11e5-8bda-c7b4e9a8f7ac_story.html; "Debate No More! Jailed for Scientific Dissent?! Twenty Climate Scientists, Including Top UN Scientist, Call for RICO Investigation of Climate Skeptics in Letter to Obama," *Climate Depot*, September 17, 2015. URL: http://www.climatedepot.com/2015/09/17/twenty-climate-scientistsits-including-top-un-scientist-call-for-rico-investigation-of-climate-skeptics-in-a-letter-to-obama

[62] Gary DeMar, "Obama Administration to Go After Retirement Accounts," Godfather Politics, November 23, 2012. URL: http://godfatherpolitics.com/8220/obama-administration-to-go-after-retirement-accounts/

[63] Jerome R. Corsi, "Now Obama Wants Your 401(K): Treasury, Labor on Path to Nationalize Retirement," *WND.com*, November 25, 2012. URL: http://www.wnd.com/2012/11/now-obama-wants-your-401k/

[64] Newt Gingrich and Peter Ferrara, "Class Warfare's Next Target: 401(K)," *Investor's Business Daily* / American Enterprise Institute, February 18, 2010. URL: http://www.aei.org/article/society-and-culture/class-warfares-next-target-401k-savings/

[65] Teresa Ghilarducci, *Guaranteed Retirement Accounts: Toward Retirement Income Security* (Briefing Paper). Washington, D.C.: Economic Policy Institute, November 20, 2007. URL: http://www.gpn.org/bp204/bp204.pdf; Karen McMahan, "Dems Target Private Retirement Accounts," *Carolina Journal*, November 4, 2008. URL: http://www.carolinajournal.com/exclusives/dems-target-private-retirement-accounts.html; Emily Cadei, "She Wants to Kill Your 401(k)," *USA Today*, March 16, 2015. URL: http://www.usatoday.com/story/money/2015/03/16/ozy-teresa-ghilarducci-revamp-retirement-savings/24842705/

[66] James Pethokoukis, "Would Obama, Dems Kill 401(k) Plans? Fears About the Stock Market May Prompt Rash Government Action." *U.S. News & World Report*, October 23, 2008. URL: http://money.usnews.com/money/blogs/capital-commerce/2008/10/23/would-obama-dems-kill- 401k-plans

[67] Nancy Thorner, "Beward: Guaranteed Retiremen Accounts (GRAs) Rise Again – Could Illinois Be Next?" *Madison-St. Clair Record*, August 8, 2013. URL: http://madisonrecord.com/ arguments/258085-beware-guaranteed-retirement-accounts-gras-rise-again-could-illinois-be-next

[68] Teresa Ghilarducci, *Guaranteed Retirement Accounts: Toward Retirement Income Security* (Briefing Paper). Washington, D.C.: Economic Policy Institute, November 20, 2007. Page 12. URL: http://www.gpn.org/bp204/bp204.pdf

[69] James Sherk and Todd Zywicki, "Obama's United Auto Workers Bailout," *Wall Street Journal*, June 13, 2012. URL: http://www.wsj.com/articles/SB10001424052702303768104577462650268680454; Daniel J. Ikenson, "Hard Lessons from the Auto Bailouts," Cato Policy Report, November/December 2009. URL: http://www.cato.org/policy-report/novemberdecember-2009/hard-lessons-auto-bailouts

[70] Avik Roy, "ACA Architect: 'The Stupidity Of The American Voter' Led Us To Hide Obamacare's True Costs From The Public," *Forbes*, November 10, 2014. URL: http://www.forbes.com/sites/theapothecary/2014/11/10/aca-architect-the-stupidity-of-the-american-voter-led-us-to-hide-obamacares-tax-hikes-and-subsidies-from-the-public/

[71] Peter J. Reilly, "President Obama Would Make Death A Taxable Event," *Forbes*, January 19, 2015. URL: http://www.forbes.com/sites/peterjreilly/2015/01/19/president-obama-would-make-death-a-taxable-event/

[72] "FACT SHEET: A Simpler, Fairer Tax Code That Responsibly Invests in Middle Class Families," Washington, D.C.: The White House, Office of the Press Secretary, January 17, 2015. URL: http://www.whitehouse.gov/the-press-office/2015/01/17/fact-sheet-simpler-fairer-tax-code-responsibly-invests-middle-class-fami; Jeanne Sahadi, "Obama Wants to Close the 'Trust Fund Loophole," *CNNMoney*, January 20, 2015. URL: http://khon2.com/2015/01/20/obama-wants-to-close-the-trust-fund-loophole/

[73] Peter J. Reilly, "President Obama Would Make Death A Taxable Event," *Forbes*, January 19, 2015. URL: http://www.forbes.com/sites/peterjreilly/2015/01/19/president-obama-would-make-death-a-taxable-event/

[74] Jonathan Weisman, "Obama Relents on Proposal to End '529' College Savings Plans," *New York Times*, January 27, 2015. URL: http://www.nytimes.com/2015/01/28/us/politics/obama-will-drop-proposal-to-end-529-college-savings-plans.html?_r=0

[75] Ewen Cameron Watt and others, *Dealing With Divergence: 2015 Investment Outlook*. New York, N.Y.: BlackRock Investment Institute, December 2014. URL: https://www.blackrock.com/corporate/en-us/literature/whitepaper/bii-2015-investment-outlook-us.pdf

[76] "Transcript: Obama and Clinton Debate," ABC News, April 16, 2008. URL: http://abcnews.go.com/Politics/DemocraticDebate/story?id=4670271&page=1&singlePage=true

Here is the referenced passage from this 2008 Hillary Clinton / Barack Obama debate:

ABC News anchor [Charles] GIBSON: ….You have, however, said you would favor an increase in the capital gains tax. As a matter of fact, you said on CNBC, and I quote, "I certainly would not go above what existed under Bill Clinton," which was 28 percent. It's now 15 percent. That's almost a doubling, if you went to 28 percent. But actually, Bill Clinton, in 1997, signed legislation that dropped the capital gains tax to 20 percent.
OBAMA: Right.
GIBSON: And George Bush has taken it down to 15 percent.
OBAMA: Right.
GIBSON: And in each instance, when the rate dropped, revenues from the tax increased; the government took in more money. And in the 1980s, when the tax was increased to 28 percent, the revenues went down. So why raise it at all, especially given the fact that 100 million people in this country own stock and would be affected?
OBAMA: Well, Charlie, what I've said is that I would look at raising the capital gains tax for purposes of fairness….

[77] David Kamin, "How to Tax the Rich," *Tax Notes*, Volume 146 Number 1 (January 5, 2015). To retrieve this eleven-page article via the Internet, go to its Abstract at the Social Science Research Network (SSRN) and click "Download This Paper." URL: http://papers.ssrn.com/sol3/papers.cfm?abstract_id=2550936

[78] Quoted in Peter Coy, "The Death of Cash," *Bloomberg Business*, April 23, 2015. URL: http://www.bloomberg.com/news/articles/2015-04-23/negative-interest-rates-may-spark-existential-crisis-for-cash

[79] Craig R. Smith & Lowell Ponte, "How Hastert's Secret Sex Scandal Touches You: Your Bank Spies On You, Too, For the Government," *Western Journalism*, June 1, 2015. URL: http://www.westernjournalism.com/how-hasterts-secret-sex-scandal-touches-you/

[80] Craig R. Smith and Lowell Ponte, *Don't Bank On It! The Unsafe World of 21ˢᵗ Century Banking*. Phoenix: Idea Factory Press, 2014. Pages 83-95.

[81] Barry Eichengreen, *Golden Fetters: The Gold Standard and the Great Depression, 1919-1939* (NBER Series on Long-Term Factors in Economic Development). Oxford: Oxford University Press, 1996.

[82] Ben S. Bernanke, "What the Fed Did and Why: Supporting the Recovery and Sustain Price Stability," *Washington Post*, November 4, 2010. URL: http://www.washingtonpost.com/wp-dyn/ content/article/2010/11/03/A R2010110307372_pf.html

[83] You can find our discussions of the "anti-stimulus" in several Craig R. Smith and Lowell Ponte books, all published by Idea Factory Press in Phoenix: *Crashing the Dollar: How to Survive a Global Currency Collapse* (2010), page 182; *The Inflation Deception: Six Ways Government Tricks Us…And Seven Ways to*

Stop It! (2011), pages 34-35, 65; and *The Great Debasement: The 100-Year Dying of the Dollar and How to Get America's Money Back* (2012), pages 113-117.

[84] Peter Coy, "The Death of Cash," *Bloomberg Business*, April 23, 2015. URL: http://www.bloomberg.com/news/articles/2015-04_23/negative-interest-rates-may-spark-existential-crisis-for-cash

[85] Peter Coy, "The Death of Cash," *Bloomberg Business*, April 23, 2015. URL: http://www.bloomberg.com/news/articles/2015-04-23/negative-interest-rates-may-spark-existential-crisis-for-cash

[86] Phoenix Capital Research, "Why Central Banks HATE Cash and Will Begin to Tax It Shortly," *Zerohedge*, May 18, 2015. URL: http://www.zerohedge.com/print/506627

[87] Our derivatives estimate nine months earlier was higher. See Craig R. Smith and Lowell Ponte, *Don't Bank On It! The Unsafe World of 21ˢᵗ Century Banking.* Phoenix: Idea Factory Press, 2014. Page 187.

[88] Phoenix Capital Research, "Why Central Banks HATE Cash and Will Begin to Tax It Shortly," *Zerohedge*, May 18, 2015. URL: http://www.zerohedge.com/print/506627

[89] Phoenix Capital Research, "Why Central Banks HATE Cash and Will Begin to Tax It Shortly," *Zerohedge*, May 18, 2015. URL: http://www.zerohedge.com/print/506627

[90] See Craig R. Smith and Lowell Ponte, *Don't Bank On It! The Unsafe World of 21ˢᵗ Century Banking.* Phoenix: Idea Factory Press, 2014. Pages 160-162.

[91] Josh Barro, "When It's a Crime to Withdraw Money From Your Bank," *New York Times*, June 5, 2015. URL: http://www.nytimes.com/2015/06/06/upshot/when-its-a-crime-to-withdraw-money-from-your-bank.html; Conor Friedersdorf, "Why Is It a Crime to Evade Government Scrutiny?" *The Atlantic*, June 2, 2015. URL: http://www.theatlantic.com/politics/archive/2015/06/when-evading-government-spying-is-a-crime/394640/

[92] Craig R. Smith and Lowell Ponte, *The Great Debasement: The 100-Year Dying of the Dollar and How to Get America's Money Back.* Phoenix: Idea Factory Press, 2012. Pages 218-219. See also: Craig R. Smith & Lowell Ponte, "How Hastert's Secret Sex Scandal Touches You: Your Bank Spies On You, Too, For the Government," *Western Journalism*, June 1, 2015. URL: http://www.westernjournalism.com/how-hasterts-secret-sex-scandal-touches-you/

[93] Craig R. Smith and Lowell Ponte, *The Great Debasement: The 100-Year Dying of the Dollar and How to Get America's Money Back.* Phoenix: Idea Factory Press, 2012. Page 219.

[94] Shaila Dewan, "Law Lets I.R.S. Seize Accounts on Suspicion, No Crime Required," *New York Times*, October 25, 2014.

[95] Nick Sibilla, "Cops Use Traffic Stops To Seize Millions From Drivers Never Charged With A Crime," *Forbes*, March 12, 2014

[96] "Small Business Owners Forced to Battle IRS Over Seized Bank Accounts," *Fox News*, February 11, 2015.

[97] Melissa Quinn, "The IRS Seized $107,000 From This North Carolina Man's Bank," *Daily Signal*, May 11, 2015.

[98] James Bovard, "The Continuing Forfeiture Scourge," *Explore Freedom* / Future of Freedom Foundation, February 1, 2013.

[99] Sarah Stillman, "Taken," *New Yorker*, August 12, 2013.

[100] Nick Sibilla, "Cops Use Traffic Stops To Seize Millions From Drivers Never Charged With A Crime," *Forbes*, March 12, 2014.

[101] Craig R. Smith and Lowell Ponte, *Don't Bank On It! The Unsafe World of 21ˢᵗ Century Banking.* Phoenix: Idea Factory Press, 2014. Pages 156-159.

[102] Joseph T. Salerno, "'The Better Than Cash Alliance": Escalating the War on Cash," Mises Institute, July 7, 2014, URL: https://mises.org/blog/better-cash-alliance-escalating-war-cash

[103] Craig R. Smith and Lowell Ponte, *The Great Debasement: The 100-Year Dying of the Dollar and How to Get America's Money Back.* Phoenix: Idea Factory Press, 2012. Page 220-221.

[104] Craig R. Smith and Lowell Ponte, *Don't Bank On It! The Unsafe World of 21ˢᵗ Century Banking.* Phoenix: Idea Factory Press, 2014. This quote appears on the book's back cover.

[105] Craig R. Smith and Lowell Ponte, *The Great Debasement: The 100-Year Dying of the Dollar and How to Get America's Money Back.* Phoenix: Idea Factory Press, 2012. Page 222.

[106] Marvin Goodfriend, "Overcoming the Zero Bound on Interest Rate Policy." Richmond, Virginia: The Federal Reserve Bank of Richmond, August 2000. Pages 12-15. URL: https://www.richmondfed.org/~/media/richmondfedorg/publications/research/working_papers/2000/pdf/wp00-3.pdf; see also Declan McCullagh, "Cash and the 'Carry Tax'," *Wired Magazine*, October 27, 1999. URL: http://archive.wired.com/politics/law/news/1999/10/32121

[107] Craig R. Smith and Lowell Ponte, *The Inflation Deception: Six Ways Government Tricks Us...And Seven Ways to Stop It!* Phoenix: Idea Factory Press, 2011. Pages 216-218.

[108] Lowell Ponte, "Big Bank 'Bail-Ins' vs. 'Bail-Outs': Bad News In Disguise Says 'Don't Bank On It' Author," *PR Buzz* URL: *https://www.prbuzz.com/personal-finance/267598-big-bank-bail-ins-vs-bail-outs-bad-news-in-disguise-says-dont-bank-on-it-author-1.html?tcode=72015-WJ1*

[109] Gregory Bresiger, "ZIRP: Or How The Fed Gave the US Financial Diabetes," DailyReckoning.com, December 18, 2013. URL: http://dailyreckoning.com/zirp-or-how-the-fed-gave-the-us-financial-diabetes/

[110] Alan Blinder, *After the Music Stopped: The Financial Crisis, The Response, and The Work Ahead.* New York: Penguin, 2013.

[111] Craig Torres and Matthew Boesler, "Fed Prepares to Maintain Record Balance Sheet for Years," Bloomberg, June 11, 2014. URL: http://www.bloomberg.com/news/articles/2014-06-11/fed-prepares-to-keep-super-sized-balance-sheet-for-years-to-come; Jon Hilsenrath, "Fed Closes Chapter On Easy Money," Wall Street Journal, October 29, 2014. URL: http://www.wsj.com/articles/fed-ends-bond-buys-sticks-to-0-rate-for-considerable-time-1414605953; Ylan Q. Mui, "Fed Looks Toward Debate On Raising Rates As Quantitative Easing Ends," Washington Post, October 29, 2014. URL: http://www.washingtonpost.com/blogs/wonkblog/wp/2014/10/29/fed-looks-toward-debate-on-raising-rates-as-quantitative-easing-ends/

[112] Michael S. Derby, "Fed's Bond Buying Yields Bonanza for Treasury," Wall Street Journal, January 9, 2015. URL: http://www.wsj.com/articles/feds-bond-buying-yields-bonanza-for-treasury-1420830368

[113] Nicole Gelinas, "Of Interest at the Fed," City Journal, Winter 2015. URL: http://www.city-journal.org/printable.php?id=11022

[114] Steve Matthews and Matthew Boesler, "Bullard Says Markets Wrong Not to Expect Mid-Year Rate Rise," Bloomberg, January 30, 2015. URL: http://www.bloomberg.com/news/articles/2015-01-30/bullard-says-investors-wrong-not-to-expect-rate-rise-by-mid-year

[115] Binyamin Appelbaum, "Federal Reserve Won't Raise Interest Rates Before June, at Earliest," New York Times, January 28, 2015. URL: http://www.nytimes.com/2015/01/29/business/federal-reserve-rate-decision.html?_r=0

[116] John Mauldin, "The Unintended Consequences of ZIRP," Thoughts from the Frontline (Newsletter), November 17, 2013. URL: http://www.mauldineconomics.com/frontlinethoughts/the-unintended-consequences-of-zirp

[117] "Why Are Interest Rates Being Kept at a Low Level?" FAQ response by the Board of Governors of the Federal Reserve System. Last updated: November 3, 2014. URL: http://www.federalreserve.gov/faqs/money_12849.htm

[118] Charles Biderman, "How The Fed Is Helping To Rig The Stock Market," Forbes, January 30, 2013. URL: http://www.forbes.com/sites/investor/2013/01/30/how-the-fed-is-helping-to-rig-the-stock-market/; for additional perspective see John Crudele, "Lessons from Stock-market Rigging History," New York Post, April 9, 2014. URL: http://nypost.com/2014/04/09/lessons-from-stock-market-rigging-history/; "How the Fed Began Rigging the Stock Market," New York Post, October 23, 2012. URL: http://nypost.com/2012/10/23/how-the-fed-began-rigging-the-stock-market/; John Crudele, "When Fed Takes Stock, Fed Really Takes Stock," New York Post, December 24, 2013. URL: http://nypost.com/2013/12/24/when-fed-takes-stock-fed-really-takes-stock/; Adam Shell, "How Much Longer Can the Fed Prop Up Stocks?" USA Today, May 2, 2013. URL: http://www.usatoday.com/story/money/markets/2013/05/02/can-fed-keep-propping-up-stocks/2129787/

[119] Michael Pento, "Fed Rigs Markets, Not the Flash Boys," Huffington Post, April 15, 2014. URL: http://www.huffingtonpost.com/michael-pento/fed-rigs-markets-not-the_b_5152500.html

[120] Bill Bonner, "Inside Ben Bernanke's Doomsday Device," Mises Canada, July 11, 2013. URL: http://mises.ca/posts/articles/inside-ben-bernankes-doomsday-device/

[121] *Ibid.*

[122] Dan Strumpf, "Companies' Stock Buybacks Help Buoy the Market," Wall Street Journal, September 15, 2014. URL: http://www.wsj.com/articles/companies-stock-buybacks-help-buoy-the-market-1410823441; Jonathan Clements, "The Downside to Stock Buybacks: There Could Be Better Uses for the Money," Wall Street Journal, October 25, 2014. URL: http://www.wsj.com/articles/the-downside-to-stock-buybacks-1414284206

[123] Charles Biderman, "How The Fed Is Helping To Rig The Stock Market," Forbes, January 30, 2013. URL: http://www.forbes.com/sites/investor/2013/01/30/how-the-fed-is-helping-to-rig-the-stock-market/

[124] BlackRock Investment Institute, *Dealing With Divergence: 2015 Investment Outlook*. New York: BlackRock Investment Institute, December 2014. Page 15. URL: https://www.blackrock.com/corporate/en-us/literature/whitepaper/bil-2015-investment-outlook-us.pdf; Tyler Durden, "Blackrock Stunner: S&P 500 Profits Are 86% Higher Than They Would Be Without Accounting Fudges," ZeroHedge, December 26, 2014. URL: http://www.zerohedge.com/print/499570

[125] Patrick Gillespie, "Making Money As The Fed Raises Rates Won't Be Easy," CNNMoney, February 3, 2015. URL: http:moneycnn.com/2015/02/03/investing/federal-reserve-rate-hike-2015/

[126] Richard Dobbs and others, "Debt and (Not Much) Deleveraging," McKinsey Global Institute, February 2015. URL: http://www.mckinsey.com/insights/Economic_Studies/Debt_and_not_much-deleveraging?cid=mckgrowth-eml-alt-mgi-mck-oth-1502 ; Ralph Atkins, "Debt Mountains Spark Fears of Another Crisis," Financial Times February 5, 2015. URL: http://www.ft.com/intl/cms/s/0/2554931c-ac85-11e4-9d32-00144feab7de.html#axzz3RNtOe4Vj

[127] Craig R. Smith and Lowell Ponte, *Don't Bank On It! The Unsafe World of 21st Century Banking.* Phoenix: Idea Factory Press, 2014. Pages 83-104.

[128] Philipp Bagus, *The ZIRP Trap: Why Low Interest Rates Are a Tax on Recovery.* (IREF Working Paper No. 201502). Paris: Institut de Recherches Economiques et Fiscales / Institute for Research in Economic and Fiscal Issues, January 2015. URL: http://de.irefeurope.org/SITES/de.irefeurope.org/IMG/pdf/bagus_2015_final.pdf

[129] *Ibid.*, page 1.

[130] Gregory Bresiger, "ZIRP: Or How The Fed Gave the US Financial Diabetes," DailyReckoning.com, December 18, 2013. URL: http://dailyreckoning.com/zirp-or-how-the-fed-gave-the-us-financial-diabetes/

[131] Eric Fry, "Financial Diabetes," DailyReckoning.com, September 19, 2012. URL: http://dailyreckoning.com/financial-diabetes/

[132] Bagus, *Op cit.*, page 7.

[133] Bagus, *Op cit.*, pages 8-9.

[134] Bagus, *Op cit.*, page 18.

[135] *Paying Taxes 2014: The Global Picture: A Comparison of Tax Systems in 189 Economies Worldwide* (Monograph). London: PricewaterhouseCoopers, 2014. URL: http://www.pwc.com/gx/ en/paying-taxes/assets/pwc-paying-taxes-2014.pdf ; Craig R. Smith and Lowell Ponte, *Don't Bank On It! The Unsafe World of 21st Century Banking.* Phoenix: Idea Factory Press, 2014. Page 138.

[136] Tim Worstall, "Why Apple Is Borrowing $6.5 Billion And What Obama's Trying To Do About It," Forbes, February 3, 2015. URL: http://www.forbes.com/sites/timworstall/2015/02/03/why-apple-is-borrowing-6-5-billion-and-what-obamas-trying-to-do-about-it/

[137] Craig R. Smith and Lowell Ponte, Don't Bank On It! The Unsafe World of 21st Century Banking. Phoenix: Idea Factory Press, 2014. Pages 105-133.

[138] Bagus, *Op cit.*, page 14.

[139] Bagus, *Op cit.*, page 14.

[140] Bagus, *Op cit.*, page 14.

[141] Carmen M. Reinhart, "Financial Repression Back to Stay," Bloomberg, March 11, 2012. URL: http://www.bloomberg.com/news/2012-03-11/financial-repression-has-come-back-to-stay-carmen-m-reinhart.html; Carmen M. Reinhart and M. Belen Sbrancia, "The Liquidation of Government Debt," National Bureau of Economic Research (NBER) Working Paper # 16893. March 2011. URL: http://www.imf.org/ external/np/seminars/eng/2011/res2/pdf/crbs.pdf; Alberto Giovanni and Martha De Melo, "Government Revenues from Financial Repression," American Economic Review, Vol. 83 #4 (September 1993). URL: http://www.jstor.org/discover/10. 2307/2117587 uid=3739560&uid=2&uid=4&uid=3739256&s id=21101221127691; Buttonwood, "Carmen Reinhart and Financial Repression," The Economist, January 10, 2012. URL: http://www.economist.com/blogs/buttonwood/2012/01/debt-crisis/print; Member of the European Parliament Nigel Farage, "Europe Is About to Impose Extreme Repression," King World News (Interview), June 22, 2012. URL: http://kingworldnews.com/kingworld- news/KWN_DailyWeb/ Entries/2012/6/22_Nigel_Farage_-_Europe_is_About_to_Impose_Extreme_Repression.html

[142] Bagus, *Op cit.*, page 21.

[143] Bagus, *Op cit.*, page 15.

[144] Bagus, *Op cit.*, page 17.

[145] Bagus, *Op cit.*, page 17.

[146] Jana Randow, ""Less Than Zero: When Interest Rates Go Negative," Bloomberg, December 18, 2014. URL: http://www.bloombergview.com/quicktake/negative-interest-rates; see also Charles Duxbury and Tommy Stubbington, "Sweden Cuts Interest Rate to Zero: Krona Falls After Riksbank Moves to Boost Inflation," Wall Street Journal, October 28, 2014. URL: http://www.wsj.com/articles/sweden-cuts-interest-rate-to-zero-1414486236; Brian Blackstone, Paul Hannon and Marcus Walker, "Aggressive ECB Stimulus Ushers In New Era for Europe," Wall Street Journal, January 22, 2015. URL: http://www.wsj.com/articles/ecb-announces-stimulus-plan-1421931011; Jason Karaian, "Welcome to Europe, Where the Bond Market Is Upside Down," Quartz / Atlantic Monthly, February 6, 2015. URL: http://qz.com/339843/welcome-to-europe-where-the-bond-market-is-upside-down/

[147] *Ibid.*

[148] Craig R. Smith and Lowell Ponte, *The Inflation Deception: Six Ways Government Tricks Us...And Seven Ways to Stop It!* Phoenix: Idea Factory Press, 2011.

[149] Leslie Shaffer, "Why Yields May Take Another Leg Down," CNBC, February 2, 2015. URL: http://www.cnbc.com/id/102387816

[150] *Ibid.*

[151] Randow, *Op cit.*

[152] "Life Below Zero Interest Must Not Become The New Normal" (Editorial), Financial Times, February 6, 2015. URL: http://www.ft.com/intl/cms/s/0/7a83595c-adf9-11e4-919e-00144feab7de.html#axzz3RBhKFm3W

[153] *Ibid.*

[154] Bagus, *Op cit.*, page 24.

[155] Sustainable Development Solutions Network: A Global Initiative For The United Nations, *World Happiness Report 2013* (press release), September 9, 2013. URL: http://unsdsn.org/resources/publications/world-happiness-report-2013/

The other two of the top five countries deemed "happiest" by this report are Switzerland and the Netherlands.

[156] "The Nordic Countries: The Next Supermodel," *The Economist*, February 2, 2013. URL: http://www.economist.com/news/leaders/21571136-politicians-both-right-and-left-could-learn-nordic-countries-next-supermodel; "The Secret of Their Success: The Nordic Countries Are Probably the Best-Governed in the World," *The Economist*, January 31, 2013. URL: http://www.economist.com/news/special-report/21570835-nordic-countries-are-probably-best-governed-world-secret-their

[157] Central Intelligence Agency, *The CIA World Factbook 2013*. New York: Skyhorse Publishing, 2012.

[158] "The Nordic Countries: The Next Supermodel," *The Economist*, February 2, 2013. URL: http://www.economist.com/news/leaders/21571136-politicians-both-right-and-left-could-learn-nordic-countries-next-supermodel; "The Secret of Their Success: The Nordic Countries Are Probably the Best-Governed in the World," *The Economist*, January 31, 2013. URL: http://www.economist.com/news/special-report/21570835-nordic-countries-are-probably-best-governed-world-secret-their

[159] The OECD is the Organisation for Economic Co-operation and Development, a Paris-based organization of 34 mostly-European nations plus the United States, the United Kingdom, Australia, New Zealand, Canada, Turkey, Israel, South Korea, Japan, Mexico and Chile. For more information, start at its Wikipedia listing at URL: https://en.wikipedia.org/wiki/Organisation_for_Economic_Co-operation_and_Development

[160] Avik Roy, "On Labor Day 2013, Welfare Pays More Than Minimum-Wage Work In 35 States," *Forbes*, September 2, 2013. URL: http://www.forbes.com/sites/theapothecary/2013/09/02/on-labor-day-2013-welfare-pays-more-than-minimum-wage-work-in-35-states/

[161] "Can Europe Stay Europe After Muslim Migrant Surge? Doubtful" (Editorial), *Investor's Business Daily*, September 11, 2015.

[162] Amy Chozick, "Campaign Casts Hillary Clinton As the Populist It Insists She Has Always Been," *New York Times*, April 21, 2015. URL: http://www.nytimes.com/2015/04/22/us/politics/hillary-clintons-quest-to-prove-her-populist-edge-is-as-strong-as-elizabeth-warrens.html?_r=0

[163] "Holder Cut Left-Wing Groups In On $17 Bil BofA Deal," *Investor's Business Daily*, August 27, 2014; Aaron Bandler, "DOJ To Give Money From Bank of America Settlement To Liberal Activist Groups," *Daily Caller*, August 28, 2014. URL: http://dailycaller.com/2014/08/28/doj-to-give-money-from-bank-of-america-settlement-to-liberal-activist-groups/

[164] Marcello Minenna, "Is Greece's Debt Worth of Risk?" *Wall Street Journal*, June 21, 2015. URL: http://www.wsj.com/articles/Is-greeces-debt-worth-the-risk-1434912649

[165] John Shmuel, "Greeks Are Rushing to Buy Cars to Protect Their Money," *Financial Post*, June 18, 2015. URL: http://business.financialpost.com/news/economy/greeks-are-rushing-to-buy-cars-to-protect-their-money

[166] Barack Obama, "Remarks by the President on the Iran Nuclear Deal" (Official transcript of speech at American University). Washington, D.C.: The White House, August 5, 2015. Page 16. URL: https://www.whitehouse.gov/the-press-office/2015/08/05/remarks-president-iran-nuclear-deal

[167] Felicia Schwartz and Nick Timiraos, "Kerry Says Rejection of Iran Nuclear Deal Could Hurt U.S. Dollar," *Wall Street Journal*, August 11, 2015. URL: http://www.wsj.com/articles/kerrry-says-rejection-of-iran-nuclear-deal-could-hurt-u-s-dollar-1439318697; Terry Atlas and Calev Ben-David, "Iran Deal Rejection Could Erode Dollar Eventually, John Kerry Says," *Bloomberg*. August 11, 2015. URL: http://www.bloomberg.com/politics/articles/2015-08-11/iran-deal-rejection-could-erode-dollar-eventually-kerry-says

[168] "Statement by Treasury Secretary Jacob J. Lew on the Joint Comprehensive Plan of Action Regarding Iran's Nuclear Program" (Official Transcript). Washington, D.C.: Press Office, U.S. Department of the Treasury, July 14, 2015. URL: http://www.treasury.gov/press-center/press-releases/Pages/jl0110.aspx

[169] Tyler Durden, "Russia Holds a 'De-Dollarization Meeting'; China, Iran Willing To Drop USD From Bilateral Trade," *ZeroHedge* May 14, 2014. URL: http://www.zerohedge.com/print/488440

[170] Peter Koenig, "Dollar Hegemony and the Iran Nuclear Issue: The Story Behind the Story," Global Research, April 9, 2015. URL: http://www.globalresearch.ca/dollar-hegemony-and-the-iran-nuclear-issue-the-story-behind-the-story/5441966

[171] Marin Katusa, "The Demise of the Petrodollar: Tehran Pushes to Ditch the US Dollar" (Undated Monograph). Stowe, Vermont: Casey Research. URL: http://www.caseyresearch.com/articles/demise-petrodollar

[172] Craig R. Smith and Lowell Ponte, *The Great Withdrawal: How the Progressives' 100-Year Debasement of America and the Dollar Ends* Phoenix: Idea Factory Press. Page 144.

[173] Craig R. Smith and Lowell Ponte, *Don't Bank On It! The Unsafe World of 21ˢᵗ Century Banking.* Phoenix: Idea Factory Press, 2014. Page 143.

[174] "Commerzbank Suggests Greece Could Sell Gold Reserves to Make Payment," *MarketPulse*, June 19, 2015. URL: http://www.marketpulse.com/20150619/commerzbank-suggests-greece-could-sell-gold-reserves-to-make-payment/; "Could Greece Sell Its Gold Reserves?" *Kitco News*, June 19, 2015. URL: http://www.kitco.com/news/2015-06-19/Could-Greece-Sell-Its-Gold-Reserves.html; Maria Petrakis and Antonis Galanopoulos, "Greek Central Bank Says Gold Reserves Worth 4.7 Billion Euros," *BloombergBusiness*, March 1, 2013. URL: http://www.bloomberg.com/news/articles/2013-03-01/greek-central-bank-says-gold-reserves-worth-4-7-billion-euros

[175] John Sfakianakis, "The Cost of Protecting Greece's Public Sector," *New York Times*, October 10, 2012. URL: http://www.nytimes.com/2012/10/11/opinion/the-cost-of-protecting-greeces-public-sector.html

[176] *Ibid.*

[177] *Ibid.*

[178] Joe Weisenthal, "Chart of the Day: Guess Which Country Has The Highest Percentage of Workers Employed By The Government," *Business Insider*, November 28, 2011. URL: http://www.businessinsider.com/chart-of-the-day-government-sector-employment-2011-11

[179] Fotis Zygoulis and Elina Zagou, "The Problems in the Greek Public Sector Cannot Be Solved Simply by Reducing the Size of Salaries or the Numbers of Staff," *London School of Economics and Political Science*, June 8, 2014. URL: http://blogs.lse.ac.uk/europpblog/2014/08/06/the-problems-in-the-greek-public-sector-cannot-be-solved-simply-by-reducing-the-size-of-salaries-or-the-numbers-of-staff/

[180] *Ibid.*

[181] Manos is quoted in John Sfakianakis, "The Cost of Protecting Greece's Public Sector," *New York Times*, October 10, 2012. URL: http://www.nytimes.com/2012/10/11/opinion/the-cost-of-protecting-greeces-public-sector.html

[182] John Sfakianakis, "The Cost of Protecting Greece's Public Sector," *New York Times*, October 10, 2012. URL: http://www.nytimes.com/2012/10/11/opinion/the-cost-of-protecting-greeces-public-sector.html

[183] "Greece Struggles to Slash Public Sector Jobs," *Deutsche Welle*, November 19, 2012. URL: http://www.dw.com/en/greece-struggles-to-slash-public-sector-jobs/a-16389443

[184] *Ibid.*

[185] Associated Press, "Greece Relaxes Capital Controls, Will Allow 500 Euro Withdrawals," *CBC*, August 18, 2015. URL: http://www.cbc.ca/news/business/greece-relaxes-capital-controls-will-allow-500-euro-withdrawals-1.3194692

[186] Craig R. Smith and Lowell Ponte, *The Great Withdrawal: How the Progressives' 100-Year Debasement of America and the Dollar Ends* Phoenix: Idea Factory Press, 2013. Page 46.

[187] "Bankrupt Cities, Municipalities List and Map," *Governing the States and Localities* (undated). URL: http://governing.com/gov-data/municipal-cities-counties-bankruptcies-and-defaults.html; "Which American Municipalities Have Filed For Bankruptcy?" *PBS Newshour*, February 8, 2014. URL: http://www.pbs.org/newshour/updates/municipalities-declared-bankruptcy/; Brad Plumer, "Detroit Isn't Alone. The U.S. Cities That Have Gone Bankrupt, In One Map," *Washington Post*, July 18, 2013.

[188] "Eight New Cities on the Verge of Bankruptcy," *Money Morning Staff Reports*, July 23, 2013. URL: http://moneymorning.com/2013/07/23/eight-new-cities-on-the-verge-of-bankruptcy/

[189] Associated Press, "City of Baltimore Is On A Path to Financial Ruin, Report Says," *Fox News*, February 6, 2013. URL: http://www.foxnews.com/politics/2013/02/08/city-baltimore-is-on-path-to-financial-ruin-report-says/; Mark Reutter, "Release of City Fiscal Forecast Sparks False Reports of Bankruptcy," *Baltimore Brew*, February 6, 2013. URL: https://www.baltimorebrew.com/2013/02/06/mayors-comments-on-city-finances-spark-false-reports-of-bankruptcy/

[190] *Ibid.*

[191] "Why Baltimore Isn't Detroit," *Baltimore Sun*, July 20, 2013. URL: http://articles.baltimoresun.com/2013-07-20/news/bs-ed-detroit-baltimore-20130720_1_baltimore-detroit-institute-city-leaders

[192] Dan Ariely and others, *The (True) Legacy of Two Really Existing Economic Systems* (Monograph). Munich, Germany: Department of Economics, University of Munich, March 19, 2015. May be downloaded in English at http://papers.ssrn.com/sol3/papers.cfm?abstract_id=2457000; "Socialism of Progressives Such As Obama Brings Out Worst in Us," *Investor's Business Daily*, August 5, 2015; Zenon Evans, "Socialists Are Cheaters, Says News Study," *Reason* Magazine, July 22, 2014;
Mark J. Perry, "Who'd a-thunk It? Socialism Is Demoralizing, Socially Corrosive, and Promotes Individual Dishonesty and Cheating?" American Enterprise Institute, July 19, 2014.

[193] *Ibid.*

[194] *Ibid.*

[195] "We Built This City" was released on The Starship's 1985 *Knee Deep In The Hoopla* album. This song was written by Bernie Taupin, Martin Page, Dennis Lambert and Peter Wolf. The band by then had evolved from Jefferson Airplane to Jefferson Starship to Starship and would soon return to the name Jefferson Starship. We include the name "Jefferson" here to reflect the spirit of the band, and as an American answer those Progressives who say "You didn't build that." To those interested in the band's evolution, see https://en.wikipedia.org/wiki/Jefferson_Airplane; https://en.wikipedia.org/wiki/Jefferson_Starship; and https://en.wikipedia.org/wiki/Starship_(band)

To see its video on YouTube, to to: https://www.youtube.com/watch?v=K1b8AhIsSYQ

[196] "Why Baltimore Isn't Detroit," *Baltimore Sun*, July 20, 2013. URL: http://articles.baltimoresun.com/2013-07-20/news/bs-ed-detroit-baltimore-20130720_1_baltimore-detroit-institute-city-leaders

[197] Alan Taylor, "Pluto Like You've Never Seen It Before," *The Atlantic*, September 17, 2015. URL: http://www.theatlantic.com/photo/2015/09/pluto-like-youve-never-seen-it-before/405904/

[198] Jonathan Corum, "NASA's New Horizons Probe Glimpses Pluto's Icy Heart," *New York Times*, September 10, 2015 (UPDATED). URL: http://www.nytimes.com/interactive/2015/07/15/science/space/new-horizons-pluto-flyby-photos.html?_r=0

[199] Tony Reichhardt, "First Photo From Space," *Air & Space Magazine*, November 2006. URL: http://www.airspacemag.com/space/the-first-photo-from-space-13721411/?no-ist=

[200] Kyle Peterson, "The Man Who Flew Mankind to Pluto," *Wall Street Journal*, July 17, 2015. URL: http://www.wsj.com/articles/the-man-who-flew-mankind-to-pluto-1437174709

[201] Christopher Cannon and others, "The Unlikely Cities That Will Power the U.S. Economy," *Bloomberg News*, September 3, 2015. URL: http://www.bloomberg.com/graphics/2015-stem-jobs/

*"We have no government, armed with power,
capable of contending with human passions,
unbridled by morality and religion.*

*Avarice, ambition, revenge and licentiousness
would break the strongest cords
of our Constitution,
as a whale goes through a net.*

*Our Constitution was made only
for a moral and religious people.*

*It is wholly inadequate
to the government of any other."*

– President John Adams
1798

*"Of all tyrannies, a tyranny exercised
for the good of its victims
may be the most oppressive.*

*It may be better to live under robber barons
than under omnipotent moral busybodies.*

*The robber baron's cruelty may sometimes sleep,
his cupidity may at some point be satiated;*

*But those who torment us for our own good
will torment us without end,
for they do so with the
approval of their consciences."*

– C.S. Lewis

Sources

Anat R. Admati and Martin Hellwig, *The Bankers' New Clothes: What's Wrong With Banking and What to Do About It.* Princeton, New Jersey: Princeton University Press, 2013.

Liaquat Ahamed, *Lords of Finance: The Bankers Who Broke the World.* New York: Penguin Books, 2009.

George A. Akerlof and Robert J. Schiller, *Animal Spirits: How Human Psychology Drives the Economy, and Why It Matters for Global Capitalism.*
Princeton, New Jersey: Princeton University Press, 2009.

Daniel Alpert, *The Age of Oversupply: Overcoming the Greatest Challenge to the Global Economy.* New York: Portfolio / Penguin, 2014.

Morris Altman, *Behavioral Economics For Dummies.* Hoboken, New Jersey: For Dummies/John Wiley & Sons, 2012.

John Anthers, *The Fearful Rise of Markets: Global Bubbles, Synchronized Meltdowns, and How to Prevent Them In The Future.* London: FT Press / Financial Times, 2010.

David Archibald, *Twilight of Abundance: Why Life in the 21ˢᵗ Century Will Be Nasty, Brutish, and Short.* Washington, D.C.: Regnery Publishing, 2014.

Tyler Atkinson, David Luttrell and Harvey Rosenblum, *How Bad Was It? The Costs and Consequences of the 2007-2009 Financial Crisis* (Staff Paper No. 20). Dallas, Texas: Federal Reserve Bank of Dallas, July 2013.

Bill Bamber and Andrew Spencer, *Bear Trap: The Fall of Bear Stearns and the Panic of 2008.* New York: Ibooks, Inc., 2008.

James R. Barth, Gerard Caprio Jr., and Ross Levine, *Guardians of Finance: Making Regulators Work for Us.* Cambridge, Massachusetts: The MIT Press, 2012.

William W. Beach and others, *Obama Tax Hikes: The Economic and Fiscal Effects* (Monograph). Washington, D.C.: Heritage Foundation, 2010.

Thorsten Beck (Editor), *The Future of Banking.* Centre for Economic Policy Research, 2011.

David Beckworth (Editor), *Boom and Bust Banking: The Causes and Cures of the Great Recession.* Oakland, California: Independent Institute, 2012.

Noah Berlatsky (Ed.), *Inflation.* Detroit: Greenhaven Press/Opposing Viewpoints Series, 2013.

Ben S. Bernanke and others, *Inflation Targeting: Lessons from the International Experience.* Princeton, New Jersey: Princeton University Press, 1999.

Peter Bernholz, *Monetary Regimes and Inflation: History, Economic and Political Relationships.* Williston, Vermont: Edward Elgar Publishing, 2006.

Peter L. Bernstein, *Against the Gods: The Remarkable Story of Risk.* Hoboken, New Jersey: John Wiley & Sons, 1998.

Mark Blyth, *Austerity: The History of a Dangerous Idea.* Oxford: Oxford University Press, 2013.

Haim Bodek, *The Problems of HFT – Collected Writings on High Frequency Trading & Stock Market Structure*. Seattle, Washington: CreateSpace / Amazon, 2013.

William Bonner and Addison Wiggin, *Financial Reckoning Day: Surviving the Soft Depression of the 21ˢᵗ Century*. Hoboken, New Jersey: John Wiley & Sons, 2004.

_____, *The New Empire of Debt: The Rise and Fall of an Epic Financial Bubble* (Second Edition). Hoboken, New Jersey: John Wiley & Sons, 2009.

Neal Boortz and John Linder, *The FairTax Book: Saying Goodbye to the Income Tax and the IRS....* New York: Regan Books / HarperCollins, 2005.

Neal Boortz, John Linder and Rob Woodall, *FairTax: The Truth: Answering the Critics*. New York: Harper, 2008.

Nick Bostrom, *Superintelligence: Paths, Dangers, Strategies*. Oxford: Oxford University Press, 2014.

Volker Bothmer and Ioannis A. Daglis, *Space Weather: Physics and Effects*. Berlin: Springer, 2010.

Donald J. Boudreaux, James Scott, Timothy B. Lee and J. Bradford DeLong, *Seeing Like a State: A Conversation with James C. Scott*. Washington, D.C.: Cato Institute / Cato Unbound, 2010.

Richard X. Bove, *Guardians of Prosperity: Why America Needs Big Banks*. New York: Portfolio/Penguin, 2013.

Jerry Bowyer, *The Free Market Capitalist's Survival Guide: How to Invest and Thrive in an Era of Rampant Socialism*. New York: Broad Side / Harper Collins, 2011.

H.W. Brands, *The Age of Gold: The California Gold Rush and the New American Dream*. New York: Doubleday / Random House, 2002.

_____, *American Colossus: The Triumph of Capitalism 1865-1900*. New York: Anchor Books / Doubleday / Random House, 2010.

_____, *The Money Men: Capitalism, Democracy, and the Hundred Years' War Over the American Dollar*. New York: W.W. Norton, 2010.

Arthur C. Brooks, *The Battle: How the Fight Between Free Enterprise and Big Government Will Shape America's Future*. New York: Basic Books/Perseus Books, 2010.

_____, *The Conservative Heart: How to Build a Fairer, Happier, and More Prosperous America*. New York: Broadside Books / HarperCollins, 2015

_____, *Gross National Happiness: Why Happiness Matters for America – and How We Can Get More of It*. New York: Basic Books, 2008.

_____, *The Road to Freedom: How to Win the Fight for Free Enterprise*. New York: Basic Books/Perseus Books, 2012.

Brendan Brown, *Euro Crash: How Asset Price Inflation Destroys the Wealth of Nations (Third Revised Edition)*. London: Palgrave Macmillan, 2014.

Ellen Hodgson Brown, *The Public Bank Solution: From Austerity to Prosperity*. Baton Rouge, Louisiana: Third Millennium Press, 2013.

_____, *Web of Debt: The Shocking Truth About Our Money System and How We Can Break Free (Fourth Edition)*. Baton Rouge, Louisiana: Third Millennium Press, 2011.

Robert Bryce, *Smaller Faster Lighter Denser Cheaper: How Innovation Keeps Proving the Catastrophists Wrong*. New York: Public Affairs / Perseus Books Group, 2014.

Dedria Bryfonski (Ed.), *The Banking Crisis*. Detroit: Greenhaven Press/Opposing Viewpoints Series, 2010.

James M. Buchanan and Richard E. Wagner, *Democracy in Deficit: The Political Legacy of Lord Keynes*. Indianapolis: Liberty Fund, 1999.

Todd G. Buchholz, *New Ideas from Dead Economists: An Introduction to Modern Economic Thought*. New York: New American Library/Penguin Books, 1989.

John Butler, *The Golden Revolution: How to Prepare for the Coming Global Gold Standard*. New York: John Wiley & Sons, 2012.

Bruce Caldwell (Editor), *The Collected Works of F.A. Hayek, Volume 2: The Road to Serfdom: Texts and Documents: The Definitive Edition*. Chicago: University of Chicago Press, 2007.

Charles W. Calomiris and Stephen H. Haber, *Fragile by Design: The Political Origins of Banking Crises and Scarce Credit*. Princeton, N.J.: Princeton University Press, 2014.

Ben Carson with Candy Carson, *America the Beautiful: Rediscovering What Made This Nation Great*. Grand Rapids, Michigan: Zondervan Publishing, 2012.

_____, *A More Perfect Union: What We The People Can Do To Reclaim Our Constitutional Liberties*. New York: Sentinel / Penguin, 2015.

_____, *One Nation: What We Can All Do To Save America's Future*. New York: Sentinel / Penguin, 2015.

Stephen G. Cecchetti and others, *The Real Effects of Debt*. BIS Working Papers No 352. Basel, Switzerland: Bank for International Settlements, September 2011. URL: http://www.bis.org/publ/work352.pdf

Central Intelligence Agency, *The CIA World Factbook 2013*. New York: Skyhorse Publishing, 2012.

Edward Chancellor, *Devil Take the Hindmost: A History of Financial Speculation*. New York: Plume (Reissue Edition), 2000.

Marc Chandler, *Making Sense of the Dollar: Exposing Dangerous Myths about Trade and Foreign Exchange*. New York: Bloomberg Press, 2009.

Ron Chernow, *The House of Morgan: An American Banking Dynasty and the Rise of Modern Finance*. New York: Grove Press, 2010.

Moorad Choudhry, *An Introduction to Banking: Liquidity Risk and Asset-Liability Management*. Hoboken, New Jersey: John Wiley & Sons, 2011.

Harold Van B. Cleveland, Charles P. Kindleberger, David P. Calleo and Lewis E. Lehrman, *Money and the Coming World Order*, Second Edition. Greenwich, Connecticut: Lehrman Institute, 2012.

Ta-Nehisi Coates, *The Beautiful Struggle: A Memoir*. New York: Spiegel & Grau / Random House, 2009.

_____, *Between the World and Me*. New York: Spiegel & Grau / Random House, 2015.

Tom A. Coburn, *The Debt Bomb: A Bold Plan to Stop Washington from Bankrupting America.* Nashville: Thomas Nelson, 2012.

Congressional Budget Office, *The Budget and Economic Outlook: Fiscal Years 2011 to 2021.* Washington, D.C.: Congressional Budget Office, January 2011. URL: http://www.cbo.gov/ftpdocs/120xx/doc12039/01-26_FY2011Outlook.pdf

Arnold Cornez, *The Offshore Money Book: How to Move Assets Offshore for Privacy, Protection, and Tax Advantage.* New York: McGraw-Hill, 2000.

Jerome R. Corsi, *America for Sale: Fighting the New World Order, Surviving a Global Depression, and Preserving U.S.A. Sovereignty.* New York: Threshold Editions / Simon & Schuster, 2009.

Jay Cost, *A Republic No More: Big Government and the Rise of American Political Corruption.* New York: Encounter Books, 2015.

Diane Coyle, *GDP: A Brief but Affectionate History.* Princeton, New Jersey: Princeton University Press, 2014.

Crews, Clyde Wayne, Jr., *Ten Thousand Commandments: An Annual Snapshot of the Federal Regulatory State.* 2014 Edition. (Monograph). Washington, D.C.: Competitive Enterprise Institute, 2014.

Mike Dash, *Tulipomania: The Story of the World's Most Coveted Flower & The Extraordinary Passions It Aroused.* Waterville, Maine: G.K. Hall & Company, Publishers, 2001.

Glyn Davies, *A History of Money: From Ancient Times to the Present Day.* Third Edition. Cardiff: University of Wales Press, 2002.

Glyn Davies and Roy Davies, *A Comparative Chronology of Money: Monetary History from Ancient Times to the Present Day.* (Monograph based on Glyn Davies and Roy Davies, above.) (2006) URL: http://projects.exeter.ac.uk/RDavies/arian/amser/chrono.html

Hernando de Soto, *The Mystery of Capital: Why Capitalism Triumphs in the West and Fails Everywhere Else.* New York: Basic Books / Perseus Books Group, 2000.

Jesus Huerta de Soto, *Money, Bank Credit, and Economic Cycles, Third Edition.* Auburn, Alabama: Ludwig von Mises Institute, 2012.

Peter H. Diamandis and Steven Kotler, *Abundance: The Future Is Better Than You Think.* New York: Free Press, 2012.

Jared Diamond, *Collapse: How Societies Choose to Fail or Succeed.* New York: Viking Press, 2005.

James D. Dilts, *The Great Road: The Building of the Baltimore and Ohio, the Nation's First Railroad, 1828-1853.* Redwood City, California: Stanford University Press, 1996.

Peter F. Drucker, *Post-Capitalist Society.* New York: Harper Business, 1993.

Dinesh D'Souza, *America: Imagine a World Without Her.* Washington, D.C.: Regnery, 2014.

_____, *Obama's America: Unmaking the American Dream.* Washington, D.C.: Regnery, 2012.

_____, *The Roots of Obama's Rage.* Washington, D.C.: Regnery, 2010.

_____, *The Virtue of Prosperity: Finding Values in an Age of Techno-Affluence.* New York: Free Press / Simon & Schuster, 2000.

Richard Duncan, *The Dollar Crisis: Causes, Consequences, Cures.* Singapore: John Wiley & Sons (Asia), 2003.

_____, *The New Depression: The Breakdown of the Paper Money Economy.* New York: John Wiley & Sons, 2012.

Gregg Easterbrook, *The Progress Paradox: How Life Gets Better While People Feel Worse.* New York: Random House, 2003.

Mary Eberstadt, *How the West Really Lost God: A New Theory of Secularization.* West Conshohocken, Pennsylvania: Templeton Press, 2013.

Nicholas Eberstadt, *A Nation of Takers: America's Entitlement Epidemic.* West Conshohocken, Pennsylvania: Templeton Press, 2012.

Gauti B. Eggertsson, *What Fiscal Policy Is Effective at Zero Interest Rate?* Staff Report No. 402 (Monograph). New York: Federal Reserve Bank of New York, November 2009. URL: http://www.newyorkfed.org/research/staff_reports/sr402.pdf

Barry Eichengreen, *Exorbitant Privilege: The Rise and Fall of the Dollar and the Future of the International Monetary System*ford: Oxford University Press, 2011.

_____, *Global Imbalances and the Lessons of Bretton Woods* (Cairoli Lectures). Cambridge, Massachusetts: MIT Press, 2010.

_____, *Globalizing Capital: A History of the International Monetary System* (Second Edition).

_____, *Golden Fetters: The Gold Standard and the Great Depression, 1919-1939* (NBER Series on Long-Term Factors in Economic Development). Oxford: Oxford University Press, 1996.

Barry Eichengreen and Marc Flandreau, *Gold Standard In Theory & History.* London: Routledge, 1997.

Kathleen C. Engel and Patricia A. McCoy, *The Subprime Virus: Reckless Credit, Regulatory Failure, and Next Steps.* New York: Oxford University Press USA, 2011.

Richard A. Epstein, *How Progressives Rewrote the Constitution.* Washington, D.C.: Cato Institute, 2006.

_____, *Takings: Private Property and the Power of Eminent* Domain. Cambridge, Massachusetts: Harvard University Press, 1985.

Federal Reserve System, Board of Governors of, *Consumers and Mobile Financial Services 2013* (Monograph). Washington, D.C.: Federal Reserve Board Division of Consumer and Community Affairs, March 2013. URL: http://www.federalreserve.gov/econresdata/consumers-and-mobile-financial-services-report-201303.pdf

Carl Feisenfeld and David Glass, *Banking Regulation in the United States, 3rd Edition.* Huntington, N.Y.: Juris Publishing, 2011.

Niall Ferguson, *The Ascent of Money: A Financial History of the World.* New York: Penguin Press, 2008.

_____, *The Cash Nexus: Money and Power in the Modern World, 1700-2000.* New York: Basic Books, 2002.

_____, *Civilization: The West and the Rest*. New York: Penguin Books, 2011.

_____, *Colossus: The Price of America's Empire*. New York: Penguin Press, 2004.

_____, *The House of Rothschild: Volume 1: Money's Prophets: 1798-1848*. New York: Penguin Books, 1999.

_____, *The House of Rothschild: Volume 2: The World's Banker: 1849-1999*. New York: Penguin Books, 2000.

_____, *The Great Degeneration: How Institutions Decay and Economies Die*. New York: Penguin Books, 2013.

Peter Ferrara, *America's Ticking Bankruptcy Bomb: How the Looming Debt Crisis Threatens the American Dream – and How We Can Turn the Tide Before It's Too Late*. New York: Broadside Books, 2011.

William Fleckenstein and Frederick Sheehan, *Greenspan's Bubbles: The Age of Ignorance at the Federal Reserve*. New York: McGraw-Hill, 2008.

Steve Forbes and Elizabeth Ames, *Money: How the Destruction of the Dollar Threatens the Global Economy – and What We Can Do About It*. New York: McGraw-Hill, 2014.

Ralph T. Foster, *Fiat Paper Money: The History and Evolution of Our Currency*. Second Edition. Shenzhen, China: Shenzhen Jinhao Publishing / Alibaba.com, 2010.

Justin Fox, *The Myth of the Rational Market: A History of Risk, Reward, and Delusion on Wall Street*. New York: Harper Business, 2009.

Kevin D. Freeman, *Economic Warfare: Risks and Responses: Analysis of Twenty-First Century Risks in Light of the Recent Market Collapse* (Monograph). Cross Consulting and Services, 2009. This can be downloaded from the Internet at no cost from http://av.r.ftdata.co.uk/files/2011/03/49755779-Economic-Warfare-Risks-and-Responses-by-Kevin-D-Freeman.pdf or at no cost from http://www.freemanglobal.com/uploads/Economic_Warfare_Risks_and_Responses.pdf

_____, *Game Plan: How to Protect Yourself from the Coming Cyber-Economic Attack*. Washington, D.C.: Regnery Publishing, 2014.

_____, *Secret Weapon: How Economic Terrorism Brought Down the U.S. Stock Market and Why It Can Happen Again*. Washington, D.C.: Regnery, 2012.

George Friedman, *The Next Decade: Where We've Been...And Where We're Going*. New York: Doubleday, 2011.

Milton Friedman, *An Economist's Protest*. Second Edition. Glen Ridge, New Jersey: Thomas Horton and Daughters, 1975. Also published as *There's No Such Thing As A Free Lunch*. La Salle, Illinois: Open Court Publishing, 1975.

_____, *Capitalism & Freedom: A Leading Economist's View of the Proper Role of Competitive Capitalism*. Chicago: University of Chicago Press, 1962.

_____, *Dollars and Deficits: Inflation, Monetary Policy and the Balance of Payments*. Englewood Cliffs, New Jersey: Prentice-Hall, 1968.

_____, *Money Mischief: Episodes in Monetary History*. New York: Harcourt Brace, 1992.

_____, *On Economics: Selected Papers*. Chicago: University of Chicago Press, 2007.

_____, *Why Government Is the Problem (Essays in Public Policy)*. Stanford, California: Hoover Institution Press, 1993.

Milton & Rose Friedman, *Free to Choose: A Personal Statement*. New York: Harcourt Brace Jovanovich, 1980.

_____, *Tyranny of the Status Quo*. San Diego, California: Harcourt Brace Jovanovich, 1984.

Milton Friedman & Anna Jacobson Schwartz, *A Monetary History of the United States, 1867-1960*. A Study by the National Bureau of Economic Research, New York. Princeton, New Jersey: Princeton University Press, 1963.

Francis Fukuyama, *The End of History and The Last Man*. New York: Free Press, 1992.

_____, *Trust: The Social Virtues and The Creation of Prosperity*. New York: Free Press, 1996.

John Fund and Hans von Spakovsky, *Obama's Enforcer: Eric Holder's Justice Department*. New York: Broadside Books, 2014.

Joseph Gagnon, Matthew Raskin, Juliew Remache and Brian Sack, *Large-Scale Asset Purchases by the Federal Reserve: Did They Work?* New York: Federal Reserve Bank of New York / *Economic Policy Review*, May 2011. URL: http://newyorkfed.org/research/epr/11v17n1/1105gagn.pdf

Joseph E. Gagnon and Brian Sack, *Monetary Policy with Abundant Liquidity: A New Operating Framework for the Federal Reserve*. Document PB 14-4 / Policy Brief. Washington, D.C.: Peterson Institute for International Economics, January 2014. URL: http://www.piie.com/publications/pb/pb14-4.pdf

James K. Galbraith, *The Predator State: How Conservatives Abandoned the Free Market and Why Liberals Should Too*. New York: Free Press, 2008.

Mark Lee Gardner, *Shot All to Hell: Jesse James, the Northfield Raid, and the Wild West's Greatest Escape*. New York: William Morrow, 2013.

John D. Gartner, *The Hypomanic Edge: The Link Between (A Little) Craziness and (A Lot of) Success in America*. New York: Simon & Schuster, 2005.

Charles Gasparino, *Bought and Paid For: The Unholy Alliance Between Barack Obama and Wall Street*. New York: Sentinel / Penguin, 2010.

Francis J. Gavin, *Gold, Dollars, and Power: The Politics of International Monetary Relations, 1958-1971 (The New Cold War History)*. Chapel Hill, North Carolina: University of North Carolina Press, 2007.

Timothy F. Geithner, *Stress Test: Reflections on Financial Crises*. New York: Crown / Random House, 2014.

Nicole Gelinas, *After the Fall: Saving Capitalism from Wall Street – and Washington*. New York: Encounter Books, 2011.

Pamela Geller and Robert Spencer, *The Post-American Presidency*. New York: Threshold Editions / Simon & Schuster, 2010.

Teresa Ghilarducci, *Guaranteed Retirement Accounts: Toward Retirement Income Security.* Washington, D.C.: Economic Policy Institute, November 20, 2007. URL: http://www.gpn.org/bp204/bp204.pdf

_____, *What You Need to Know About the Economics of Growing Old (But Were Afraid to Ask): A Provocative Reference Guide to the Economics of Aging.* Notre Dame, Indiana: University of Notre Dame Press, 2004.

_____, *When I'm Sixty-Four: The Plot Against Pensions and the Plan to Save Them.* Princeton, New Jersey: Princeton University Press, 2008.

George Gilder, *Knowledge and Power: The Information Theory of Capitalism and How It Is Revolutionizing Our World.* Washington, D.C.: Regnery Publishing, 2013.

_____, *Wealth and Poverty.* New York: Basic Books, 1981.

Jonah Goldberg, *Liberal Fascism: The Secret History of the American Left, From Mussolini to the Politics of Meaning.* New York: Doubleday, 2008.

_____, *The Tyranny of Cliches: How Liberals Cheat in the War of Ideas.* New York: Sentinel / Penguin, 2012.

David P. Goldman, *How Civilizations Die (And Why Islam Is Dying Too).* Washington, D.C.: Regnery, 2011.

Jason Goodwin, *Greenback: The Almighty Dollar and The Invention of America.* New York: John Macrae / Henry Holt and Company, 2003.

William M. Gouge, *A Short History of Paper Money and Banking in the United States.* Auburn, Alabama: Ludwig von Mises Institute, 2011.

Charles Goyette, *The Dollar Meltdown: Surviving the Impending Currency Crisis with Gold, Oil, and Other Unconventional Investments.* New York: Portfolio / Penguin, 2009.

Michael Grabell, *Money Well Spent? The Truth Behind the Trillion-Dollar Stimulus, the Biggest Economic Recovery Plan in History.* New York: PublicAffairs / Perseus Books Group, 2012.

David Graeber, *Debt: The First 5,000 Years. Brooklyn, New York: Melville House Books, 2012.*

Thomas Greco, *The End of Money and the Future of Civilization.* White River Junction, Vermont: Chelsea Green Publishing, 2009.

_____, *Money: Understanding and Creating Alternatives to Legal Tender.* White River Junction, Vermont: Chelsea Green Publishing, 2012.

Andy Greenberg, *This Machine Kills Secrets: How WikiLeakers, Cypherpunks, and Hacktivists Aim to Free the World's Information.* New York: Dutton Adult, 2012.

Alan Greenspan, *The Age of Turbulence: Adventures in a New World.* New York: Penguin Books, 2007.

William Greider, *Secrets of the Temple: How the Federal Reserve Runs the Country.* New York: Simon & Schuster, 1989.

G. Edward Griffin, *The Creature from Jekyll Island: A Second Look at the Federal Reserve.* Third Edition. Westlake Village, California: American Media, 1998.

Mary Katherine Ham and Guy Benson, *End of Discussion: How the Left's Outrage Industry Shuts Down*

Debate, Manipulates Voters, and Makes America Less Free (and Fun). New York: Crown Forum, 2015.

Alexander Hamilton, James Madison and John Jay, *The Federalist Papers.* New York: Mentor Books / New American Library, 1961. For an online version of James Madison's Federalist Paper No. 44, go to this URL: http://www.constitution.org/fed/federa44.htm

Bob Harris, *The International Bank of Bob: Connecting Our Worlds One $25 Kiva Loan At A Time.* New York: Walker & Company, 2013.

Keith Hart, *Money in an Unequal World.* New York: Texere, 2001.

David Harvey, *Seventeen Contradictions and the End of Capitalism.* Oxford: Oxford University Press, 2014.

Friedrich A. Hayek (Editor), *Capitalism and the Historians.* Chicago: Phoenix Books / University of Chicago Press, 1963.

_____, *Choice in Currency: A Way to Stop Inflation.* London: Institute of Economic Affairs, 1976. This can be downloaded from the Internet at no cost from http://www.iea.org.uk/sites/default/files/publications/files/upldbook409.pdf

_____, *The Counter-Revolution of Science: Studies On The Abuse of Reason.* New York: The Free Press / Macmillan / Crowell-Collier, 1955.

_____, *The Constitution of Liberty.* The Definitive Edition, Edited by Ronald Hamowy. Chicago: University of Chicago Press, 2011.

_____, *Denationalisation of Money: The Argument Refined: An Analysis of the Theory and Practice of Concurrent Currencies. Third Edition.* London: Institute of Economic Affairs, 1990. This can be downloaded from the Internet at no cost from http://mises.org/books/denationalisation.pdf

_____, *The Fatal Conceit: The Errors of Socialism.* Chicago: University of Chicago Press, 1991.

_____, *The Road to Serfdom.* Chicago: Phoenix Books / University of Chicago Press, 1944.

Henry Hazlitt, *The Failure of the "New Economics": An Analysis of The Keynesian Fallacies.* New Rochelle, New York: Arlington House, 1959.

_____, *From Bretton Woods to World Inflation: A Study of Causes & Consequences.* Chicago: Regnery Gateway, 1984. This can be downloaded from the Internet at no cost from http://mises.org/books/brettonwoods.pdf

Robert L. Hetzel, *The Great Recession: Market Failure or Policy Failure? (Studies in Macroeconomic History).* New York: Cambridge University Press, 2012.

_____, *The Monetary Policy of the Federal Reserve.* New York: Cambridge University Press, 2008.

David Horowitz and Jacob Laksin, *The New Leviathan: How the Left-Wing Money-Machine Shapes American Politics and Threatens America's Future.* New York: Crown Forum, 2012.

Philip K. Howard, *The Rule of Nobody: Saving America from Dead Laws and Broken Government.* New York: W.W. Norton, 2014.

Timothy Howard, *The Mortgage Wars: Inside Fannie Mae, Big-Money Politics, and the Collapse of the*

American Dream. New York: McGraw-Hill Education, 2014.

Glenn Hubbard and Tim Kane, *Balance: The Economics of Great Powers From Ancient Rome to Modern America.* New York: Simon & Schuster, 2013.

Michael Hudson, *The Bubble and Beyond: Fictitious Capital, Debt Deflation and Global Crisis.* ISLET / Open Library, 2012.

W.H. Hutt, *The Keynesian Episode: A Reassessment.* Indianapolis: Liberty*Press*, 1979.

Bob Ivry, *The Seven Sins of Wall Street: Big Banks, Their Washington Lackeys, and the Next Financial Crisis.* New York: PublicAffairs Press / Perseus Group, 2014.

Andrew Jackson and Ben Dyson, *Modernising Money: Why Our Monetary System Is Broken and How It Can Be Fixed.* Positive Money, 2013.

Steven H. Jaffe, Jessica Lautin and the Museum of the City of New York, *Capital of Capital: Money, Banking, and Power in New York City, 1784-2012.* New York: Columbia University Press, 2014.

Simon Johnson and James Kwak, *13 Bankers: The Wall Street Takeover and the Next Financial Meltdown.* New York: Pantheon Books, 2010.

Robert Kagan, *The World America Made.* New York: Vintage / Random House, 2012.

Craig Karmin, *Biography of the Dollar: How the Mighty Buck Conquered the World and Why It's Under Siege.* New York: Crown Business, 2008.

Margrit Kennedy, *People Money: The Promise of Regional Currencies.* London: Triarchy Press, 2012.

Charles R. Kesler, *I Am the Change: Barack Obama and the Crisis of Liberalism.* New York: Broadside Books, 2012.

John Maynard Keynes, *Essays in Persuasion.* New York: W.W. Norton, 1963.

_____, *The General Theory of Employment, Interest, and Money.* New York: Harcourt, Brace & World, 1935.

Charles P. Kindleberger and Robert Z. Aliber, *Manias, Panics and Crashes: A History of Financial Crises (Sixth Edition).* London: Palgrave Macmillan, 2011.

Arnold Kling, *The Case for Auditing the Fed Is Obvious.* (Monograph / Briefing Paper). Washington, D.C.: Cato Institute, April 27, 2010. URL: http://www.cato.org/pubs/bp/bp118.pdf

Knowledge @ Wharton and Ernst & Young, *Global Banking 2020: Foresight and Insights.*

Gabriel Kolko, *Railroads and Regulation 1877-1916.* New York: W.W. Norton, 1970. Originally published in 1965 by Princeton University Press.

Laurence J. Kotlikoff, *Jimmy Stewart Is Dead: Ending the World's Ongoing Financial Plague with Limited Purpose Banking.* Hoboken, New Jersey: John Wiley & Sons, 2011.

Laurence J. Kotlikoff and Scott Burns, *The Clash of Generations: Saving Ourselves, Our Kids, and Our Economy.* Cambridge, Massachusetts: The MIT Press, 2012.

_____, *The Coming Generational Storm: What You Need to Know*

About America's Economic Future. Cambridge, Massachusetts: MIT Press, 2005.

Laurence J. Kotlikoff, Philip Moeller and Paul Solman, *Get What's Yours: The Secrets to Maxing Out Your Social Security.* New York: Simon & Schuster, 2015.

Paul Krugman, *The Return of Depression Economics and The Crisis of 2008.* New York: W.W. Norton, 2009.

Stanley Kurtz, *Spreading the Wealth: How Obama Is Robbing the Suburbs to Pay for the Cities.* New York: Sentinel / Penguin, 2012.

Joel Kurtzman, *The Death of Money: How the Electronic Economy Has Destabilized the World's Markets and Created Financial Chaos.* New York: Simon & Schuster, 1993.

Kwasi Kwartyeng, *War and Gold: A Five-Hundred-Year History of Empires, Adventures and Debt.* London: Bloomsbury Publishing, 2014.

Arthur B. Laffer, Stephen Moore and Peter J. Tanous, *The End of Prosperity: How Higher Taxes Will Doom the Economy – If We Let It Happen.* New York: Threshold Editions / Simon & Schuster, 2008.

Arthur B. Laffer, Stephen Moore, Rex A. Sinquefield and Travis H. Brown, *An Inquiry into the Nature and Causes of the Wealth of States: How Taxes, Energy, and Worker Freedom Change Everything.* Hoboken, New Jersey: John Wiley & Sons, 2014.

Arthur B. Laffer and Stephen Moore, *Return to Prosperity: How America Can Regain Its Economic Superpower Status.* New York: Threshold Editions / Simon & Schuster, 2010.

George Lakoff, *The Political Mind: A Cognitive Scientist's Guide to Your Brain and Its Politics.* New York: Penguin Books, 2009.

George Lakoff and Elizabeth Wehling, *The Little Blue Book: The Essential Guide to Thinking and Talking Democratic.* New York: Free Press, 2012.

John Lanchester, *I.O.U.: Why Everyone Owes Everyone and No One Can Pay.* New York: Simon & Schuster, 2010.

David S. Landes, *The Wealth and Poverty of Nations: Why Some Are So Rich and Some So Poor.* New York: W.W. Norton, 1998.

Vincent Lannoye, *The Story of Money For Understanding Economics.* Seattle: CreateSpace Independent Publishing / Amazon, 2011.

Jonathan V. Last, *What to Expect When No One's Expecting: America's Coming Demographic Disaster.* New York: Encounter Books, 2013.

Adam Lebor, *Tower of Basel: The Shadowy History of the Secret Bank that Runs the World.* New York: PublicAffairs / Perseus Group, 2013.

Lewis E. Lehrman, *Money, Gold and History.* Greenwich, Connecticut: The Lehrman Institute, 2013.

_____, *The True Gold Standard – A Monetary Reform Plan Without Official Reserve Currencies.* Greenwich, Connecticut: The Lehrman Institute, 2011.

Gwendolyn Leick (Editor), *The Babylonian World.* London: Routledge, 2009. See chapter "The Egibi Family" by Cornelia Wunsch.

George Lekatis, *Understanding Basel III: What Is Different After March 2013*. Washington, D.C.: Basel III Compliance Professionals Association (BiiiCPA), 2013.

Lawrence Lessig, *Republic, Lost: How Money Corrupts Congress – and a Plan to Stop It*. Twelve / Hachette Book Group, 2011.

Louise Levathes, *When China Ruled the Seas: The Treasure Fleet of the Dragon Throne, 1405-1433*. Oxford: Oxford University Press, 1997.

Mark Levin, *Plunder and Deceit*. New York: Threshold Editions / Simon & Schuster, 2015.

Hunter Lewis, *Crony Capitalism in America: 2008-2012*. Charlottesville, Virginia: AC2 Publishing, 2013.

Michael Lewis, *Boomerang: Travels in the New Third World*. New York: W.W. Norton, 2011.

_____, *Flash Boys: A Wall Street Revolt*. New York: W.W. Norton, 2014.

_____, *Panic: The Story of Modern Financial Insanity*. New York: W.W. Norton, 2009.

Naphtali Lewis and Meyer Reinhold (Editors), *Roman Civilization: Sourcebook II: The Empire*. New York: Harper Torchbooks, 1966.

Nathan Lewis and Addison Wiggin, *Gold: The Once and Future Money*. Hoboken, New Jersey: John Wiley & Sons, 2007.

Qiao Liang and Wang Xiangsui, *Unrestricted Warfare*. Panama City, Panama: Pan American Publishing Company, 2002.

Bernard Lietaer and Stephen Belgin, *New Money for a New World*. Qiterra Press, 2011.

Bernard Lietaer and Jacqui Dunne, *Rethinking Money: How New Currencies Turn Scarcity Into Prosperity*. San Francisco: Berrett-Koehler Publishers/BK Currents, 2013.

Charles A. Lindbergh, Sr., *Lindbergh on the Federal Reserve* (Formerly titled: *The Economic Pinch*). Costa Mesa, California: Noontide Press, 1989.

Julia Lovell, *The Great Wall: China Against the World, 1000 BC-AD 2000*. New York: Grove Press, 2007.

David Lukas, *Whose Future Are You Financing? What the Government And Wall Street Don't Want You To Know*. Little Rock, Arkansas: Race Publishing, 2014.

Deirdre N. McCloskey, *Bourgeois Dignity: Why Economics Can't Explain the Modern World*. Chicago: University of Chicago Press, 2010.

Heather MacDonald, *The Burden of Bad Ideas: How Modern Intellectuals Misshape Our Society*. Chicago: Ivan R. Dee, 2000.

Robert D. McHugh, *The Coming Economic Ice Age: Five Steps To Survive and Prosper*. London: Thomas Noble Books, 2013.

Bethany McLean and Joe Nocera, *All the Devils Are Here: The Hidden History of the Financial Crisis*. New York: Portfolio / Penguin, 2010.

John McWhorter, *Winning the Race: Beyond the Crisis in Black America*. New York: Gotham / Penguine,

2006.

Michael Magnusson, *The Land Without A Banking Law: How to Start a Bank With a Thousand Dollars*. York, England: Opus Operis Publishing, 2013.

_____, *Offshore Bank License: Seven Jurisdictions*. York, England: Opus Operis Publishing, 2013.

Michael P. Malloy, *Principles of Bank Regulation, 3rd (Concise Hornbook)*. Eagan, Minnesota: West Publishing/Thompson Reuters, 2011.

Felix Martin, *Gold: The Unauthorized Biography*. New York: Knopf, 2014.

James A. Marusek, *Solar Storm Threat Analysis* (Monograph). Bloomfield, Indiana: Impact, 2007. URL: http://www.breadandbutterscience.com/SSTA.pdf.

Karl Marx and Friedrich Engels, *The Communist Manifesto*. London: Penguin Classics, 1985.

Paul Mason, *Postcapitalism: A Guide to Our Future*. New York: Farrar, Straus and Girous, 2016.

Philip Matyszak, *Ancient Rome on 5 Denarii a Day*. London: Thames & Hudson, 2008.

John Mauldin and Jonathan Tepper, *Code Red: How to Protect Your Savings From the Coming Crisis*. Hoboken, New Jersey: John Wiley & Sons, 2013.

_____, *Endgame: The End of the Debt Supercycle and How It Changes Everything*. Hoboken, New Jersey: John Wiley & Sons, 2011.

Martin Mayer, *The Fed: The Inside Story of How the World's Most Powerful Financial Institution Drives the Markets*. New York: Free Press, 2001.

Michael Medved, *The 5 Big Lies About American Business: Combating Smears Against the Free-Market Economy*. New York: Crown Forum, 2009.

David I. Meiselman and Arthur B. Laffer (Editors), *The Phenomenon of Worldwide Inflation*. Washington, D.C.: American Enterprise Institute, 1975.

Mary Mellor, *The Future of Money: From Financial Crisis to Public Resource*. London: Pluto Press, 2010.

Gavin Menzies, *1421: The Year China Discovered America*. New York: Harper Perennial, 2002.

_____, *1434: The Year a Magnificent Chinese Fleet Sailed to Italy and Ignited the Renaissance*. New York: Harper Perennial, 2009.

Atif Mian and Amir Sufi, *House of Debt: How They (and You) Caused the Great Recession, and How We Can Prevent It from Happening Again*. Chicago: University of Chicago Press, 2014.

Norbert J. Michel, *The Financial Stability Oversight Council: Helping to Enshrine "Too Big to Fail"* (Monograph / *Backgrounder*). Washington, D.C.: The Heritage Foundation, April 1, 2014.

Willem Middlekoop, *The Big Reset: War on Gold and the Financial Endgame*. Amsterdam: Amsterdam University Press, 2014.

James D. Miller, *Singularity Rising: Surviving and Thriving in a Smarter, Richer, and More Dangerous World*. Dallas, Texas: BenBella Books, 2012.

Terry Miller, Anthony B. Kim and Kim R. Holmes, *2014 Index of Economic Freedom*. Washington, D.C.: Heritage Foundation / *Wall Street Journal*, 2014. URL for free download: http://www.heritage.org/index/download

Gregory J. Millman, *The Vandals' Crown: How Rebel Currency Traders Overthrew the World's Central Banks*. New York: Free Press, 1995.

Brendan Miniter (Ed.), *The 4% Solution: Unleashing the Economic Growth America Needs*. New York: Crown Business / George W. Bush Institute, 2012.

Hyman P. Minsky, *John Maynard Keynes*. New York: McGraw-Hill, 2008.

_____, *Stabilizing an Unstable Economy*. New York: McGraw-Hill, 2008.

Ludwig von Mises, *The Anti-Capitalist Mentality*. Princeton, New Jersey: Van Nostrand Company, 1956.

_____, *Human Action: A Treatise on Economics*. Third Revised Edition. Chicago: Contemporary Books, 1966.

_____, *On the Manipulation of Money and Credit*. Dobbs Ferry, New York: Free Market Books, 1978.

_____, *The Theory of Money and Credit*, New Edition. Irvington-on-Hudson, NY: Foundation for Economic Education, 1971.

Frederic S. Mishkin, *The Economics of Money, Banking and Financial Markets: The Business School Edition, 3rd Edition*. New York: Prentice-Hall, 2012.

Kelly Mitchell, *Gold Wars: The Battle for the Global Economy*. Atlanta, Georgia: Clarity Press, 2013.

Stephen Moore, *How Barack Obama Is Bankrupting the U.S. Economy* (Encounter Broadside No. 4). New York: Encounter Books, 2009.

_____, *Who's the Fairest of Them All? The Truth About Opportunity, Taxes, and Wealth in America*. New York: Encounter Books, 2012.

Charles R. Morris, *The Trillion Dollar Meltdown: Easy Money, High Rollers, and the Great Credit Crash*. New York: Public Affairs/Perseus, 2008.

Alan D. Morrison and William J. Wilhelm, Jr., *Investment Banking: Institutions, Politics, and Law*. New York: Oxford University Press, USA, 2008.

Warren Mosler, *Soft Currency Economics II: What Everyone Thinks That They Know About Monetary Policy Is Wrong*. Seattle: Amazon Digital Services, 2012.

Cullen Murphy, *Are We Rome? The Fall of an Empire and the Fate of America*. Boston: Mariner Books/Houghton Mifflin, 2007.

Robert P. Murphy, *The Politically Incorrect Guide to Capitalism*. Washington, D.C.: Regnery, 2007.

Charles Murray, *Coming Apart: The State of White America, 1960-2010*. New York: Crown Forum, 2012.

_____, *What It Means to Be a Libertarian: A Personal Interpretation*. New York: Broadway Books, 1997.

Ralph Nader, *Unstoppable: The Emerging Left-Right Alliance to Dismantle the Corporate State*. New York: Nation Books, 2014.

Andrew P. Napolitano, *Lies the Government Told You: Myth, Power, and Deception in American History.* Nashville: Thomas Nelson, 2010.

_____, *Theodore and Woodrow: How Two American Presidents Destroyed Constitutional Freedom*. Nashville: Thomas Nelson, 2012.

Sylvia Nasar, *Grand Pursuit: The Story of Economic Genius*. New York: Simon & Schuster, 2011.

R. Nelson Nash, *Becoming Your Own Banker (Sixth Edition). Infinite Banking Concepts, 2012.*

Paul Nathan, *The New Gold Standard: Rediscovering the Power of Gold to Protect and Grow Wealth*. Hoboken, New Jersey: Wiley & Sons, 2011.

Karen Rhea Nemet-Nejat, *Daily Life in Ancient Mesopotamia*. Ada, Michigan: Baker Academic Publishing, 2001.

Maxwell Newton, *The Fed: Inside the Federal Reserve, the Secret Power Center that Controls the American Economy*. New York: Times Books, 1983.

Johan Norberg, *Financial Fiasco: How America's Infatuation with Home Ownership and Easy Money Created the Economic Crisis.* Washington, D.C.: Cato Institute, 2009.

Grover Norquist and John R. Lott, Jr., *Debacle: Obama's War on Jobs and Growth and What We Can Do Now to Regain Our Future.* Hoboken, New Jersey: John Wiley & Sons, 2012.

Barack Obama, *The Audacity of Hope: Thoughts on Reclaiming the American Dream*. New York: Crown, 2006.

Mancur Olson, *The Logic of Collective Action: Public Goods and the Theory of Groups*, Revised Edition. Cambridge, Massachusetts: Harvard University Press, 1971.

_____, *Power and Prosperity: Outgrowing Communist and Capitalist Dictatorships.* New York: Basic Books, 2000.

_____, *The Rise and Decline of Nations: Economic Growth, Stagflation, and Social Rigidities.* New Haven, Connecticut: Yale University Press, 1984.

James Ostrowski, *Progressivism: A Prime on the Idea Destroying America*. Cazenovia, N.Y.: Cazenovia Books, 2014.

Ronen Palan, Richard Murphy and Christian Chavagneux, *Tax Havens: How Globalization Really Works*. Ithaca, New York: Cornell University Press / Cornell Studies in Money, 2009.

Scott Patterson, *Dark Pools: The Rise of the Machine Traders and the Rigging of the U.S. Stock Market*. New York: Crown Business / Random House, 2012.

Ron Paul, *End The Fed*. New York: Grand Central Publishing / Hachette, 2009.

_____, *Liberty Defined: 50 Essential Issues That Affect Our Freedom*. New York: Grand Central Publishing / Hachette, 2011.

_____, *Pillars of Prosperity: Free Markets, Honest Money, Private Property.* Ludwig von Mises Institute, 2008.

_____, *The Revolution: A Manifesto.* New York: Grand Central Publishing / Hachette, 2008.

Ron Paul and Lewis Lehrman, *The Case for Gold: A Minority Report of the U.S. Gold Commission.* Ludwig von Mises Institute, 2007. This can be downloaded from the Internet at no cost from http://mises.org/books/caseforgold.pdf

John Peet and Anton La Guardia, *Unhappy Union: How the Euro Crisis – and Europe – Can Be Fixed.* London: Economist Books, 2014.

Michael G. Pento, *The Coming Bond Market Collapse: How to Survive the Demise of the U.S. Debt Market.* Hoboken, New Jersey: John Wiley & Sons, 2013.

Peter G. Peterson, *Running On Empty: How the Democratic and Republican Parties Are Bankrupting Our Future and What Americans Can Do About It.* New York: Farrar, Straus and Giroux, 2004.

Kevin Phillips, *Bad Money: Reckless Finance, Failed Politics, and the Global Crisis of American Capitalism.* New York: Viking Press, 2008.

_____, *Boiling Point: Democrats, Republicans, and the Decline of Middle-Class Prosperity.* New York: Random House, 1993.

James Piereson, *Shattered Consensus: The Rise and Decline of America's Postwar Political Order.* New York: Encounter Books, 2015.

Thomas Piketty, *Capital in the Twenty-First Century.* Cambridge, Massachusetts: Harvard University Press, 2014.

Federico Pistono, *Robots Will Steal Your Job, But That's OK: How to Survive the Economic Collapse and Be Happy.* Seattle, Washington: CreateSpace / Amazon, 2014.

Lowell Ponte, *The Cooling.* Englewood Cliffs, New Jersey: Prentice-Hall, 1976.

Richard A. Posner, *The Crisis of Capitalist Democracy.* Cambridge, Massachusetts: Harvard University Press, 2010.

_____, *A Failure of Capitalism: The Crisis of '08 and the Descent into Depression.* Cambridge, Massachusetts: Harvard University Press, 2009.

Virginia Postrel, *The Future and Its Enemies: The Growing Conflict Over Creativity, Enterprise, and Progress.* New York: Free Press, 1998.

Sidney Powell, *Licensed to Lie: Exposing Corruption in the Department of Justice.* Dallas: Brown Books Publishing, 2014.

Kirsten Powers, *The Silencing: How the Left is Killing Free Speech.* Washington, D.C.: Regnery Publishing, 2015.

Eswar S. Prasad, *The Dollar Trap: How the U.S. Dollar Tightened Its Grip on Global Finance.* Princeton, New Jersey: Princeton University Press, 2014.

Nomi Prins, *All the Presidents' Bankers: The Hidden Alliances That Drive American Power.* New York: Nation Books, 2014.

John Quiggin, *Zombie Economics: How Dead Ideas Still Walk Among Us*. Princeton, New Jersey: Princeton University Press, 2012.

Raghuram G. Rajan, *Fault Lines: How Hidden Fractures Still Threaten the World Economy*. Princeton, New Jersey: Princeton University Press, 2010.

Joshua Cooper Ramo, *The Age of the Unthinkable: Why the New World Disorder Constantly Surprises Us And What We Can Do About It*. New York: Little Brown / Hachette, 2009.

Ayn Rand, *Capitalism: The Unknown Ideal (With additional articles by Nathaniel Branden, Alan Greenspan, and Robert Hessen)*. New York: Signet / New American Library, 1967.

Carmen M. Reinhart and Kenneth S. Rogoff, *This Time Is Different: Eight Centuries of Financial Folly*. Princeton, New Jersey: Princeton University Press, 2009.

James Rickards, *Currency Wars: The Making of the Next Global Crisis*. New York: Portfolio/Penguin, 2011.

_____, *The Death of Money: The Coming Collapse of the International Monetary System*. New York: Portfolio / Penguin, 2014.

Jeremy Rifkin, *The Age of Access: The New Culture of Hypercapitalism, Where All of Life Is a Paid-for Experience*. New York: Jeremy P. Tarcher / Penguin, 2000.

_____, *The End of Work: The Decline of the Global Labor Force and the Dawn of the Post-Market Era*. New York: Jeremy P. Tarcher / G.P. Putnam's Sons, 1995.

_____, *The Zero Marginal Cost Society: The Internet of Things, the Collaborative Commons, and the Eclipse of Capitalism*. New York: Palgrave Macmillan, 2014.

Barry Ritzholtz with Aaron Task, *Bailout Nation: How Greed and Easy Money Corrupted Wall Street and Shook the World Economy*. Hoboken, New Jersey: John Wiley & Sons, 2009.

Keith Roberts, *The Origins of Business, Money and Markets*. New York: Columbia University Press / Columbia Business School Publishing, 2011.

Wilhelm Roepke, *A Humane Economy: The Social Framework of the Free Market*. Chicago: Henry Regnery Company, 1960. This can be downloaded from the Internet at no cost from http://mises.org/books/Humane_ Economy_Ropke.pdf

Murray N. Rothbard, *America's Great Depression*. Fifth Edition. Auburn, Alabama: Ludwig von Mises Institute, 2000. This can be downloaded from the Internet at no cost from http://mises.org/rothbard/agd.pdf

_____, *The Case Against the Fed*. Second Edition. Auburn, Alabama: Ludwig von Mises Institute, 2007. A version of this book can be downloaded from the Internet at no cost from http://mises.org/ books/Fed.pdf

_____, *A History of Money and Banking in the United States: The Colonial Era to World War II*. Auburn, Alabama: Ludwig von Mises Institute, 2002. This can be downloaded from the Internet at no cost from http://mises.org/Books/HistoryofMoney.pdf

_____, *The Mystery of Banking*. Second Edition. Auburn, Alabama: Ludwig von Mises Institute, 2010. This can be downloaded from the Internet at no cost from http://mises.org/Books/ MysteryofBanking.pdf

_____, *What Has Government Done to Our Money?* Auburn, Alabama: Ludwig von Mises Institute, 2008. This can be downloaded from the Internet at no cost from http://mises.org/Books/Whathasgovernmentdone.pdf

_____, *For a New Liberty: The Libertarian Manifesto* (Revised Edition). New York: Collier Books / Macmillian, 1978.

Michael Rothschild, *Bionomics: The Inevitability of Capitalism.* New York: John Macrae / Henry Holt and Company, 1990.

Nouriel Roubini and Stephen Mihm, *Crisis Economics: A Crash Course in the Future of Finance.* New York: Penguin Books, 2010.

Robert J. Samuelson, *The Good Life and Its Discontents: The American Dream in the Age of Entitlement 1945-1995.* New York: Times Books, 1995.

_____, *The Great Inflation and Its Aftermath: The Transformation of America's Economy, Politics and Society.* New York: Random House, 2008.

Peter D. Schiff and Andrew J. Schiff, *How an Economy Grows and Why It Crashes.* Hoboken, New Jersey: John Wiley & Sons, 2010.

Detlev S. Schlichter, *Paper Money Collapse: The Folly of Elastic Money and the Coming Monetary Breakdown.* New York: John Wiley & Sons, 2011.

Peter H. Schuck, *Why Government Fails So Often: And How It Can Do Better.* Princeton, New Jersey: Princeton University Press, 2014.

Peter H. Schuck and James Q. Wilson (Eds.), *Understanding America: The Anatomy of an Exceptional Nation.* New York: PublicAffairs / Perseus Books Group, 2009.

Robert L. Schuettinger and Eamonn F. Butler, *Forty Centuries of Wage and Price Controls: How NOT to Fight Inflation.* Washington, D.C.: Heritage Foundation, 1979. This can be downloaded from the Internet at no cost from http://mises.org/books/fortycenturies.pdf

Barry Schwartz, *The Paradox of Choice: Why More Is Less.* New York: Ecco / Harper Collins, 2004.

Peter Schweizer, *Architects of Ruin: How Big Government Liberals Wrecked the Global Economy – and How They Will Do It Again If No One Stops Them.* New York: HarperCollins, 2009.

James C. Scott, *Seeing Like A State: How Certain Schemes to Improve the Human Condition Have Failed.* New Haven, Connecticut: Yale University Press, 1998.

George Selgin and others, *Has the Fed Been a Failure?* Revised Edition. (Monograph). Washington, D.C.: Cato Institute, 2010.

Hans F. Sennholz (Editor), *Inflation Is Theft.* Irvington-on-Hudson, New York: Foundation for Economic Education, 1994. A copy of this book may be downloaded at no cost from FEE's website at http://fee.org/wp-content/uploads/2009/11/InflationisTheft.pdf See also: Hans F. Sennholz, "Inflation Is Theft," *LewRockwell.com*, June 24, 2005. URL: http://www.lewrockwell.com/orig6/sennholz6.html

Judy Shelton, *Fixing the Dollar Now: Why US Money Lost Its Integrity and How We Can Restore It.* Washington, D.C.: Atlas Economic Research Foundation, 2011.

_____, *Money Meltdown: Restoring Order to the Global Currency System*. New York: The Free Press / Macmillan, 1994.

Amity Shlaes, *The Forgotten Man: A New History of the Great Depression*. New York: Harper Collins, 2007.

_____, *The Greedy Hand: How Taxes Drive Americans Crazy And What to Do About It*. New York: Random House, 1999.

Fred Siegel, *The Revolt Against the Masses: How Liberalism Has Undermined the Middle Class*. New York: Encounter Books, 2014.

Julian L. Simon, *The Ultimate Resource*. Princeton, New Jersey: Princeton University Press, 1981.

Chris Skinner, *Digital Bank: Strategies to Launch or Become a Digital Bank*. Singapore: Marshall Cavendish International (Asia-Singapore) / Times Publishing, 2014.

_____, *The Future of Banking in a Globalised World*. Hoboken, New Jersey: Wiley Finance Series, 2007.

Mark Skousen, *Economics of a Pure Gold Standard*. Seattle: CreateSpace, 2010.

_____, *The Making of Modern Economics: The Lives and Ideas of the Great Thinkers*. Second Edition. Armonk, New York: M.E. Sharpe, 2009.

Nick Smicek and Alex Williams, *Inventing the Future: Postcapitalism and a World Without Work*. London: Verso, 2015.

Craig R. Smith, *Rediscovering Gold in the 21ˢᵗ Century*. Sixth Edition. Phoenix: Idea Factory Press, 2007.

_____, *The Uses of Inflation: Monetary Policy and Governance in the 21ˢᵗ Century* (Monograph). Phoenix: Swiss America Trading Corporation, 2011.

Craig R. Smith and Lowell Ponte, *Crashing the Dollar: How to Survive a Global Currency Collapse*. Phoenix: Idea Factory Press, 2010.

_____, *The Great Debasement: The 100-Year Dying of the Dollar and How to Get America's Money Back*. Phoenix: Idea Factory Press, 2012.

_____, *The Great Withdrawal: How the Progressives' 100-Year Debasement of America and the Dollar Ends*. Phoenix: Idea Factory Press, 2013.

_____, *The Inflation Deception: Six Ways Government Tricks Us...And Seven Ways to Stop It!* Phoenix: Idea Factory Press, 2011.

_____, *Re-Making Money: Ways to Restore America's Optimistic Golden Age*. Phoenix: Idea Factory Press, 2011.

Helen Smith, *Men on Strike: Why Men Are Boycotting Marriage, Fatherhood, and the American Dream – and Why It Matters*. New York: Encounter Books, 2012.

Roy C. Smith, Ingo Walter and Gayle DeLong, *Global Banking* (Third Edition). Oxford: Oxford University Press, 2012.

Vera C. Smith, *The Rationale of Central Banking and the Free Banking Alternative*. Indianapolis, Indiana: Liberty Press / Liberty Fund, 1990.

Jacob Soll, *The Reckoning: Financial Accountability and the Rise and Fall of Nations*. New York: Basic Books, 2014.

Guy Sorman, *Economics Does Not Lie: A Defense of the Free Market in a Time of Crisis*. New York: Encounter Books, 2009.

George Soros, *The Age of Fallibility: Consequences of the War on Terror*. New York: Public Affairs, 2007.

_____, *The Bubble of American Supremacy: the Costs of Bush's War in Iraq*. London: Weidenfeld & Nicolson, 2004.

_____, *George Soros on Globalization*. New York: Public Affairs, 2005.

_____, *The New Paradigm for Financial Markets: The Credit Crisis of 2008 and What It Means*. New York: Public Affairs, 2008.

_____, *Open Society: Reforming Global Capitalism*. New York: Public Affairs, 2000.

_____, *The Soros Lectures at the Central European University*. New York: Public Affairs, 2010.

Thomas Sowell, *Basic Economics: A Common Sense Guide to the Economy*. Third Edition. New York: Basic Books/Perseus Books Group, 2007.

_____, *A Conflict of Visions: Ideological Origins of Political Struggles*. New York: William Morrow, 1987.

_____, *Dismantling America*. New York: Basic Books, 2010.

_____, *Economic Facts and Fallacies*. Second Edition. New York: Basic Books, 2011.

_____, *The Housing Boom and Bust*. Revised Edition. New York: Basic Books, 2010.

_____, *Intellectuals and Society*. New York: Basic Books/Perseus Books, 2009.

_____, *Marxism: Philosophy and Economics*. New York: William Morrow, 1985.

_____, *On Classical Economics*. New Haven, Connecticut: Yale University Press, 2007.

_____, *The Quest for Cosmic Justice*. New York: Free Press/Simon & Schuster, 1999.

_____, *The Vision of the Anointed: Self-Congratulation as a Basis for Social Policy*. BasicBooks/HarperCollins, 1995.

Dimitri Speck, *The Gold Cartel: Government Intervention on Gold, the Mega Bubble in Paper, and What This Means for Your Future*. New York: Palgrave Macmillan, 2013.

Paul Sperry, *The Great American Bank Robbery: The Unauthorized Report About What Really Caused the Great Recession*. Nashville, Tennessee: Thomas Nelson / HarperCollins Christian Publishing, 2011.

Henry William Spiegel and Ann Hubbard (Editors), *The Growth of Economic Thought (3rd Edition)*. Durham, North Carolina: Duke University Press, 1991.

Mark Steyn, *After America: Get Ready for Armageddon*. Washington, D.C.: Regnery, 2011.

_____, *America Alone: The End of the World As We Know It*. Washington, D.C.: Regnery, 2008. *[Full Disclosure: Steyn quotes Lowell Ponte in this book.]*

Joseph E. Stiglitz, *Freefall: America, Free Markets, and the Sinking of the World Economy*. New York: W.W. Norton, 2010.

_____, *Globalization and Its Discontents*. New York: W.W. Norton, 2002.

David A. Stockman, *The Great Deformation: The Corruption of Capitalism in America*. New York: PublicAffairs/Perseus Books Group, 2013.

John F. Stover, *History of the Baltimore and Ohio Railroad*. West Lafayette, Indiana: Purdue University Press, 1995.

Paola Subacchi and John Driffill (Editors), *Beyond the Dollar: Rethinking the International Monetary System*. London: Chatham House / Royal Institute of International Affairs, 2010. URL: http://www. chathamhouse.org/sites/default/files/public/Research/International%20Economics/r0310_ims.pdf

Cass R. Sunstein, *A Constitution of Many Minds: Why the Founding Document Doesn't Mean What It Meant Before*. Princeton, New Jersey: Princeton University Press, 2011.

_____, *Simpler: The Future of Government*. New York: Simon & Schuster, 2013.

Ron Suskind, *Confidence Men: Wall Street, Washington, and the Education of a President*. New York: Harper Collins, 2011.

Bob Swarup, *Money Mania: Booms, Panics, and Busts from Ancient Rome to the Great Meltdown*. London: Bloomsbury Press, 2014.

Charles J. Sykes, *A Nation of Moochers: America's Addiction to Getting Something for Nothing*. New York: St. Martin's Press, 2012.

Nassim Nicholas Taleb, *Antifragile: Things That Gain from Disorder*. New York: Random House, 2012.

_____, *The Bed of Procrustes: Philosophical and Practical Aphorisms*. New York: Random House, 2010.

_____, *The Black Swan: Second Edition: The Impact of the Highly Improbable: With a New Section: "On Robustness and Fragility."* New York: Random House, 2010.

_____, *Fooled by Randomness: The Hidden Role of Chance in Life and in the Markets*. New York: Random House, 2005.

Peter J. Tanous and Jeff Cox, *Debt, Deficits and the Demise of the American Economy*. Hoboken, New Jersey: John Wiley & Sons, 2011.

Daniel K. Tarullo, *Banking on Basel: The Future of International Financial Regulation*. Washington, D.C.: The Peterson Institute for International Economics, 2008.

Richard H. Thaler and Cass R. Sunstein, *Nudge: Improving Decisions About Health, Wealth, and Happiness*. New York: Penguin Books, 2009.

J.A. Thompson, *The Bible and Archeology*. Grand Rapids, Michigan: William B. Eerdmans Publishing, 1962.

James Turk and John Rubino, *The Money Bubble: What to Do Before It Pops*. Moscow, Idaho: DollarCollapse

Press, 2013.

Walter Tyndale, *Fundamentals of Offshore Banking: How to Open Accounts Almost Anywhere.* Seattle, Washington: CreateSpace/Amazon Publishing, 2009.

United States Government Accountability Office, *Offshore Tax Evasion: IRS Has Collected Billions of Dollars, but May be Missing Continued Evasion* (Report). Washington, D.C.: GAO, March 2013. URL: http://www.gao.gov/assets/660/653369.pdf

Richard Vague, *The Next Economic Disaster: Why It's Coming and How to Avoid It.* Philadelphia: University of Pennsylvania Press, 2014.

Johan Van Overtveldt, *Bernanke's Test: Ben Bernanke, Alan Greenspan and the Drama of the Central Banker.* Chicago: B2 Books/Agate Publishing, 2009.

Harry C. Veryser, *It Didn't Have to Be This Way: Why Boom and Bust Is Unnecessary – and How the Austrian School of Economics Breaks the Cycle.* Wilmington, Delaware: ISI Books / Intercollegiate Studies Institute, 2012.

Damon Vickers, *The Day After the Dollar Crashes: A Survival Guide for the Rise of the New World Order.* Hoboken, New Jersey: John Wiley & Sons, 2011.

William Voegeli, *Never Enough: America's Limitless Welfare State.* New York: Encounter Books, 2010.

M.W. Walbert, *The Coming Battle: A Complete History of the National Banking Money Power in the United States.* Chicago: W.B. Conkey Company, 1899. Reprinted by Walter Publishing & Research, Merlin, Oregon, 1997.

David M. Walker, *Comeback America: Turning the Country Around and Restoring Fiscal Responsibility.* New York: Random House, 2009.

Jude Wanniski, *The Way the World Works.* New York: Touchstone / Simon & Schuster, 1978.

Jack Weatherford, *The History of Money: From Sandstone to Cyberspace.* New York: Crown Publishers, 1997.

Carolyn Webber and Aaron Wildavsky, *A History of Taxation and Expenditure in the Western World.* New York: Simon & Schuster, 1986.

Janine R. Wedel, *Shadow Elite: How the World's New Power Brokers Undermine Democracy, Government and the Free Market.* New York: Basic Books / Perseus Books Group, 2009.

Eric J. Weiner, *The Shadow Market: How a Group of Wealthy Nations and Powerful Investors Secretly Dominate the World.* New York: Scribner, 2010.

David Wessel, *In Fed We Trust: Ben Bernanke's War on the Great Panic: How the Federal Reserve Became the Fourth Branch of Government.* New York: Crown Business, 2009.

Diana West, *American Betrayal: The Secret Assault on Our Nation's Character.* New York: St. Martin's Press, 2013.

_____, *The Death of the Grown-Up: How America's Arrested Development Is Bringing Down Western Civilization.* New York: St. Martin's Press, 2007.

Drew Westen, *The Political Brain: The Role of Emotion in Deciding the Fate of the Nation.* Washington,

D.C.: PublicAffairs / Perseus Books Group, 2008.

R. Christopher Whalen, *Inflated: How Money and Debt Built the American Dream.* Hoboken, New Jersey: John Wiley & Sons, 2010.

Lawrence H. White, *The Clash of Economic Ideas: The Great Policy Debates and Experiments of the Last Hundred Years.* Cambridge: Cambridge University Press, 2012.

_____, *Is The Gold Standard Still the Gold Standard among Monetary Systems?* (Monograph). Washington, D.C.: Cato Institute, February 8, 2008. URL: http://www.cato.org/pubs/bp/bp100.pdf

Meredith Whitney, *Fate of the States: The New Geography of American Prosperity.* New York: Portfolio, 2013.

Peter C. Whybrow, *American Mania: When More Is Not Enough.* New York: W.W. Norton, 2005.

Addison Wiggin and William Bonner, *Financial Reckoning Day Fallout: Surviving Today's Global Depression.* Hoboken, New Jersey: John Wiley & Sons, 2009.

Addison Wiggin and Kate Incontrera, *I.O.U.S.A.: One Nation. Under Stress. In Debt.* Hoboken, New Jersey: John Wiley & Sons, 2008.

Benjamin Wiker, *Worshipping the State: How Liberalism Became Our State Religion.* Washington, D.C.: Regnery, 2013.

Aaron Wildavsky, *How to Limit Government Spending...,* Berkeley, California: University of California Press, 1980.

John Williams, *Hyperinflation 2012: Special Commentary Number 414. Shadow Government Statistics (Shadowstats),* January 25, 2012. URL: http://www.shadowstats.com/article/no-414-hyperinflation-special-report-2012

Jonathan Williams (Editor), *Money: A History.* New York: St. Martin's Press, 1997.

David Wolman, *The End of Money: Counterfeiters, Preachers, Techies, Dreamers – and the Coming Cashless Society.* Boston: Da Capo Press / Perseus Books, 2012.

Gordon S. Wood, *Empire of Liberty: A History of the Early Republic, 1789-1815.* New York: Oxford University Press, 2009.

Thomas E. Woods, Jr., *Meltdown: A Free-Market Look at Why the Stock Market Collapsed, the Economy Tanked, and Government Bailouts Will Make Things Worse.* Washington, D.C.: Regnery Publishing, 2009.

_____, *Nullification: How to Resist Federal Tyranny in the 21st Century.* Washington, D.C.: Regnery Publishing, 2010.

_____, *Rollback: Repealing Big Government Before the Coming Fiscal Collapse.* Washington, D.C.: Regnery Publishing, 2011.

Thomas E. Woods, Jr., and Kevin R.C. Gutzman, *Who Killed the Constitution?: The Federal Government vs. American Liberty From WWI to Barack Obama.* New York: Three Rivers Press, 2009.

Bob Woodward, *Maestro: Greenspan's Fed and the American Boom.* New York: Simon & Schuster, 2000.

_____, *The Power of Politics.* New York: Simon & Schuster, 2012.

L. Randall Wray, *Modern Money Theory: A Primer on Macroeconomics for Sovereign Monetary Systems.* London: Palgrave Macmillan, 2012.

_____, *Understanding Modern Money: The Key to Full Employment and Price Stability.* Northampton, Massachusetts: Edward Elgar Publishing, 2006.

Pamela Yellen, *The Bank On Yourself Revolution: Fire Your Banker, Bypass Wall Street, and Take Control of Your Own Financial Future.* Ben Bella Books, 2014.

Fareed Zakaria, *The Future of Freedom: Illiberal Democracy at Home and Abroad.* New York: W.W. Norton, 2003.

_____, *The Post-American World.* New York: W.W. Norton, 2009.

Luigi Zingales, *A Capitalism for the People: Recapturing the Lost Genius of American Prosperity.* New York: Basic Books / Perseus Books Group, 2012.
Todd J. Zywicki, *The Economics and Regulation of Network Branded Prepaid Cards* (Working Paper). Arlington, Virginia: Mercatus Center / George Mason University, January 2013. URL: http://mercatus.org/sites/default/files/Zywicki_Prepaid_v2.pdf

"We have rights, as individuals, to give as much of our own money as we please to charity; but as members of Congress we have no right so to appropriate a dollar of public money."

– David "Davy" Crockett
Congressman 1827-1835

"I cannot undertake to lay my finger on that article of the Constitution which grant[s] a right to Congress of expending, on objects of benevolence, the money of their constituents."

– James Madison
1794